COMPUTER BOOK SERIES FROM IDG

Lotus Notes® Releas...
For Dummies®

MW00716524

Enhancing Text

Action	SmartIcon	PC Keyboard	Mac Keyboard	Menu Commands
Italic	*I*	Ctrl+I	⌘+I	Text⇨Italic
Bold	**B**	Ctrl+B	⌘+B	Text⇨Bold
Underline	U	Ctrl+U	⌘+U	Text⇨Underline
Strikethrough	◇	Alt+Enter	⌘+K	Text Properties, first tab
Superscript	◇	Alt+Enter	⌘+K	Text Properties, first tab
Subscript	◇	Alt+Enter	⌘+K	Text Properties, first tab
Normal style	No icon	Ctrl+T	⌘+T	Text⇨Normal Text
Delete		Delete	Delete	Edit⇨Clear
Cut to Clipboard	✂	Ctrl+X	⌘+X	Edit⇨Cut
Copy to Clipboard		Ctrl+C	⌘+C	Edit⇨Copy
Paste		Ctrl+V	⌘+V	Edit⇨Paste
Append to Clipboard	No icon	Ctrl+Shift+Insert	None	No menu item
Change font	◇	Alt+Enter	⌘+K	Text Properties, first tab
You may also use the Status bar to change this feature				
Change font size	◇	F2/Shift+F2	⌘+K	Text Properties, first tab
You may also use the Status bar to change this feature				
Change font color	◇	Alt+Enter	None	Text Properties, first tab
Align paragraph	☰ ☰	Alt+Enter	⌘+J	Text Properties, second tab
Indent paragraph	⇥ ☰	F7/F8	F7/F8	Text Properties, second tab
***Note:** F7 for first line only, F8 for all lines*				
Outdent paragraph	No icon	Shift+F7/F8	Shift+F7/F8	Text Properties, second tab
***Note:** Shift+F7 for first line only, F8 for all lines*				

IDG BOOKS WORLDWIDE

...For Dummies: #1 Computer Book Series for Beginners

Lotus Notes® Release 4 For Dummies®

Cheat Sheet

FOR DUMMIES
COMPUTER BOOK SERIES FROM IDG

Working with Documents

Task	Keyboard	Mouse or Menu
Read selected document	Enter	Double-click
Delete selected document	Delete	Edit⇨Clear
Clear document from screen button	Esc	Double-click right mouse
Edit document	Ctrl+E	Double-click open document
Send a message	Esc and then Send, or Actions⇨Send	Click Send button
Forward a document	Actions⇨Forward	
Send a memo when you're in another database	Create⇨Mail⇨Memo	
Update a view	F9	View⇨Refresh

Conquering Categories

To Do This	Keyboard	Mouse or Menu
Expand a category	+ (Keypad)	View⇨Expand/Collapse⇨Expand Selected Level
Collapse a category	- (Keypad)	View⇨Expand/Collapse⇨Collapse Selected Level
Expand all categories	Shift+ + (Keypad)	View⇨Expand All
Collapse all categories	Shift+ - (Keypad)	View⇨Collapse All

For the Security-Minded

To Do This	Use
Password-protect your Notes ID	File⇨Tools⇨User ID⇨Set Password
Log off all Notes servers	F5
Encrypt the body of a memo	Actions⇨Delivery Options, Encrypt

Get Help Quick

To Do This	Use
Get help on current task	F1
Find a help topic	Help⇨Help Topics
Get help on error messages	F1 when message appears
Get Release 3 equivalent commands	Help⇨Release 3 Menu Finder

Selecting Text

To Select This	Do This
A word	Double-click it
Next several words (Edit mode)	Ctrl+right-arrow key
Previous several words (Edit mode)	Ctrl+left-arrow key
All text in current field	Edit⇨Select All
A large chunk of text	Position cursor at beginning, Shift+click at end of chunk
From cursor to beginning of field	Shift+Ctrl+Home
From cursor to end of field	Shift+Ctrl+End

Navigating among Documents

To Go To	Keyboard	Icon
Next unread document	Tab or F4	
Previous unread document	Shift+Tab or Shift+F4	
Next document	Enter	
Previous document	Backspace	

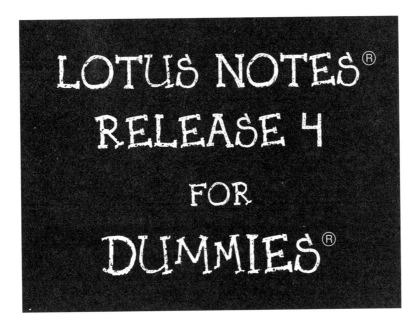

LOTUS NOTES® RELEASE 4 FOR DUMMIES®

by Steve Londergan

and Pat Freeland

Foreword by Mike Zisman

IDG Books Worldwide, Inc.
An International Data Group Company

Foster City, CA ♦ Chicago, IL ♦ Indianapolis, IN ♦ Southlake, TX

Lotus Notes® Release 4 For Dummies®

Published by
IDG Books Worldwide, Inc.
An International Data Group Company
919 E. Hillsdale Blvd.
Suite 400
Foster City, CA 94404
http://www.idgbooks.com (IDG Books Worldwide Web site)
http://www.dummies.com (Dummies Press Web site)

Library of Congress Catalog Card No.: 96-75122

ISBN: 1-56884-934-6

Printed in the United States of America

10 9 8 7 6 5 4

1O/QS/QU/ZX/IN

Distributed in the United States by IDG Books Worldwide, Inc.

Distributed by Macmillan Canada for Canada; by Transworld Publishers Limited in the United Kingdom and Europe; by WoodsLane Pty. Ltd. for Australia; by WoodsLane Enterprises Ltd. for New Zealand; by Longman Singapore Publishers Ltd. for Singapore, Malaysia, Thailand, and Indonesia; by Simron Pty. Ltd. for South Africa; by Toppan Company Ltd. for Japan; by Distribuidora Cuspide for Argentina; by Livraria Cultura for Brazil; by Ediciencia S.A. for Ecuador; by Addison-Wesley Publishing Company for Korea; by Ediciones ZETA S.C.R. Ltda. for Peru; by WS Computer Publishing Company, Inc., for the Philippines; by Unalis Corporation for Taiwan; by Contemporanea de Ediciones for Venezuela. Authorized Sales Agent: Anthony Rudkin Associates for the Middle East and North Africa.

For general information on IDG Books Worldwide's books in the U.S., please call our Consumer Customer Service department at 800-762-2974. For reseller information, including discounts and premium sales, please call our Reseller Customer Service department at 800-434-3422.

For information on where to purchase IDG Books Worldwide's books outside the U.S., please contact our International Sales department at 415-655-3023 or fax 415-655-3299.

For information on foreign language translations, please contact our Foreign & Subsidiary Rights department at 415-655-3021 or fax 415-655-3281.

For sales inquiries and special prices for bulk quantities, please contact our Sales department at 415-655-3200 or write to the address above.

For information on using IDG Books Worldwide's books in the classroom or for ordering examination copies, please contact our Educational Sales department at 800-434-2086 or fax 817-251-8174.

For press review copies, author interviews, or other publicity information, please contact our Public Relations department at 415-655-3000 or fax 415-655-3299.

For authorization to photocopy items for corporate, personal, or educational use, please contact Copyright Clearance Center, 222 Rosewood Drive, Danvers, MA 01923, or fax 508-750-4470.

is a trademark under exclusive license to IDG Books Worldwide, Inc., from International Data Group, Inc.

About the Authors

Stephen Londergan has been explaining how computers work for more than ten years — and the funny part is that sometimes people listen. This is Steve's second book for IDG. He works for Lotus Development, where he helps people figure out how to use Notes.

Steve lives in oh-so-lovely Braintree, Massachusetts, with his wife Robyn and his two sons, Michael and Richard. (At press time, the Londergans were expecting their third child.) Readers of the original *Lotus Notes For Dummies* will be surprised to learn that the Londergan family is now keeping company with a beagle by the name of Katie.

Steve and Pat (the other author of this book) have been colleagues for more than 20 years. This feat is only possible because Pat Freeland was Steve's sixth-grade math teacher.

Pat Freeland is a member of the senior technical staff at HTR, Inc., where he does training, writing, and consulting. Formerly, while at Lotus, Pat was editor of *Lotus Notes Knowledge Base*.

Pat lives in Hingham, Massachusetts, with his wife and two children, a cat and two dogs. He has written several books and magazine articles on Notes and other computer products.

ABOUT IDG BOOKS WORLDWIDE

Welcome to the world of IDG Books Worldwide.

IDG Books Worldwide, Inc., is a subsidiary of International Data Group, the world's largest publisher of computer-related information and the leading global provider of information services on information technology. IDG was founded more than 25 years ago and now employs more than 8,500 people worldwide. IDG publishes more than 275 computer publications in over 75 countries (see listing below). More than 60 million people read one or more IDG publications each month.

Launched in 1990, IDG Books Worldwide is today the #1 publisher of best-selling computer books in the United States. We are proud to have received eight awards from the Computer Press Association in recognition of editorial excellence and three from *Computer Currents'* First Annual Readers' Choice Awards. Our best-selling *...For Dummies®* series has more than 30 million copies in print with translations in 30 languages. IDG Books Worldwide, through a joint venture with IDG's Hi-Tech Beijing, became the first U.S. publisher to publish a computer book in the People's Republic of China. In record time, IDG Books Worldwide has become the first choice for millions of readers around the world who want to learn how to better manage their businesses.

Our mission is simple: Every one of our books is designed to bring extra value and skill-building instructions to the reader. Our books are written by experts who understand and care about our readers. The knowledge base of our editorial staff comes from years of experience in publishing, education, and journalism — experience we use to produce books for the '90s. In short, we care about books, so we attract the best people. We devote special attention to details such as audience, interior design, use of icons, and illustrations. And because we use an efficient process of authoring, editing, and desktop publishing our books electronically, we can spend more time ensuring superior content and spend less time on the technicalities of making books.

You can count on our commitment to deliver high-quality books at competitive prices on topics you want to read about. At IDG Books Worldwide, we continue in the IDG tradition of delivering quality for more than 25 years. You'll find no better book on a subject than one from IDG Books Worldwide.

John J. Kilcullen

John Kilcullen
CEO
IDG Books Worldwide, Inc.

Eighth Annual Computer Press Awards ≥1992

Ninth Annual Computer Press Awards ≥1993

Tenth Annual Computer Press Awards ≥1994

Eleventh Annual Computer Press Awards ≥1995

IDG Books Worldwide, Inc., is a subsidiary of International Data Group, the world's largest publisher of computer-related information and the leading global provider of information services on information technology. International Data Group publishes over 275 computer publications in over 75 countries. Sixty million people read one or more International Data Group publications each month. International Data Group's publications include: **ARGENTINA:** Buyer's Guide, Computerworld Argentina, PC World Argentina; **AUSTRALIA:** Australian Macworld, Australian PC World, Australian Reseller News, Computerworld, IT Casebook, Network World, Publish, Webmaster; **AUSTRIA:** Computerwelt Osterreich, Networks Austria, PC Tip Austria; **BANGLADESH:** PC World Bangladesh; **BELARUS:** PC World Belarus; **BELGIUM:** Data News; **BRAZIL:** Annuário de Informática, Computerworld, Connections, Macworld, PC Player, PC World, Publish, Reseller News, Supergamepower; **BULGARIA:** Computerworld Bulgaria, Network World Bulgaria, PC & MacWorld Bulgaria; **CANADA:** CIO Canada, Client/Server World, ComputerWorld Canada, InfoWorld Canada, NetworkWorld Canada, WebWorld; **CHILE:** Computerworld Chile, PC World Chile; **COLOMBIA:** Computerworld Colombia, PC World Colombia; **COSTA RICA:** PC World Centro America; **THE CZECH AND SLOVAK REPUBLICS:** Computerworld Czechoslovakia, Macworld Czech Republic, PC World Czechoslovakia; **DENMARK:** Communications World Danmark, Computerworld Danmark, Macworld Danmark, PC World Danmark, Techworld Denmark; **DOMINICAN REPUBLIC:** PC World Republica Dominicana; **ECUADOR:** PC World Ecuador; **EGYPT:** Computerworld Middle East, PC World Middle East; **EL SALVADOR:** PC World Centro America; **FINLAND:** MikroPC, Tietoverkko, Tietoviikko; **FRANCE:** Distributique, Hebdo, Info PC, Le Monde Informatique, Macworld, Reseaux & Telecoms, WebMaster France; **GERMANY:** Computer Partner, Computerwoche, Computerwoche Extra, Computerwoche FOCUS, Global Online, Macwelt, PC Welt; **GREECE:** Amiga Computing, GamePro Greece, Multimedia World; **GUATEMALA:** PC World Centro America; **HONDURAS:** PC World Centro America; **HONG KONG:** Computerworld Hong Kong, PC World Hong Kong, Publish in Asia; **HUNGARY:** ABCD CD-ROM, Computerworld Szamitastechnika, Internetto online Magazine, PC World Hungary, PC-X Magazin Hungary; **ICELAND:** Tolvuheimur PC World Island; **INDIA:** Information Communications World, Information Systems Computerworld, PC World India, Publish in Asia; **INDONESIA:** InfoKomputer PC World, Komputek Computerworld, Publish in Asia; **IRELAND:** ComputerScope, PC Live!; **ISRAEL:** Macworld Israel, People & Computers/Computerworld; **ITALY:** Computerworld Italia, Macworld Italia, Networking Italia, PC World Italia; **JAPAN:** DTP World, Macworld Japan, Nikkei Personal Computing, OS/2 World Japan, SunWorld Japan, Windows NT World, Windows World Japan; **KENYA:** PC World East African; **KOREA:** Hi-Tech Information, Macworld Korea, PC World Korea; **MACEDONIA:** PC World Macedonia; **MALAYSIA:** Computerworld Malaysia, PC World Malaysia, Publish in Asia; **MALTA:** PC World Malta; **MEXICO:** Computerworld Mexico, PC World Mexico; **MYANMAR:** PC World Myanmar; **NETHERLANDS:** Computer! Totaal, LAN Internetworking Magazine, LAN World Buyers Guide, Macworld Netherlands, Net, WebWereld; **NEW ZEALAND:** Absolute Beginners Guide and Plain & Simple Series, Computer Buyer, Computer Industry Directory, Computerworld New Zealand, MTB, Network World, PC World New Zealand; **NICARAGUA:** PC World Centro America; **NORWAY:** Computerworld Norge, CW Rapport, Datamagasinet, Financial Rapport, Kursguide Norge, Macworld Norge, Multimediaworld Norge, PC World Ekspress Norge, PC World Nettverk, PC World Norge, PC World ProduktGuide Norge; **PAKISTAN:** Computerworld Pakistan; **PANAMA:** PC World Panama; **PEOPLE'S REPUBLIC OF CHINA:** China Computer Users, China Computerworld, China InfoWorld, China Telecom World Weekly, Computer & Communication, Electronic Design China, Electronics Today, Electronics Weekly, Game Software, PC World China, Popular Computer Week, Software Weekly, Software World, Telecom World; **PERU:** Computerworld Peru, PC World Profesional Peru, PC World SoHo Peru; **PHILIPPINES:** Click!, Computerworld Philippines, PC World Philippines, Publish in Asia; **POLAND:** Computerworld Poland, Computerworld Special Report Poland, Cyber, Macworld Poland, Networld Poland, PC World Komputer; **PORTUGAL:** Cerebro/PC World, Computerworld/Correio Informático, Dealer World Portugal, Mac*In/PC*In Portugal, Multimedia World; **PUERTO RICO:** PC World Puerto Rico; **ROMANIA:** Computerworld Romania, PC World Romania, Telecom Romania; **RUSSIA:** Computerworld Russia, Mir PK, Publish, Seti; **SINGAPORE:** Computerworld Singapore, PC World Singapore, Publish in Asia; **SLOVENIA:** Monitor; **SOUTH AFRICA:** Computing SA, Network World SA, Software World SA; **SPAIN:** Communicaciones World España, Computerworld España, Dealer World España, Macworld España, PC World España; **SRI LANKA:** Infolink PC World; **SWEDEN:** CAP&Design, Computer Sweden, Corporate Computing Sweden, Internetworld Sweden, it.branschen, Macworld Sweden, MaxiData Sweden, MikroDatorn, Natverk & Kommunikation, PC World Sweden, PCaktiv, Windows World Sweden; **SWITZERLAND:** Computerworld Schweiz, Macworld Schweiz, PCtip; **TAIWAN:** Computerworld Taiwan, Macworld Taiwan, NEW ViSiON/Publish, PC World Taiwan, Windows World Taiwan; **THAILAND:** Publish in Asia, Thai Computerworld; **TURKEY:** Computerworld Turkiye, Macworld Turkiye, Network World Turkiye, PC World Turkiye; **UKRAINE:** Computerworld Kiev, Multimedia World Ukraine, PC World Ukraine; **UNITED KINGDOM:** Acorn User UK, Amiga Action UK, Amiga Computing UK, Apple Talk UK, Computing, Macworld, Parents and Computers UK, PC Advisor, PC Home, PSX Pro, The WEB; **UNITED STATES:** Cable in the Classroom, CIO Magazine, Computerworld, DOS World, Federal Computer Week, GamePro Magazine, InfoWorld, I-Way, Macworld, Network World, PC Games, PC World, Publish, Video Event, THE WEB Magazine, and WebMaster; online webzines: JavaWorld, NetscapeWorld, and SunWorld Online; **URUGUAY:** InfoWorld Uruguay; **VENEZUELA:** Computerworld Venezuela, PC World Venezuela; and **VIETNAM:** PC World Vietnam.   2/14/97

Dedications

Stephen Londergan

My efforts here are dedicated to my late uncle Bobby Stone, who taught me how and why hard work is important.

Pat Freeland

To my family, Vicki, Cavi, and Michael — my best friends and the light of my life. Thanks for your love and patience.

Acknowledgments

We'd like to both acknowledge and thank the great Bethann Cregg, our technical editor, for her incredible insight and attention to detail; and the incomparable Shannon Ross from IDG, who acted as both our project editor and copy editor (two jobs, one salary). Thanks also go to William A. Barton, Leah P. Cameron, Suzanne Packer, and Kelly Ewing for their editorial help.

Publisher's Acknowledgments

We're proud of this book; please send us your comments about it by using the Reader Response Card at the back of the book or by e-mailing us at feedback/dummies@idgbooks.com. Some of the people who helped bring this book to market include the following:

Acquisitions, Development, and Editorial

Associate Project Editor: Shannon Ross

Assistant Acquisitions Editor: Gareth Hancock

Product Development Manager: Mary Bednarek

Technical Reviewer: Bethann Cregg

Editorial Managers: Kristin A. Cocks,
   Mary C. Corder

Editorial Assistant: Chris H. Collins

Production

Project Coordinator: J. Tyler Connor

Layout and Graphics: E. Shawn Aylsworth,
   Brett Black, Cameron Booker, Linda M. Boyer,
   Elizabeth Cárdenas-Nelson, Angela F. Hunckler,
   Todd Klemme, Jill Lyttle, Jane E. Martin,
   Mark Owens, Carla Radzikinas, Gina Scott

Proofreaders: Mary C. Oby, Christine Meloy Beck,
   Dwight Ramsey, Carl Saff, Robert Springer

Indexer: David Heiret

General and Administrative

IDG Books Worldwide, Inc.: John Kilcullen, CEO; Steven Berkowitz, President and Publisher

IDG Books Technology Publishing: Brenda McLaughlin, Senior Vice President and Group Publisher

Dummies Technology Press and Dummies Editorial: Diane Graves Steele, Vice President and Associate Publisher; Judith A. Taylor, Brand Manager; Kristin A. Cocks, Editorial Director

Dummies Trade Press: Kathleen A. Welton, Vice President and Publisher; Stacy S. Collins, Brand Manager

IDG Books Production for Dummies Press: Beth Jenkins, Production Director; Cindy L. Phipps, Supervisor of Project Coordination, Production Proofreading, and Indexing; Kathie S. Schutte, Supervisor of Page Layout; Shelley Lea, Supervisor of Graphics and Design; Debbie J. Gates, Production Systems Specialist; Tony Augsburger, Supervisor of Reprints and Bluelines; Leslie Popplewell, Media Archive Coordinator

Dummies Packaging and Book Design: Patti Sandez, Packaging Specialist; Lance Kayser, Packaging Assistant; Kavish + Kavish, Cover Design

◆

The publisher would like to give special thanks to Patrick J. McGovern,
without whom this book would not have been possible.

◆

Contents at a Glance

Cartoons at a Glance

By Rich Tennant • Fax: 508-546-7747 • E-mail: the5wave@tiac.net

page 319

page 291

page 7

page 165

page 223

page 35

page 95

Table of Contents

Part IV: Getting the Most out of Notes *165*

Foreword

● ●

*R*elease 3 of Notes was a great product; Release 4 is even better. We've added great user-interface features, completely rewritten the mail system, expanded programmability, added forms, improved performance, and just made life a lot easier for millions of present and future Notes users. We've also tightly integrated Notes with the Internet — the Notes client can access Web servers, and Notes servers can be accessed by Web browsers.

With all this capability, it can be challenging to get started; after all, it's easier to master riding a bicycle than a sleek new automobile. That's where this book comes in. *Lotus Notes Release 4 For Dummies* unravels most of the Notes mysteries and makes the program easy to understand in a simple, step-by-step way. Read it. Better yet, read it while you're at your Notes workstation, trying things out each step of the way. You'll be glad you did. And you'll have a great time getting to know Notes. This is a book that's not only useful but also enjoyable.

Notes will keep you connected to your organization and to your friends even when you're not connected to your network. Give it a try, and you'll be hooked — just like me. Good luck and good reading.

Mike Zisman
Executive V.P. and CEO
Lotus Development

Introduction

*Y*our company just decided to use Lotus Notes. Suddenly you're faced with the prospect of interacting with your fellow human beings by means of your computer, instead of via paper and the telephone. The prospect of going online may be as frightening as being forced to sit through Acts III & IV of *Hamlet* at your local high school. Or perhaps you've been online forever (you trendsetter, you!), but now you're going to start using Lotus Notes — and that's a new program to you.

Who needs Notes anyway? For what seems like ages, you've been sending memos on paper, calling people in distant offices on the phone and jotting little notes to yourself as you talk, and then filing these shreds of paper in the "In" box on your desk. Company policies, sales projections, marketing strategies, and other miscellaneous information are right at your fingertips — until the cleaning crew arrives and "cleans up" your desk. Now where *is* that sales sheet from last quarter?!

And how often have you been frustrated and delayed by something silly, like having to make copies of that memo you want to send to 25 people? Ensuring that up-to-date information is available to everyone who needs it is a big, time-consuming, and not-altogether-enticing task.

So who needs Notes? You may not know it yet, but *you* do! Notes can make your life easier with a capital E!

Notes is the program to use when you begin to realize that there has to be a better way — a way to get your work done more efficiently, a way to communicate and share information with people more quickly.

Notes is a program for getting information into the hands of the people who need it . . . and also for keeping that same information out of the hands of the people who *shouldn't* see it (no matter how much they want to snoop). With Notes, you don't have to worry about silly things like what kind of computer people have, or where they are, or what kind of network or modem they use.

Yeah, sounds great. But is it worth it? Do you have all kinds of time to invest in learning this (allegedly) wonderful program? Fear not. The book you're holding in your hot little hands will get you up and running as quickly as possible.

This book is for anyone who's using or planning to use Lotus Notes. You may be a relative Notes novice (or even a computer neophyte). Or maybe you're a cc:Mail jock who is about to launch into the wonderful world of Notes. Either way, you've come to the right place.

About This Book

We know that you're busy and that you hate to read computer manuals. So we designed this book to tell you what you need to know and to get you rolling as quickly and as painlessly as possible.

Among other things, you'll find the following:

- ✔ How to send an electronic message to one person or to a group of people — forget the copy machine, interoffice envelopes, and the like
- ✔ How to read, reply to, and (occasionally) ignore all the e-mail that you'll soon be receiving
- ✔ How to organize, print, save, and forward messages
- ✔ How to read and contribute to Notes databases, and how to store information in those databases so others can see it
- ✔ How to hide sensitive and confidential information from prying eyes
- ✔ How to create attractive documents
- ✔ How to communicate with the home office from your house or a hotel room
- ✔ How to cruise the Internet without leaving your chair (or Notes, for that matter)

Foolish Assumptions

Without so much as a phone call, we are making the following assumptions about you, dear reader:

- ✔ You want to know *what*, but not necessarily *why*. We'll leave the why to the computer nerds and concentrate on what's important to getting you working with Notes ASAP.
- ✔ You already have a computer that's had Notes installed on it (although you can use Appendix A if you really need to know how to install the program).
- ✔ You're willing to send a check for $357 to your beloved *Lotus Notes Release 4 For Dummies* authors. (Just kidding, although tips are appreciated.)

How to Use This Book

You have a choice: either read this book from cover to cover (you don't have to do it in one sitting!) or pick the particular topics that interest you and read just those parts in the order that makes the most sense for you. Either way, you'll get the information you need. In general, the concepts are straightforward, so you won't have any trouble jumping from chapter to chapter or from section to section.

We strive to avoid techno-babble and "geek speak" as much as we can. If a particular term is unfamiliar to you, you can always check the glossary at the end of the book. You can also use the Index and Table of Contents to find more information about any particular concept.

If we want you to type something, we'll put it in bold, like this:

Type this and then press Enter.

(In which case, you'd type "Type this" but not "and then press Enter." But you probably already figured that out.)

Sometimes we refer to text that you see on-screen. When we refer to the exact wording as it appears on the monitor, it will look like this: `Some words on your screen`. If the text's longer than a few words, it'll look like this:

```
This is how exact on-screen text or computer code will look.
```

We frequently tell you to make menu selections or use the SmartIcons (whatever those are). There will be a picture of the SmartIcon you should use in the margin. Menu items are presented like this: Choose File⇨Database⇨New. You simply click the first menu, then click the second one from the drop-down list, and so on. Or you can press Ctrl and then the underlined letter.

If a dialog box appears as you use a command, we'll reproduce it right in the book (in brilliant black and white) and tell you how to use it.

How This Book Is Organized

The arrangement and order of the chapters in this book reflect the way most people learn Notes.

Part I: Getting Acquainted with Notes

Here, we get the inevitable definitions out of the way and then jump right into getting Notes set up on your computer. Think of it as finding out what all those dials on the dashboard do before you try driving a car.

Part II: E-Mail for Everyone

This part deals with the most common thing you'll be doing on Notes: sending, receiving, and working with e-mail and memos.

Part III: The Brave New World of Notes Databases

The chapters in this section of the book show you how to get at the databases that your company has, how to read and create documents, how to create your own databases, and some other cool things that will expand your already dazzling command of the program.

Part IV: Getting the Most out of Notes

Eventually, you'll need to type special characters (like the © copyright symbol, among others), to modify the style of paragraphs, to customize and personalize the way Notes works on your computer, to use Notes with other programs, or to use Notes when you're away from the office. When that time comes, you'll want to peruse this part of the book.

Part V: Notes in the Fast Lane

When you're ready to move into high gear and take your Notes knowledge with you into the 21st century, turn (without delay) to Part V. In this part, we show you how to take Notes with you on your business trips, how to hop from Notes straight onto the Internet, and how to search through all your Notes databases at warp speed. Buckle up!

Part VI: The Part of Tens

Every single one of the books in the ...*For Dummies* series has a Part of Tens. Why should this book be any different? Here, we present an assortment of factoids that you'll find useful. This treasure trove of tips includes ten new features in Notes Release 4, ten cool tricks you can use to impress your friends, ten things you should never, ever do, and other cool tidbits. It's nowhere near as exciting as the Part of Tens in Dr. Ruth's *Sex For Dummies,* but it'll hold your interest!

Part VII: Appendixes

Appendix A takes you through installing Notes on your computer. Check out Appendix B for information about the database templates that come ready-made with Notes. For you world travelers, Appendix C details setting up Notes for use away from the office (AKA *remote setup*). Appendix D has some special tips for people who use Notes on Macintosh. We finish up the Appendixes with a glossary of the terms and concepts explained elsewhere in the book.

What You Don't Need to Read

We, of course, consider every last word in this book to be informative, insightful, and often quite humorous, and we can't think of a reason why you wouldn't want to read every one of the scintillating sentences contained herein. You, on the other hand, probably have better things to do. So we've marked the especially trivial details with a special Technical Stuff icon, so you know what you can (or can't) skip.

Icons Used in This Book

You'll see lots of little pictures (we call them *icons*) scattered amongst the pages of this book. Read on to see what each signifies.

This icon alerts you to information that's especially interesting to, uh, *nerds.* You know, the kind of people who always made your high-school math classes run late because they were asking so many questions? In some high schools, this person was all too often the victim of something known as a *wedgie,* but that's a separate book. We're not saying a bunch of football players will give you a wedgie if you read these sections, but then again. . . .

This icon tells you that some little shard of knowledge is coming that will make your life with Notes just a bit easier. Definitely worth reading.

As you stumble along the pathway of life, these little commandments are things that you should never forget. For example, you should always . . . well, it had something to do with, ummm. . . . We'll come back to this later.

Ignore this icon at your own peril. You've been warned.

So, Off You Go!

Get going, you have a lot of reading to do. Don't be afraid to experiment, and remember to check out the Help feature early and often.

Part I
Getting Acquainted with Notes

The 5th Wave   By Rich Tennant

"I requested an e-mail system for our office, and this is what we got."

In this part...

The first thing to do when you're using a new program is to find out the basic information. (Of course, most people install the program, make lots of mistakes, get mad, and then finally, after they have sputtered and fumed, turn to the instructions.) Notes is a really powerful and complex program. This part prepares you for Notes so that you can use it to its full potential, don't waste a lot of time, develop good habits, and don't curse the program because you couldn't figure out how to do something that just may not be that easy.

So, here in the first section of the book, we present the information you need to know to get started. We have attempted to avoid the technobabble where possible, but sometimes it actually helps to know the official terms. If you call your administrator and say, "The thingie next to the hinkyminky returns a box that says something when I clunk it," you can expect to be classified as someone who needs lots of help — next month. In the meantime, you're on your own.

Chapter 1

Just What Is Notes, Anyway?

. . . .

. . . .

*L*otus Notes is a computer program that lets you communicate and interact electronically with other people. You can use Notes to send people e-mail (whether or not they use Lotus Notes) and to share other kinds of information with them — like spreadsheets, word processing documents, and other stuff like that.

If you're a loner who doesn't like to talk to people, if you think "information is power" and don't like to share, well, then, you probably won't like Notes. If, on the other hand, your work means interacting with other people, and you want (or need) to share information with coworkers, customers, and the like, you'll be a Notes junkie in no time! You'll be sharing information and interacting with people in ways you probably haven't yet imagined.

The ultra-cool thing about Notes is that it's easy to use. You get to jump on the *electronic superhighway* (bet you haven't heard that expression before) with little or no knowledge of the messy underside of computers. If you find expressions like *local area network, ISDN,* and *HTML* scary (or even downright boring), Notes is the program for you! Leave all that technical jargon to the geeks and get to work! You can concentrate on the important things — like sending flattering e-mail to your boss, responding to your customers, and sounding lofty and knowledgeable at meetings.

And what's better, you don't even have to be at the office to participate in the aforementioned technological fiesta. If you have a modem, you can do all your work from home, the hotel, or even from an airplane; and your colleagues won't ever know that you're home goofing off!

What the Heck Is Groupware?

Groupware is software that allows you to work together with a group of other people. That was easy, wasn't it? Groupware won't make you a better golfer or help you win friends and influence people (use Dale Carnegie for that), but it can help you do the following:

- Send e-mail documents to individuals and groups.
- Create databases and put information into them that you, everyone, or only people you choose can read and edit.
- Be sure that the same information on a particular subject is available to everyone who is supposed to see it — regardless of where they are and without having to worry about what kind of computer or network they use.
- Allow everyone in the organization to communicate with each other as quickly as possible, whether the communication is gossip, news, or vital corporate data (assuming you can tell the difference).
- Be sure that forms and documents used in your organization are standard so that you all seem organized, even if you're not.
- Keep information in a safe and readily available place, rather than in piles on everyone's desk.
- Prevent prying, nosy, unauthorized busybodies from rummaging around in places where they have no business.
- Collect information from widely scattered sources.
- Eliminate the need to buy reams of former trees; instead, electronically store mountains of documents in a space smaller than a bread box.
- Combine data, graphics, text, and tables from many different places such as spreadsheet programs, word processors, and even the World Wide Web and the Internet.
- Hold information and e-mail for users who are only occasionally connected.

I mail, you mail, we all mail e-mail

Unless you've been living under a rock, you've heard of e-mail, and you probably know that the *e* stands for *electronic*. So, take away the *e* and you have *mail*, and that's all there is to it.

Most people prefer e-mail to p-mail (the *p* stands for *paper*) because e-mail is so fast; you can get a five-page e-mail to a coworker in Japan in just a few minutes. The post office can't compete with that! Plus, you don't need to hunt for stamps or walk down to the post office. You send e-mail right from your desk, without even leaving your chair. Just put a name at the top of a memo and click the Send button. Put several names at the top of the memo, and the memo goes to everyone. (Of course, there is the *little* matter of someone buying a computer for everyone, connecting them all together, and then buying Notes. But that's beside the point.)

In Notes, the e-mail you send goes to everyone you address it to and *only* to those people. If you write a nasty note about the boss and send it to a friend two floors down, you don't have to worry that the boss will see it — unless your (former) friend decides to forward it to the boss or to print it and hang it on the bulletin board.

In Notes e-mail, unlike some other e-mail systems I could mention, you can add text enhancements like boldface, italics, or underlining; you can change colors and fonts; you can add tables, links (whatever that means), and graphics. Instead of sending messages that make people yawn, you can make people sit up and take notice.

And, barring the rare (and expensive) system breakdown, you can be confident that your Notes e-mail message will be delivered. Contrast this assurance with a memo slipped into a company mailer and left to languish in the quagmire of interoffice mail. Figure 1-1 shows a memo addressed to Rich Lanchantin, with a courtesy copy (cc) to Leslie Igoe and one to a group called the Planning Department. All these people will receive the memo in time to act on the schedule changes.

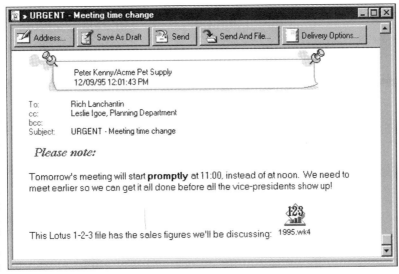

Figure 1-1:
You can send short memos like this to many people quickly and easily, without leaving the comfort of your chair.

This being the 1990s and all, more and more people around the world are hooked up with all sorts of e-mail programs. With Notes, you can send an e-mail message to your friend (who works at another company), your cousin (who's studying art in Paris), or even to your kid (who's at home using America Online).

Databasically

The most important concept in Notes is the *database*. In fact, the entire program is organized around databases. A *database* is just a bunch of information grouped together. The Sears Roebuck catalog is really a database — it's organized in alphabetic order, with the name, description, picture, and price of each item kept nice and neat. But the only way to find an item in the Sears catalog is to turn the pages and let your fingers do the walking. That's where electronic databases are much more useful.

When you use Notes, you create *documents:* memos, company policy statements, sales records, or listings of baseball statistics. These documents are all stored in databases with other documents of the same type. You can select information from that database without ever turning pages or scanning long lists. Ask your database to show you all sales contacts in Alabama, for example, and, as quickly as the electrons can arrange themselves, the list of Alabama sales contacts appears on-screen. (How y'all doin'?)

A good example of a Notes database is a *discussion database,* which is the electronic equivalent of the backyard fence. You can express your opinion on a particular subject by composing a main document. Then someone in the Singapore office may compose a reply to your statement telling you that you're all wet. Someone in Stockholm can compose a response to that response, telling the Singapore person to lay off you. And so on. Others may sound off about their own opinions by writing entries to the discussion database. People anywhere and everywhere in your organization can respond to these opinions.

You can write your opinion using Notes working in Windows, while one person's response is created on a Macintosh, and others are using UNIX or OS/2. Everyone can read all the documents, regardless of what kind of computer the documents were composed on. All of you can share not only your highly-sought-after opinions, but also drawings, enhanced text, and even information from other sources like Excel or the Internet.

In Notes, databases contain *views.* Views contain *documents.* Documents contain *fields.* And fields contain individual pieces of data. See, the whole concept is based on data, and that's why it's called a *data*base. Don't let all these new words bog you down. We get into what they mean for you and how you can put them to good use in future chapters. For now, we just want to give you the big picture.

You Can't Be All Things to All People

So Notes is groupware with amazing e-mail and database capabilities. But, for all its power and glory, there are some things that Notes isn't.

What Notes isn't

Notes is a database program, that's for sure. But it isn't a true *relational database*. Relational databases allow you to enter data in a field in one database and then use that same field in another database. Notes can't do that. Unless you're a database design jockey, you probably don't give two toots about whether a database is relational. But the fact that Notes isn't relational translates into some good news and some bad news for you.

The good news is that Notes is not rigid. Unlike other databases, Notes doesn't require you to set the size of a field and then limit entries in that field to your specified maximum size. (*Fields,* as you may or may not yet know, are the little bits of information, like a person's last name, that make up a document.) You can enter any amount of data in a Notes database field without having to redesign your database. For example, in other programs, you would have to decide how many characters a Last Name field would accept. Suppose you allow 20 characters, and then you hire John-Jacob Jingleheimerschmidt. You would either have to be satisfied with "J J Jingleheimerschm," or you would have to go through the nail-breaking procedure of redesigning the database. With Notes, you just type away, secure in the knowledge that Notes will accept anything and everything that you type.

Because it isn't rigid, Notes allows you to create *rich text fields*. A rich text field is one in which you can add such fancy stuff as character formats (boldface and italics, for instance), linked or embedded objects, or video clips and pictures of your (no doubt) lovely children.

So, if that's the good news, what's the bad news? If you need to use your computer to track customer orders, and you have 92,000 of them to track, Notes isn't the best choice. (Kind of like using a nail file as a screw driver.) Applications that require the care and management of thousands and thousands of records of information probably *don't* belong in Notes.

Not only is Notes not a relational database, it also isn't the program to use for *transaction-based systems*, such as airline ticketing. Imagine lots of offices (all in different cities) selling lots of tickets for a particular flight and recording the data on their local copy of the reservations database. Later, at flight time, a huge crowd appears, everyone with tickets for the same seat on the same plane. When you need *immediate* sharing of information everywhere, you should use terminals connected to a single gigantic computer somewhere. Notes allows periodic, but not immediate, sharing of updates to databases.

But don't worry, it's probably not your decision whether you use Notes, anyway. Let the geeks in MIS decide whether Notes is the right tool for your company. Just make sure that you tell them to buy lots of copies of this book — whatever they decide!

What Notes is

Notes is a truly useful and powerful program because of its ability to send e-mail *and* create databases of all sorts that every person in the organization can share, add to, and read. This pair of abilities makes Notes able to leap tall buildings in a single bound, more powerful than . . . well, more powerful than programs that allow you only to send e-mail or only to create databases.

Rich text fields and other Notes fields have an advantage over those in regular databases: they don't have a field size limit. In other database programs, changing the size of a field in a large database can be a heck of a lot of work and, if not done correctly, can corrupt your database. Whether you put one word or a whole book in a Notes field makes no difference to Notes.

Fields in other databases are, in a word, *blah*. No boldface, no variety in fonts, and no possibility for attachments or embedded objects. Not so with rich text fields, because they contain more than just information. Rich text fields can contain anything your heart desires to put there in order to set them apart from the mundane, to educate and excite the readers, and to allow you to express yourself as the creative genius that you are.

With Notes, you can create databases for any of the following uses:

- **Reference:** Members of your organization seeking knowledge can find what they need to know, contributed by those who have knowledge to share — from each according to his or her ability, to each according to his or her need. Kind of brings a tear to your eye.

- **Workflow:** Those charged with a broad task can record the individual assignments and proclaim the completion of each, documenting progress toward a job well done.

- **E-mail:** Anyone in the organization can communicate privately or publicly with anyone they choose.

- **Fax:** One of the means by which valuable data stored in your organization's databases can be distributed to a needy and grateful public.

This, then, is Notes. More than just a program, more than just a database, more than just an e-mail facility — Notes is a dynamic tool allowing the sharing of knowledge throughout the organization. Because, when all is said and done, knowledge *is* power.

What Makes Notes So Special?

A couple of additional features that distinguish Notes from mere e-mail programs or database programs are its ability to make compound documents and to replicate databases.

Compound documents — feel that power

You've heard of compound fractures, right? Well, compound documents are nothing like them. Does that help? No? Well, they're not like the compound eye on an insect either. Getting clearer? Well, how about this.

Normally, when you're busy using Notes, you are typing a memo or filling in a form or writing some text to be included with other similar entries in a database. Sometimes, however, you need to put more than just text in your document.

To emphasize a point you're making about sales figures, you may want to include a spreadsheet that you created in Lotus 1-2-3. A graph that you made in Freelance would help — and maybe even a link to a related home page that you found on the World Wide Web. So you copy and paste them all into your document.

The result? A *compound document*, containing data, graphics, or other features from other programs. Figure 1-2 is a simple example of a compound document containing a small spreadsheet and a graph. (We discuss compound documents in greater detail in Chapter 16.)

Figure 1-2:
This is an example of a compound document; it has a table, a pie chart from Lotus 1-2-3, and some bold and italicized text.

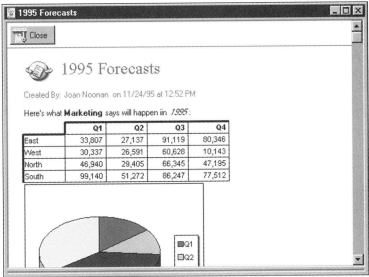

1995 Forecasts

Created By: Joan Noonan on 11/24/95 at 12:52 PM

Here's what **Marketing** says will happen iin *1995*:

	Q1	Q2	Q3	Q4
East	33,807	27,137	91,119	80,346
West	30,337	26,591	60,628	10,143
North	46,940	29,405	66,345	47,195
South	99,140	51,272	86,247	77,512

Replication: an explanation

Replication is what makes Notes the great program that it is. Oh sure, other programs allow you to send e-mail, but they don't replicate. As we explained earlier, your mail database is only one kind of database that can exist in Notes. Chances are that other databases have been created throughout your organization. *Replicas*, copies of those databases, may be on many servers in your organization around the world. This magic is how your colleague in France can see what you've been working on. He looks at a *replica copy* of the database in question on his server in Paris while you look at a copy of the same database on your server in, say, Chicago.

One example of this technological feat is a database listing each employee's name, employee number, location, shoe size, and other important data. At each location, these replicas are updated as people are hired, fired, or change their shoe sizes. Obviously, employees at each location will enter different information into the database. Replication enables Notes to make all the databases contain the same information.

When the replication is complete, all replicas have the same information so that up-to-date information is available everywhere. Every so often, the server in France "talks to" your server in Chicago so that the two servers can synchronize their copy of the database. That way, the Chicago server ends up with the documents that your French colleague has been composing, while at the same time the server computer *en France* gets the documents that you've been adding to the database. Pretty cool, *non?* Don't get too worried about this, because it's not your job to set it up and make it happen!

But replication is also the process by which remote workstations update their own local databases, including your mail database. So, when you take your laptop on a trip to Denver, you'll *replicate* with the server back at the home office, too. The frequency of replication is a decision that the owner of the remote workstation makes. In a database that has a rapid turnover of information, replicating several times a day might be necessary. In a database that doesn't change often, such as one listing corporate policies, replicating may only be necessary about once a month.

Who's the Boss?

Notes uses computers all hooked together in a *network*. In some ways, a network is like a department in a corporation, because it has individual workers and someone in charge. The individual computers need to be connected to a *boss* computer in order to be able to work together. No doubt your boss serves the same vital role in your department.

Service with a smile: Notes servers

By a curious twist of fate, the computer in charge of a Notes network is called the *server*. The server acts as a central, shared computer for the others, storing the mail databases for all the people whose computers are hooked to it and regulating the flow of information. It may also store other databases created by users who want the information for others to share. The server usually is a more powerful computer with more storage than the ones connected to it, and it's kept in a physically secure and remote location. Is this beginning to sound like your boss — powerful, having the best equipment, remote, and in charge? The server may also be like your boss in that it's not where the regular work in Notes is done. The actual work is done on the individual computers connected to the server.

In large organizations, many servers (all around the world), each with their own bunch of attached computers, are connected together over the company-wide network.

Down by the workstation

In the wonderful world of Notes, your computer is known as a *workstation*. This is where individual users get the real work done. Workstations usually contain the Notes program files for each individual user, as well as any databases that the users create for their own personal use.

Not all workstations are always connected to a server. If you go on a business trip and take your laptop computer, you would need a long network cable to connect directly to the office, unless your business trip only takes you to the parking lot. When you use your computer to connect to the server by phone line and modem, your computer is called a *remote workstation*. Some workstations are both LAN and remote. If you have a laptop, you can hook it to the LAN when you are at the office and then use its modem for a remote hookup when you are on the road.

No matter how fast your modem is, you'll find that using it is slower than using Notes on the LAN. So plan on taking extra time with the modem and be sure your teenager won't need the phone for a while.

Your User ID — The Key to Notes

When you were born, the hospital gave your mother a copy of your birth certificate. When you graduated from high school, you got a diploma. And when you learned to drive, you got a driver's license. When you start using Notes, someone is going to give you what's known as a *User ID*.

Don't expect to get a copy of Notes, install it on your computer, and then be able to tap into the nerve center of your company. Even if you're the company president and have a fistful of Notes disks, even if you *do* lunch rather than eat it, even if you have the fanciest car in the lot, until you get that User ID, you don't have a prayer of being able to use Notes.

When you get your User ID, you have the key that gets you access to your own mail database and the other databases in the company. Figure 1-3 shows some information about a User ID. To you, this may only look like a series of numbers and letters, but to the servers, it's what makes you a legitimate user of Notes in your organization.

Those last three words are very important, by the way. Your User ID makes you a member of *your* organization. You can't sneak into your competitors' offices down the street and use your User ID in their Notes network, because your User ID is created by and recognized only by your own organization.

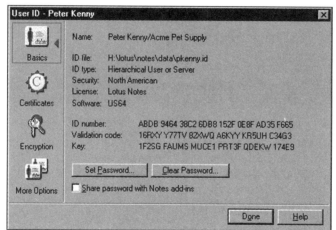

Figure 1-3:
This is a
sample
User ID.

Keep a copy of your Notes User ID on a floppy disk so that you'll be able to copy it back to your hard disk if you accidentally delete your Notes program files, or if you experience the heartbreak of computer failure. Remember, if your computer breaks down, your User ID enables you to use another person's computer as if it were your own. For this reason, you should keep your Notes User ID in a secure place (under lock and key).

When push comes to shove, your User ID is just another (small) file on your computer. You'll need your User ID each and every time you use Notes. Most people keep their User ID file on their hard disk. If you want to use your computer at home to do some work, you'll have to make a copy of your User ID file and bring that copy home with you. You can't use Notes without a copy of that User ID. Never, ever — no fooling.

Chapter 2

Get Rolling with Notes!

So, your company just got Lotus Notes, and you're all excited about the idea that you'll be using this powerful, state-of-the-art program that you've heard so much about. Alternately, maybe you aren't so thrilled. Your boss told you that you had to start using Notes, and you're not exactly overjoyed at the prospect of installing and learning yet another software program. In either case, the good news is that learning how to set up, start, and stop the program isn't all that difficult.

This is the one and only chapter in this whole book where you have to be careful to follow the steps exactly as they're outlined. (Sometimes, you just gotta play by the rules. . . .)

Before You Start Notes for the First Time: Stuff You Need to Ask Your Administrator

You may be used to programs that let you just install them, start them, and get to work. Not Notes. When you start Notes for the very first time, you need to be prepared to answer a few questions, and the best way to get the answers is to ask someone. Your Notes administrator will be able to provide you with the information that you need for your first date with Notes. Don't even bother trying to use the program until you've gotten the answers.

Get on the phone, call your administrator, and ask for the answers to the questions in Table 2-1. And don't worry if you don't understand the answers (or the questions)!

Table 2-1	Stuff to Ask Your Friendly Notes Administrator
The Question	*The Answer*
How will I be connecting to my Notes server?	Pick one: ( ) By the network ( ) By a modem ( ) Both ways ( ) Neither way
How will I get my User ID?	Pick one: ( ) From the Name and Address Book ( ) On a disk
User ID filename:	( )
What is my password?	( )
What is my exact User Name?	( )
What is the name of my home server?	( )
What is my network type?	( )
Some Time Info:	
What is my time zone?	( )
Do we follow Daylight Savings Time?	Pick one: ( ) Yes ( ) No

Notes administrators are important people because they can make your life with Notes nothing but smooth sailing, or they can make your life with Notes an absolute nightmare. So we advise being very nice to them. Be polite and be courteous to them on the phone — and don't rule out a small cash gift from time to time, just to keep them cheerful. You'll thank yourself for this fore-thought when you need your adminstrator to dig you out of a problem.

When you start Notes for the first time, there's a little bit of work the program has to do — such as find your mail database, set up your desktop, and so on. How Notes handles this setup depends on how you'll be connecting to your Notes server. The steps are quite different if you're using Notes on a network than if you're using it *remotely* (at home, in a hotel room, or in any other place that's not connected to a network). If you're starting Notes for the first time from a remote location, you need to check out Appendix A.

Starting the Program

First things first: you need to start the program. To do so, double-click the Notes program icon. Where is this mysterious Notes icon? Well, that all depends on where you put it when you installed the program. (Refer to Appendix A for more information on how to install the program.) The icon you're trying to find looks like Figure 2-1. It's hard to say exactly where it will be on your computer, because a lot depends on whether you're using Windows 95, Macintosh, or whatever. If you're using Windows 95, for example, you'll find the Notes program icon in the Start Programs menu.

Figure 2-1:
The Notes program icon.

When you finally find the icon, double-click it to start the program. Notes starts, and you see what's called the *splash screen,* shown in Figure 2-2. (Don't worry if the splash screen you see is a little different from the one pictured here!)

Figure 2-2:
You'll see this screen every time you start Lotus Notes.

Don't even think about starting Notes unless you have answers to all the questions in Table 2-1.

Setting Up Notes

After showing you the splash screen, Notes is smart enough to figure out that this is your first time using the program. Here comes the tricky part: the set-up questions. To answer them, make sure you have the worksheet in Table 2-1 handy.

You will not be able to set up Notes without first consulting with your Notes administrator. Read the beginning of this chapter if you haven't done so yet.

The first time you start Notes, the program leads you through the dreaded setup. Notes is going to create your desktop, build a Personal Name and Address Book for you, and much, much more. The good news is that this laborious process only has to happen once — the very first time you start Notes. Next time, Notes won't have to ask you all these questions. That's a promise!

The very first thing you see after the splash screen is a dialog box that looks like Figure 2-3. Here, you tell Notes how you'll be connecting to your Notes server and where your User ID is coming from.

Figure 2-3:
Use the
worksheet
in Table 2-1
to complete
this dialog
box.

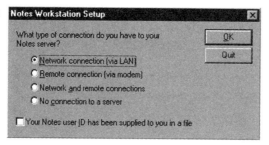

Your User ID is a file that was created for you by your administrator, and you need it to run the program — this time and every time. If you don't know what a User ID is (never mind where it's coming from!), refer to this book's Introduction.

What you see after you click OK in the dialog box shown in Figure 2-3 depends on whether you clicked the box that says `Your Notes user ID has been supplied to you in a file.`

If your User ID was supplied to you in a file (in other words, your administrator gave you a disk with your ID), Notes will ask you if you want to Copy your User ID to your data directory. If you choose Yes, Notes copies your User ID to your hard disk and will look there every time you run the program. If you choose No, you'll have to insert the floppy disk that you got from your administrator each and every time you want to use the program. (More secure, but less convenient.) Most people choose Yes.

After you've told Notes where your User ID is and what your home server's name is, you have to prove to Notes that you are who you say you are by entering your password in the dialog box shown in Figure 2-4.

Figure 2-4:
This dialog
box (with
cool
hieroglyphics)
appears
each time
you enter
your
password.

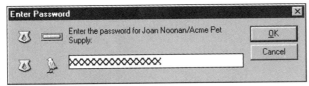

Get used to entering your password, because Notes will ask you for it every time you use the program, day in and day out. Later on, you should change your password to something that your administrator won't know. But, for now, you can enter the one that your administrator assigned to you.

When you change your password, make it something easy to remember but not too obvious. Forgetting your password or using an easily guessable password is a Very Bad Thing.

Don't be surprised to see a bunch of Xs as you type your password; Notes displays Xs in place of letters so anyone who might be looking over your shoulder can't figure out what your password is. (Consequently, we do not recommend making your password a bunch of Xs.)

After you've entered your name, User ID, and home server name, Notes has a little work to do. Be patient; the work shouldn't take more than five minutes.

Don't be surprised if your administrator tells you that your User Name has a bunch of slashes in it. Notes names are things like "Robert Donnelly/Sales/NTS Associates," or maybe "William Beer/IDG." His mother and friends might call him Billy, but to Notes he's "William Beer/IDG."

The last dialog box you'll have to deal with during Setup asks you about your time zone. Pick the appropriate time zone, tell Notes whether you observe DST, and click OK. Hey, congratulations — Notes Setup is complete! Remember, starting the program next time won't be so arduous — it was only painful because this was your first time. Your reward for completing this long, drawn-out, painful process is the dialog box you see in Figure 2-5.

After the setup's complete, you'll notice (pay attention!) that Notes has automatically added three database icons to your workspace, as shown in Figure 2-6. These three icons represent your own personal mail database, your own Personal Name and Address Book, and your company's Public Name and Address Book. (We discuss how you actually use each of these databases in Chapters 4 and 5.)

Figure 2-5:
Notes tells
you when
you're done
setting up
for the
first time.

You might find that your new Notes workspace has more or fewer icons than the standard three. As usual, it depends on how your administrator has set up Notes at your company, so don't be alarmed if what you see on your computer is a little different from what you see in Figure 2-6.

Figure 2-6:
Three icons
appear
on-screen
when you
start for the
first time.

Understanding the Workspace

Now that Notes is running, how do you get started? At the starting gun, you should see something that looks like Figure 2-7 — it's your *workspace*. You need to know about the five main elements of the Notes workspace:

- ✔ The menus
- ✔ The SmartIcons
- ✔ The database icons
- ✔ The workspace tabs
- ✔ The Status bar

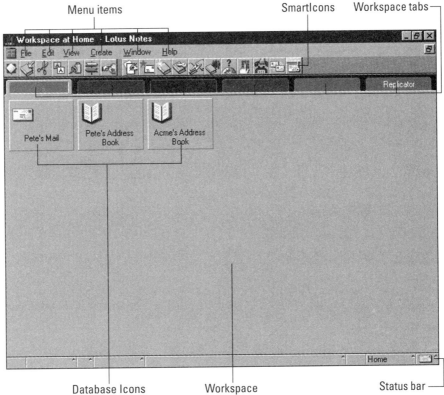

Figure 2-7:
The Notes
workspace.

What's on the menu?

More good news: the menus work exactly the way you'd expect them to. You're probably already familiar with many of the options available on the Notes menu, because many are the same as the options in other programs you may use. For example, you save a document in Notes the same way you save a spreadsheet in Lotus 1-2-3, which is the same way you save a document in Microsoft Word.

If you are a mouse user, you can open any menu item by clicking it. If you don't like to (and don't want to) use the mouse, you can press Alt and then use the right- and left-arrow keys to select the menu you want. (Press Enter when you've got it selected.) You can use the same strategy to actually pick any of the items in a menu; use the arrow keys to select the item you want to choose and then press Enter, or just click it.

You'll notice that some of the words in the menus are gray, and others are black. You can only choose the black ones because, when a menu option is grayed out, that means that the choice isn't appropriate right now. For example, if you were in the middle of editing a document and took a look at the Edit menu, you'll see that the Select by Date... option is gray. That just means that Selecting by Date (whatever that means!) is not an option while you're editing a document.

You'll also notice that some menu items have a little triangle after them. (Check out the Edit menu for an example.) Whenever you see a menu item followed by one of these little triangle things, you know that this menu item leads to another menu item, as shown in Figure 2-8. (Mac users see ellipses [...] instead of triangles in their menus.)

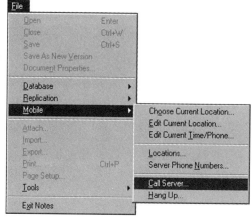

Figure 2-8:
Triangles in the menu are your cue that there's a submenu associated with that choice.

In addition to seeing triangles all over the place, have you noticed that some menu options are followed by an ellipsis (like the Call Server item in Figure 2-8)? Those three dots tell you that that item leads not to another menu, but to a dialog box.

Wise up with SmartIcons

If you've ever used any of the Lotus SmartSuite applications before, you should recognize the row of small pictures that's stretched across the top of the screen; these pictures are what Lotus calls *SmartIcons*. SmartIcons are just a way for you to execute certain commands very quickly — without having to use the menus. For example, if you want to print the document that's on-screen, you can choose File⇨Print, but it's easier and faster to click the Print SmartIcon, shown in Figure 2-9. (Lotus probably wouldn't like to admit it, but their SmartIcons are an awful lot like the buttons found on Microsoft's Button Bar. Or maybe Microsoft's buttons are an awful lot like Lotus's SmartIcons. . . .)

Figure 2-9:
Using a
SmartIcon is
often the
quickest
and easiest
way to do
something.

Some SmartIcons are obvious — or relatively obvious, anyway. For example, you can probably guess that the one that looks like a small jar of library paste is the one you use to paste from the Clipboard. Some of the SmartIcons aren't so obvious, though. What about the sixth one from the left — the one with red and green arrows that sort of look like a traffic sign? (Incidentally, that's one of the Help SmartIcons.) Fear not, though, you don't have to be an Egyptologist to use the SmartIcons.

If you can't guess what a SmartIcon is going to do for you, just point to it and then wait a second or two. A cute little balloon thingy appears like magic to tell you what's what — like Figure 2-10. (Okay, so even some of the balloon hints don't make sense, but a lousy hint is better than no hint, right?) If you want to see the SmartIcon hints on your Mac, you'll have to choose Balloon Help⇨Show Balloons (that's the little question mark in the upper-right corner of the screen).

More SmartIcons exist than first appear — in fact, probably more than you'll ever use. (There's probably a SmartIcon for just about every item in every menu.) Because so many SmartIcons are available, Lotus has collected them into palettes. The idea here is that the SmartIcons you'll use when you read a message are probably not the best ones to have around when you compose a message. So don't be surprised if you notice the SmartIcons changing; they're *context-sensitive*. That means that the SmartIcons you see in one context (like reading your e-mail) are different from the ones you see in a different context (like setting up your modem).

Dealing with database icons

The workspace is the part of the screen that you use more than any other part. It is made up of a series of six pages, each of which can hold many database icons. We'll discuss exactly what these pages are all about in the upcoming section "Keeping tabs on your pages." For now, think of each page as being a place to hold a bunch of database icons.

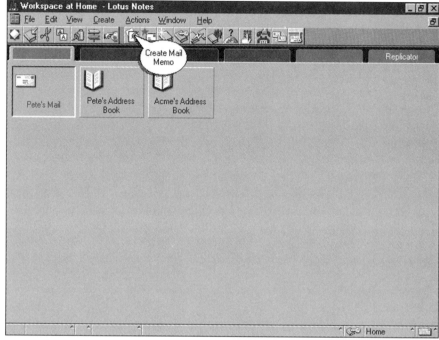

Figure 2-10:
You can get a hint for any SmartIcon by putting the mouse pointer on it and waiting a second.

"So," you ask, "just what *is* a database icon, anyway?" Each of the little blocks in your workspace is called a *database icon* and represents a Notes database. The icon usually has a little picture (your mail database has a picture of an envelope) and a title (your mail database's title probably isn't "Stephen Londergan's Mail," but we know of at least one person whose is).

Opening a database

When you want to open a database to read the documents it contains, just double-click the icon for that database. For example, if you, Jane Q. Public, want to read your mail, just double-click the icon that says `Jane Q. Public's Mail` and Presto! You've just opened that database, and there's your mail.

If you have mouse-a-phobia, use the arrow keys instead to select the icon you want and then press Enter. Or, to open a database the really hard way, use the arrow keys to select the icon you want and then choose File⇨Open.

Closing a database

Closing a database is one of the simplest things in the world. If you're in a database and you want to close it and return to the desktop, choose File⇨Close. You can also close a database (or any open window, for that matter) by pressing Esc.

Making those icons more informative

You can change the way database icons look in two different ways.

- ✔ You can have each icon tell you how many new, unread documents are in the database.
- ✔ You can have the database icons tell you where the database is located.

If you choose <u>V</u>iew⇨Re<u>f</u>resh Unread Count, the icons expand to show you the number of new, unread documents in each database, as you can see in Figure 2-11.

Whenever you want Notes to update the number of unread documents that appear in the icons, press F9 or choose <u>V</u>iew⇨Re<u>f</u>resh Unread Count. Notes then checks each database to see whether any new documents have been added to the databases since you started the program (or since the last time you selected <u>V</u>iew⇨Re<u>f</u>resh Unread Count).

If you choose <u>V</u>iew⇨Show <u>S</u>erver Names, the icon titles change to include the location of the database. Try <u>V</u>iew⇨Show <u>S</u>erver Names and then look at your icons for the Name and Address Books. (If you're not sitting in front of your computer, just take a look at Figure 2-12.)

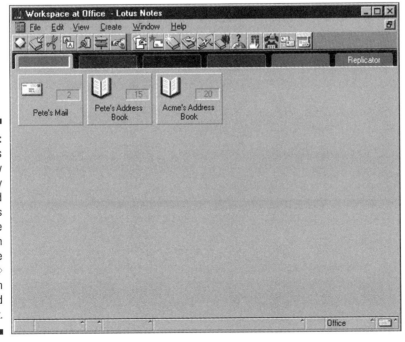

Figure 2-11:
Notes tells you how many Unread documents a database has when you choose <u>V</u>iew⇨ Re<u>f</u>resh Unread Count.

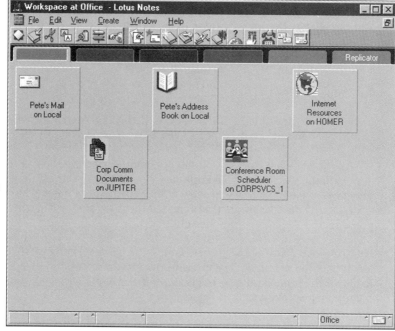

Figure 2-12:
Notes
database
icons can
tell you
where each
database is
located.

In our example, one of the databases is named Internet Resources on HOMER, and the other is named Pete's Address Book on Local. Because the first database's title includes the words "on HOMER," you know that it is actually located on a Notes server named HOMER. Because the other database says "on Local," you know that that database is stored right on your own hard disk. When Notes tells you a database is Local, it really means that the database is on your hard disk, on your computer.

But you really don't have to worry about where a database is stored. You open them, close them, and use them exactly the same way, no matter where they are.

Moving, arranging, and deleting database icons

Besides opening a database, you can do two other things with the database icons: move 'em and delete 'em.

To move a database icon to another part of the page or to another page altogether, do the following:

1. **Point to the database icon with the mouse.**

2. **Press and hold down the left (primary) mouse button.**

3. **Drag the icon to its new home. Welcome to the neighborhood!**

   (If you want to drag the icon to a new page altogether, drop it on that page's tab.)

You can also choose View⇨Arrange Icons to have Notes make all the icons on the current workspace nice and neat.

To delete a database icon, follow these steps:

1. **Select the database icon that you want to delete by clicking it once or by using the cursor keys.**

2. **Press Delete (or choose Edit⇨Clear).**

Deleting an icon just means that you don't want that database on your screen every day; it does *not* delete the actual database from the server (or from your hard disk, if it's a local database).

If you blow it and end up deleting an icon that you shouldn't have deleted, just select File⇨Database⇨Open to get it right back again.

Keeping tabs on your pages

If you refer back to Figure 2-7, you can see that the Notes desktop comes ready-made with six pages, each with a tab sticking up just below the menu bar. You use these pages to store and organize database icons. For example, you may decide to put all the database icons from your marketing project on one page, all your icons related to mail on another page, and so on.

If you want to see the icons that are on a different page than the one you're on, you just click that page's tab. The screen then changes to show you the icons on that page.

You can even choose a name and a color for each of your page tabs.

1. **Double-click a page tab.**

   You'll get a dialog box like the one in Figure 2-13.

2. **Type the name (up to 32 letters) which you'd like to appear on the tab.**

3. **Choose the tab's color.**

4. **Click OK.**

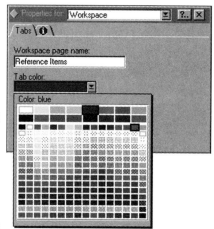

Figure 2-13:
Naming a
workspace
tab and
choosing a
color for it.

Your Notes workspace comes complete with six pages (no assembly required), but you can have more or fewer pages, if you want.

✔ To add a new workspace page, choose Create⮞Workspace Page. (That's easy, huh?)

✔ To remove a page, click the page's tab and choose Edit⮞Clear (or just press Del).

When you remove a workspace page, you also remove all the database icons on that page. It's usually a good idea to move database icons off of a page before you delete the page.

Now that you know how to add and remove pages, you should also know that most people don't bother. Because any one page can have as many databases as you want on it, why bother with all these extra pages? Take a look at Figure 2-14. Pretty silly, huh?

Checking your Status bar

Last but not least, we have the Status bar. (If you use any other Lotus products, you already recognize this feature, because all of Lotus's SmartSuite products have it.) The Status bar is that band that runs along the bottom of the screen and is another shortcut of sorts. It displays information for you (that's where you'll see the `New mail has been delivered to you` messages), and you can also use it to change fonts and type sizes. Refer to Chapter 12 for more information about the Status bar. For now, just bask in the knowledge that you've seen it.

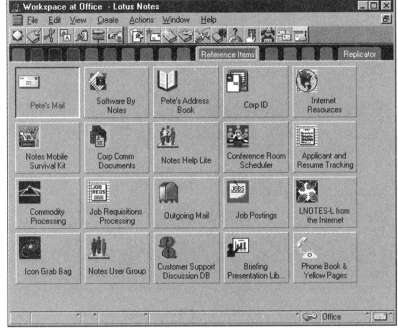

Figure 2-14:
Don't get carried away with adding too many workspace pages!

Multitasking (It's Not as Hard as It Sounds)

One of the advantages to using Windows, OS/2, Macintosh, or UNIX is that these operating systems can multitask. *Multitask* is a $25 computer word for an operating system that can run more than one program at the same time.

What does that mean to you? Let's say that you're using Notes to read e-mail. After you've finished reading your e-mail, you have to do some work in your spreadsheet program. Sure, you could exit Notes and then start Excel, but what happens when you want to check your e-mail again in a half-hour? Are you going to shut down Excel, start Notes, and then, after you've read your new e-mail, shut down Notes to start Excel again? Of course not! You're going to multitask. (Sounds exciting, doesn't it?)

If you want to temporarily leave your Notes session to start a different program, don't exit Notes. Use your operating system command to leave Notes "up and running" while you go do your other work. (As always, the way you do this depends on the operating system.) If you leave Notes running while you're in that other program, you'll be able to switch back and forth between the programs much more quickly and easily.

The really cool thing about leaving Notes running while you're in another program is that Notes is able to notify you when you've received new mail, even though you may be typing a letter in WordPerfect. You'll occasionally hear a sort of "beep beep beep" message, which is Notes' way of telling you that you have new mail.

If you want to get the "beep beep beep — New mail has been delivered to you" messages while you're using some other program, you have to leave Notes running while using other programs. You will not get this notification if you shut down Notes the instant you're finished with it. In fact, most people leave Notes up and running all day long.

The way you switch from one active program to another depends on the operating system you use.

- ✔ **In Windows:** Press Ctrl+Esc to get the Start menu, choose the program you want to switch to, and click OK.

- ✔ **On a Macintosh:** From the Application menu, choose the program you want to switch to. To start a new program, choose Finder from the Application menu and then start the program as you normally would.

- ✔ **In OS/2:** Press Ctrl+Esc to get the task list and then choose the program you want to switch to. To start a new program, choose Main from the dialog box and then start the other program as you normally would.

When It's Time to Say Good-bye . . .

When you're finished using Notes (is it time to go home already?), exit Notes the way you exit any other program. The easiest way to tell Notes that you're done is to choose File⇨Exit. Depending on your operating system, you may have other, snazzier ways to end the program. For example, with Windows 95 you can press Alt+F4 to end the Notes task. There's a similar process in OS/2. So, if you're a techno-jock and you know some other fancy way to shut down Notes, we say go for it. But when you're done showing off, the easiest way to stop Notes will always be to choose File⇨Exit.

Part II
E-Mail for Everyone

"Dang it. I told you switching to groupware would disrupt the workflow around here."

In this part...

*A*fter you know what Notes is and what it isn't, and you can use random bits of Notes terminology to the amazement of your friends and/or coworkers, you're ready to actually send a memo. Maybe you can already read a message if someone sends you one. Then again, maybe there are fifty memos crowding your mail database, each with things you should have done yesterday, the boss is drumming her fingers, and here you are reading this little introduction.

This section explains the e-mail part of Notes and makes you wonder why the heck any office ever bothers with paper and phone calls.

Chapter 3
Gotta Get My E-Mail!

. . . .

In This Chapter

▶ Opening your mail database

▶ Reading your mail

. . . .

*Y*our regular mail arrives in a mailbox at the end of your driveway. Your mailbox for e-mail, on the other hand, is shaped remarkably like a computer. Actually, although you read your e-mail while sitting at your computer, your e-mail database is really on the server computer, not your own computer. To get at your e-mail, you need to have an icon in your desktop for your mail database. (If you can't find that icon, consult Chapter 2.)

May I Have the Envelope, Please

To open your e-mail database, either double-click your mail database icon or select the database and press Enter. You should see something that looks very much like Figure 3-1. There, in a list, is your very own, personal, for-your-eyes-only e-mail.

We should mention right up front that nobody but you can open *your* mail database. (And you can't open anyone else's, either. Not that you'd even think of doing it.)

Actually, as you can see in Figure 3-1, there's more than just your mail on-screen when you open your e-mail database. In fact, the screen is divided into four parts.

✔ The first pane (as you can see in the figure) is called the *Navigation pane.* You use this pane to sort the messages in your mail database.

✔ On the right-hand side of the screen is the *View pane.* This is a summary of the messages in your mail database.

The View pane

The Action bar

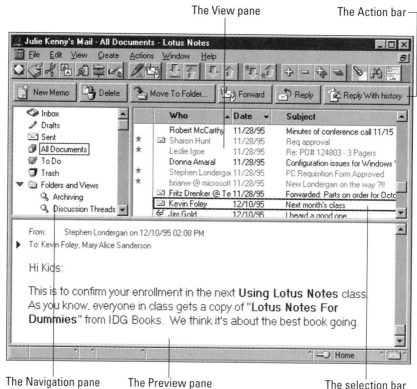

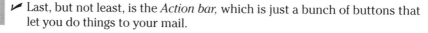

Figure 3-1:
Your e-mail
database
looks a lot
like this one.

The Navigation pane   The Preview pane   The selection bar

✔ Beneath the Navigation and View panes is the *Preview pane,* in which is displayed an actual e-mail message, sent to you by an actual person. (If your mail database doesn't have a Preview pane, choose <u>V</u>iew⇨Document Preview.)

✔ Last, but not least, is the *Action bar,* which is just a bunch of buttons that let you do things to your mail.

A rose is a rose is a memo is a message! The words *memo, document, message,* or even *e-mail* are often used interchangeably. They all mean the same thing.

Using Your Mail

Onward, upward, and e-ward! Get ready to see how you can adjust the panes, rearrange your messages, and (most important) read your messages.

Having it your way

Although the Action bar at the top of the screen isn't going anywhere, you can pick a couple of different ways to arrange the rest of your e-mail database.

When you choose View⇨Arrange Preview, you see the dialog box like this:

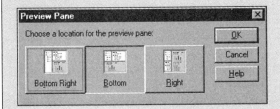

Pick the layout that turns you on and click OK.

We suggest you try each of the Layout options in the Preview Pane dialog box to find out which one works best for you.

The Navigation pane

The Navigation pane gives you a way to sort and rearrange all the messages in your mail database; each of the items in the Navigation pane is called a *folder*. For example, the Inbox folder shows you all the messages that have been sent to you (and not the messages you have sent to other people).

There are eight (count 'em) important folders in the Navigation pane — listed, for your browsing convenience, in Table 3-1.

Table 3-1	Eight Important Folders in Your Navigation Pane	
Folder Icon	*Folder Name*	*What the Folder or View Contains*
◈ Inbox	Inbox	Messages that have been sent to you
✎ Drafts	Drafts	Messages that you composed, but haven't (yet) mailed off
⊡ Sent	Sent	Messages that you wrote and sent to other people
⊡ All Documents	All Documents	Pretty obvious

(continued)

Table 3-1 *(continued)*		
Folder Icon	**Folder Name**	**What the Folder or View Contains**
🖋 To Do	Tasks	Things to keep you busy
🗑 Trash	Trash	Documents that you're going to delete
🔍 Archiving	Archive Data	Old messages you've put away to save space
🔍 Discussion Threads	Discussion Threads	Messages listed together based on their subject

There are, of course, other items listed in the Navigation pane, such as *Agents* and *Design.* You use the Agents folder to create a little mini-computer program in your mail database. You use the Design folder to change the ways your mail database works. Read Chapter 14 to find out more.

To see the contents of a folder in the Navigation pane, just click the folder you want. Don't be surprised if a couple of the folders are empty!

The View pane

The View pane presents you with a summary of the documents in a given folder. When you press the up-arrow and down-arrow keys (↑ ↓), you'll see the selection bar move from one message to the next. (The *selection bar* is that big black bar that highlights the message in the View pane.) And, as you press ↑ and ↓, you'll also see a preview of that document in the Preview pane.

Each row of information in the View pane represents information about an individual message. Each message is divided into columns of information, such as the name of the person who sent the message, the date when it was sent, and the subject of the message. Aside from just looking at the pane to see who sent you what messages, you can do a couple of other things. . . .

Changing the column widths

Sometimes, the contents of a column are wider than the column itself, which means that you can't see all the information. This problem (unlike world hunger) is easily remedied, because you can change any column's width, right here and right now.

To change a column's width, move your mouse so that the pointer is on the horizontal line representing the right side of the too-narrow column. When you get the mouse right where you want it, the pointer changes to a two-headed monster, as you can see in Figure 3-2. Then all you do is drag the column to its new size. That's easy, huh?

The two-headed monster

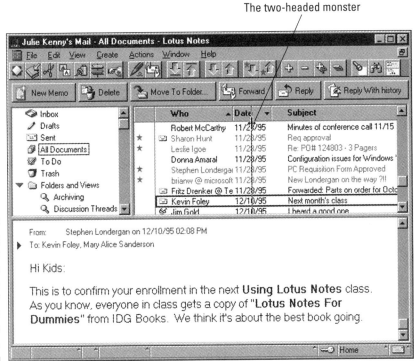

Figure 3-2:
You can
easily make
a column
bigger or
smaller by
dragging its
right edge.

Sorting your mail

Did you notice in Figure 3-2 that the headings for the Who column and the Date column have little triangles in them? Those triangles tell you that those columns are set up to *sort on the fly,* which is a fancy way of saying (no, this doesn't involve an airplane) that you can re-sort the documents by clicking the column heading.

For example, if you want to rearrange the documents in this column so that they're listed from newest to oldest, click right on the word Date in the column heading. Before your very eyes, the documents rearrange themselves. Click the word Date again, and the documents shuffle into the opposite order — oldest to newest. You can do the same thing with the Who column to realphabetize the documents based on the person's name.

Anytime you see a little triangle in a column heading, you can click it to rearrange the documents listed in that column.

Reading your mail

As you press up-arrow and down-arrow keys to move the selection bar in the View pane, the Preview pane changes to give you a preview of what's in each message.

But, when you want to read the message *in its entirety,* you can either double-click the message in question, or highlight it with the selection bar and press Enter. Bye-bye panes; the document you selected fills the screen. After you've opened a document, you can use the up-arrow and down-arrow keys (or the vertical scroll bar) to move through the document.

Closing a message

When you're done reading your message, you can close it and return to the View pane:

- ✔ Press Esc. The memo disappears, and you're back to the View pane.
- ✔ Choose File➪Close. The memo disappears, and you're back to the View pane.

Or you can move immediately to another message:

- ✔ Press Enter and the next message appears.
- ✔ Press Backspace and the previous message appears.
- ✔ Press Tab to move to the next unread message or press Shift+Tab to move to the previous unread message, if you have one.
- ✔ Press F4 to see the next unread document or press Shift+F4 to see the previous unread message.
- ✔ Click any of the four SmartIcons pictured here:

 • The down arrow without the star opens the next memo.

 • The up arrow opens the previous document in the list.

 • The down arrow with the star opens the next unread memo.

 • The up arrow with the star opens the previous unread document.

If you're getting a little worried about remembering all these options, don't bother trying. Pick the one that works best for you and forget the others. Enter and Backspace are pretty easy to remember.

If you're especially observant, you may have noticed that, *before you opened* the document, it had a little star next to it in the View pane, where now it has none. You may have also noticed that the name of the document in the View pane changed colors after you opened it. It used to be red, now it's black. What gives?

Notes keeps track of which documents you have read and which you haven't. If, in the View pane, a document has a star next to it and is red, you know that it's brand-spanking-new — or at least that you haven't read it yet. On the other hand, if the document in question doesn't have a star and is black, you *have* read it.

R-E-D documents haven't been R-E-A-D.

Aren't those pictures just the cutest things . . .

You'll see lots of little icons in the View pane. Each one tells you something about the message beside it. So wouldn't it be appropriate, at this point in the book, to include a little table explaining what they all mean? (Enter Table 3-2, stage left.)

Table 3-2	Icons in Your Mail Database
The Icon	**What It Means**
�writing	A message you have saved, but not sent yet
▪	A message that's been marked as High Importance - probably from your boss
▣	A message that's been marked as Normal or Low Importance
☑	A task you haven't completed - get to work!
✓	A task you have completed
✐	A message that has an attached file, or an embedded object (whatever that means!)

That distracting Preview pane

The Preview pane is at the bottom of the screen, and it shows you the beginning of whichever message you've highlighted with the selection bar. There really isn't too much you can do with the Preview pane, other than read the document displayed there.

If you don't like the fact that each document is previewed for you in the Preview pane, you can always choose <u>V</u>iew⇨Document <u>P</u>review. Each time you select this command from the menu, Notes switches back and forth between opening and closing the Preview pane. Some people prefer to keep the Preview pane closed all the time.

The Action bar

Last, but not least, the *Action bar* is that strip of big buttons at the top of your mail database window. These buttons aren't much different from the SmartIcons; if you see one you want to use, just click it with the mouse. You might notice that the buttons change, depending on what you're doing. (In other words, the buttons in the Action bar while you're previewing a message are different from the ones you'll see up there whilst reading a message.

Get Me Outta Here!

When you want to close your mail and return to the Notes workspace, choose File⇨Close or press Esc. You may have to do this twice, if you're reading a message when you decide to close your mail. The first time closes your message; the second time closes your mail database.

Chapter 4

Making a Message

*H*ooray! You opened your e-mail database and read all your messages. You called your boss back to confirm that power lunch (So what if you had to use the telephone because you didn't know how to use Notes to answer an e-mail?), and you didn't miss that emergency 3:00 staff meeting. Still, there are a couple of messages remaining in your e-mail that deserve an answer — and maybe the phone isn't the best way to respond. Perhaps you'd even like to compose a few messages of your own. It's time to get on board the Notes e-mail wagon.

The purpose of this chapter is not to turn you into a Shakespeare or a Hemingway. What you say in your memos is up to you. We just want to give you some pointers so that your message gets to where it's going.

Good Memo Manners

This will probably come as no surprise, but you shouldn't use e-mail for some things:

- ✔ Vicki and I are giving a little wedding for our daughter next week. Can you make it? Bring your own champagne.

- ✔ I'm sorry your parakeet died; hope it wasn't anything serious — or catching.

- ✔ Hey, J. B. Here are a few suggestions about how to get this company turned around. First, fire all your vice presidents.

✔ Smedley, you're fired. Be out of your office in five minutes. We've already hired a replacement.

✔ Fire! Everyone leave the building as quickly as possible!

✔ Don't you think the president is a jerk? I sure do. What a moron! I could do the job better than that idiot.

✔ I just found out that Rogers is making $90,000.

Each of the preceding points may have its place in some form of communication, but not in e-mailed memos. Before you put fingers to keyboard, pause to ponder the following points:

✔ There are times when more formal styles of communication (such as paper documents) are desirable.

✔ There are also times when talking face-to-face is preferable.

✔ Don't go over your boss's head in writing if you wouldn't consider doing it under other circumstances.

✔ Resist the temptation to include the whole world in your cc: list.

✔ A message may be *delivered* almost instantly, but that doesn't mean everyone is going to *read* it instantly.

✔ Although Notes is a secure e-mail system (a message only goes to the person you address it to), there's nothing to stop that person from sending it on to other people.

✔ If you have composed a nasty-gram, sleep on it before sending it.

✔ Rogers is only making $70,000.

Sending an e-mail to too many people is called *spamming,* as in: "Jim really spammed his complaints around, huh? What an idiot! I wonder how soon he'll get fired?" Don't include too many people in your cc: lists!

Your New, Outgoing Memo

Having dispensed with the indispensable lesson in memo manners, you are ready to compose an actual, honest-to-goodness, real-life memo. One of the nice things about Notes is that you can always compose a new mail message, anytime and anywhere. You could be reading a discussion database or looking at your company's phone-book database when the urge to write an e-mail strikes you. No matter where you are or what you're doing, a new e-mail message is just a menu choice away.

When you want to write a new e-mail message, choose Create➪Mail➪Memo, or click the Create Mail Memo SmartIcon, and the blank memo form in Figure 4-1 appears. If you're one of those people who has trouble writing, think of writing a memo as filling in the fields in a record in a database.

As you can see in Figure 4-1, your new memo has four parts:

- ✔ **The Action bar:** which contains some buttons you'll use while composing your memo

- ✔ **Your name:** whatever that may be

- ✔ **The Address and Subject fields:** where you enter the names of your memo's recipients and a short description of the memo

- ✔ **The Body field:** where you type the body of your message

Writing a new message involves three basic steps:

1. **Figure out the people to whom you'll be sending your message.**

2. **Enter the body of the message.**

3. **Save the message and/or send it off.**

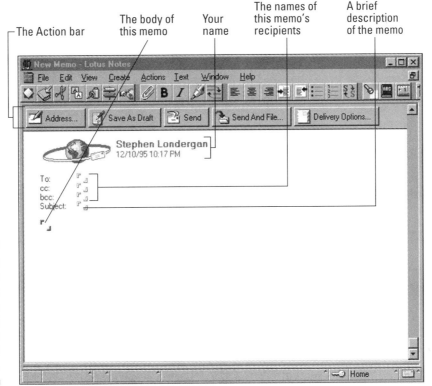

Figure 4-1:
This is the form you use to create and send a new mail message.

The fine print

At this point, we think it's a good idea to tell you that what you're reading here may not be true. Or this section may be true, but later in the book you may notice that what we describe is not what you see on your screen. If there's a discrepancy between what you are reading and what you are seeing, one of the following excuses may apply:

✔ Your company's Notes administrator may have altered the memo form to customize it for your organization.

✔ Your company may not be set up to use Notes mail — it is possible to use Notes for its database capabilities but use a separate program to send e-mail. If this is the case, you probably want to stop reading this chapter and skip ahead to Chapter 5.

✔ You can't always believe everything you read.

Before we get carried away explaining each of these three steps in mind-numbing detail, it's worth mentioning that you can simply enter a recipient's name in the To: field, enter some text in the Body field, and then click the Send button (up there in the Action bar) to dispatch your message.

Step #1: Addressing a message

In the simplest case, you know the name of the person (or persons) to whom you'll be sending a memo (or memos), so you simply type the name (or names) in one or more of the address fields. As you may have noticed in Figure 4-1, you have three address fields to choose from: *To:*, *cc:*, and *bcc:*. What's the difference, you ask?

✔ **To:** is the field where you enter the name of the primary recipient of your memo. If you have more than one name, separate each with a comma.

✔ **cc:** is the field where you enter the name of anyone to whom you want to send a *courtesy copy* of your memo. Again, if you have more than one name, separate each with a comma.

✔ **bcc:** is the field you use to send a *blind courtesy copy* of the memo — that is, to send someone a copy without the rest of the recipients knowing about it. Imagine, for instance, that you send a memo to a coworker asking to have a certain job done. You want your manager to know that you have made the request, but you don't want the coworker to know that your manager is aware of what's going on. Send the memo To: the coworker with a bcc: to your manager. When your coworker receives the message, the bcc: field won't be visible, so your secret is safe. Your coworker won't know that you sent a copy of this same message to your boss. Pretty devious, huh?

Of course, spelling is important, so you want to be pretty careful to spell the names correctly. Fear not, though; if you misspell a name, Notes will catch your mistake and let you correct it. You may also notice that, as you type a recipient's name, Notes does its best to help you get it right. If you're typing a name and want to accept the guess that Notes offers, just press Enter to accept the suggestion. (See Chapter 19 for more about the type-ahead feature.)

If you're not sure how to spell a person's name, there's an easy way to find out. You can use the Address button on the Action bar, or choose Actions⇨Address, and let your fingers do the walking.

You have two Name and Address Book icons on your desktop — your very own *personal* N&A Book and your company's *public* N&A Book. These are the two databases that Notes uses when you select Actions⇨Address. Each of these databases contains the e-mail addresses of various people: Your personal N&A Book has the names of your friends (usually people who don't work at your company), and the public N&A Book has the names of everyone at your company. (You can find out more about Name and Address books in Chapter 2.)

When you choose Actions⇨Address, you see the dialog box in Figure 4-2. Use the Address Book drop-down list at the top left of this dialog box to select your personal N&A book or the company's public N&A Book.

Figure 4-2: Use this Mail Address dialog box to pick and choose the names of people you want to receive your memo.

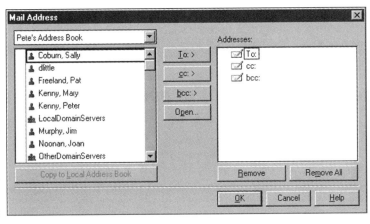

On the left side of the Mail Address dialog box, you see the names of the people in your Personal N&A Book. If you want to send your memo to someone on this list, select that person's name and then click the To:, cc:, or bcc: button, depending on how you want the message to be addressed. When you do, the name of the person you selected appears in the right side of the dialog box. (If you make a mistake, use the Remove or Remove All buttons to start over.)

TIP

If you are a mouse aficionado, you can drag the name from the left window into the right window, as you can see depicted so nicely in Figure 4-3.

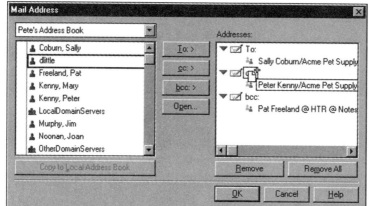

Figure 4-3:
You can also drag the names to address a message.

When you're done using the Mail Address dialog box to pick your recipient names, choose OK.

REMEMBER

After choosing the recipients' names, be sure to type a brief description of what your memo is about in the subject field. Keep your description short and make it interesting. What you enter here will show up in the View pane of your recipient's mail database.

Step #2: Writing the body of the message

And now on to the important stuff. You've typed (or chosen) all of the names of the people who will (soon) be receiving your little pearl of wisdom. In the Body field of the message (on your screen, the Body fields enclosed in those little red brackets), you get to say whatever it is that you want to say.

You may wonder how you're going to fit all that you have to say between those two end markers. Rest assured that the field expands (just like all the other fields in the memo), so you can fill it with as much information as you want.

TECHNICAL STUFF

Speaking of those little corner markers, notice that they are red, even though all the other fields have black end markers (unless you have a monochrome monitor, in which case, all your markers look just the same). The red corners mean that the Body field is an *encryptable* field. We discuss encryptable fields in Chapter 6, but we'll tell you here that the body field is the only field in the memo form that you can scramble so that it is absolutely unreadable until the intended recipient opens the memo.

You can enter any text you want, and you can get as fancy as you want, too. You can make the text **bold**, or *italicized,* or even χηανγε τηε φοντ ανδ σιζε . Because the Body field on an e-mail is what's known as a *rich text field*, you can make its contents pretty elaborate. In addition to all these crazy things you can do with the text, you can even include other cool features like files and objects. Read more about that in Chapter 6.

Step #3: Adding a special touch

Before dispatching a message, you can ask for some special delivery options. When you're done with the Body field, consider the Actions⇨Delivery Options menu (or the Delivery Options button in the Action bar). Either one leads to the dialog box shown Figure 4-4.

Figure 4-4:
Use these
options to
do some
special
things with
your
outgoing
message.

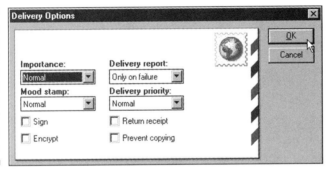

Importance

You have three settings for your message's importance: Normal, High, and Low. As we discuss in Chapter 3, Notes flags messages that have been marked as High Importance with a special red envelope in the recipients' mail database. Use this feature if you want to alert your recipient to an especially important or urgent message.

Mood Stamp

The Mood stamp list is a way to get in touch with your (electronic) inner child. This is the 90s, after all. A *mood stamp* is actually a picture that Notes adds right at the top of a message, so that your reader knows what frame of mind you were in as you sent the message. A message with a mood stamp is also marked as such in the View pane of the recipient's mail database.

You have twelve mood stamps to choose from; try each to see what they look like. The Joke selection is especially useful if you want to send a message that's just a little sarcastic, and you need to make sure that your reader realizes that, yes, you were just kidding! If you don't want any mood stamp in your outgoing message, choose Normal. Figure 4-5 shows a mail memo that has been marked as a Joke.

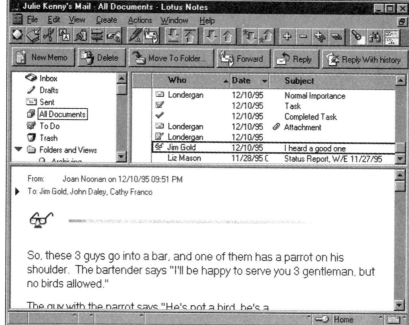

Figure 4-5:
If you mark your message as a joke, your reader will know not to take you too seriously.

Delivery report

The four choices regarding a Delivery report are: Only on failure, Confirm delivery, Trace entire path, and None.

- ✔ If you choose Delivery report: Only on failure, you can assume that no news is good news; in other words, Notes will tell you if your outgoing message couldn't be delivered for some reason.

- ✔ If you're a little less of an optimist, choose to Confirm delivery, in which case Notes tells you exactly when and where your message was delivered.

- ✔ Trace entire path tells you where (and at what times) your message stopped on its way to your recipient (you probably don't care).

- ✔ None means that you're throwing caution to the wind, and don't care to know whether your message gets delivered or not.

If you do choose a Delivery report option other than None, you'll receive the report back (as an e-mail message to you) as soon as the message you sent arrives. When that will be depends on your network and on your network administrator. If your recipient is far away, it might take a couple of hours, or maybe even an entire day, for the message to get delivered. Check out Figure 4-6 to see an example Delivery report.

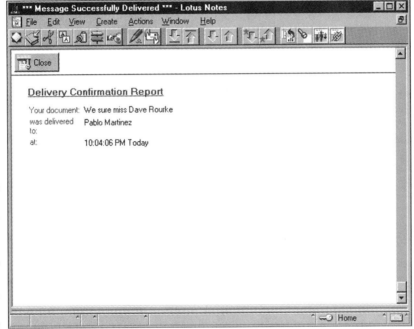

Figure 4-6:
A Delivery report tells you when your message arrived at its destination.

If you're sending a message to someone who doesn't use Notes, or if your message is going through the Internet, you may not be able to get Delivery or Receipt reports.

Delivery priority

Your next decision in the Delivery Options dialog box relates to how quickly Notes will deliver your message.

- ✔ **Low:** sends the message late at night, when the network isn't so busy.
- ✔ **Normal:** sends the message as soon as possible, based on the mail delivery schedules your administrator has crafted.
- ✔ **High:** sends your message _right now_ — step aside, coming through!

If you're sending a huge attachment in an e-mail message, consider marking it as Low priority. The message won't be delivered until you're home fast asleep, but it'll probably cost your company less money to send it so late at night. Maybe this is a way to earn that Employee of the Month award!

Sign

The company president calls you and complains about a memo you sent demanding shorter working hours and a raise for the whole department. Try as you may, you can't remember sending a memo like that. Are you losing your marbles? Memory blackout? That may be, but it's more likely that someone sent a memo in your name. A mischievous Notes administrator, for example, can write a memo that has your name in the From: field, even though it isn't really from you.

The way to avoid being blamed for messages that aren't really from you is to *sign* them. You sign messages for the same reason that you sign checks or official documents: to show that they're really from you. You don't need to sign a meet-me-for-coffee memo, but when you send a message with crucial or sensitive information, you may want Notes to prove that the message really came from you.

We're talking computers here — obviously you can't scratch your signature on the screen at the bottom of a memo. (Well, actually, you can, but we don't think your boss would appreciate it.) You sign a message by choosing Actions⇨ Delivery Options and then selecting Sign from the dialog box.

The signature you use in Notes is even more difficult to forge than your own John Hancock, because it's a numeric computer code added to the message when you send it and checked by the recipient's computer when the message is opened. The memo doesn't have an actual signature on it, but this message appears at the bottom of the screen:

```
Signed by Alan Dunkel/Eastisle on 09-11-96 08:30:46, accord-
              ing to Eastisle.
```

Encrypt

Sure enough, the world is crawling with busybodies, bad guys, and spies — and you may be sending your messages over less-than-secure media. If you use the modem, you're sending your messages over phone lines, where a person up to no good may be able to read them. This is no problem for your meet-me-for-coffee messages, but if you send a message that includes information such as sensitive corporate data, employee performance appraisals, or *really, really* good gossip that you don't want anyone else to read, you had better *encrypt* it.

Encrypting a message is easy. Notes does all the work to scramble the body of a message so that only the people you send it to can read it. From the time the message leaves your mail database until the recipient opens it, the message is encrypted. So, if some low-life snooper does intercept your message, the only things he or she will be able to read are the addresses and the subject line.

When you create a memo, choose Actions➪Delivery Options, or click the Delivery Options button in the Action bar. You get the Delivery Options dialog box. Click the Encrypt check box at the bottom of the Delivery Options dialog box, and select OK to close the dialog box when you're finished.

When you send an encrypted message, Notes does the scrambling for you — behind the scenes. When the recipients open the message, they'll see the plain text just as you wrote it. Only the intended recipients with the proper User IDs can read the encrypted part of the message. The only one who will see the actual jumbled-up version is the poor spy who intercepts the message in transit.

You can encrypt messages only to other Notes users. If you're sending e-mail to a person who uses a different e-mail program, or if you're sending your message through the Internet, don't bother with the Encrypt button.

Think about it — who can read your e-mail if it's open and visible on your screen and you're away from your desk? If you guessed "anyone who walks near your computer," you may have a bright future in the spy business, because you're absolutely right. If you leave a highly sensitive message visible and go for a cup of coffee, forget about your bright future in the spy business. The message is decrypted while it is open. So when you leave your desk, close the message and then press F5 to disable your access to Notes. That way, the next time you try to use Notes you'll have to enter your password — and so will anyone else. Get it? To learn how to set a password, check out "Some IDeas" in Chapter 14.

Return Receipt

If you use the Delivery Options dialog box to request a Return receipt, Notes will notify you when the recipient *reads* your message. This is different from a Delivery report, which tells you when the message arrived in the recipient's mail database. Request a Receipt report to prevent the "I never saw your message" excuse; use Delivery reports to eliminate the "I never got your message, the network must have lost it" excuse.

Prevent copying

Should you choose to Prevent copying, you can be certain that the person who receives your message will not be able to forward it to anyone else. In fact, they won't even be able to Edit➪Copy your memo to the clipboard, in case they're intent on a little illicit Edit➪Pasting. This is a way to make sure that what you say to one person doesn't get spammed all over your company.

When you're done with the Delivery Options, choose OK to get back to your document. In most cases, once you've made up your mind vis-à-vis these options, you'll then click the Send and File button to be done with it.

If your head is spinning from all these delivery options, you may be happy to read that you only need to use them under special circumstances. In fact, for most messages, you'll blow right by the Delivery Options altogether. What a relief!

Step #4: Sending off the message

After successfully choosing the address and entering the text, you're ready to dispatch your message. When it's time to let 'er rip, choose Actions➪Send, or click the Send button on the Action bar. Off the memo goes, with barely a whisper.

If you change your mind and decide not to send a message (what were you thinking?), press Esc and then choose to Discard changes. If you want to send your message later, and just save it for now (maybe you want to take a little break first), click the Save As Draft button in the Action bar.

What happens when you send your memo? It gets handed off to your mail server, the computer down in the basement that's responsible for shuttling the message to its recipients. And you? You're right back where you were when you started composing the message in the first place. Rest assured that your memo will be delivered to the recipients; Notes notifies you if, for some reason, it can't deliver your message.

The only possible downside to using Actions➪Send is that the memo is *not* saved for you. It goes to the recipients all right, but you'll have no record of what you sent. This is why you might consider using Actions➪Send and File (or clicking the Send and File button in the Action bar) to dispatch your documents. This choice really does two things: (1) saves your message, and (b) sends it off. That way, you get a record of what you sent.

When you choose to send and file your message, you get the dialog box in Figure 4-7. Click the folder into which you want to save your outgoing message and then choose Add.

When you're not sure where you should save an outgoing message, it's always safe to Add it to your Inbox folder.

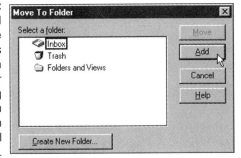

Figure 4-7:
The Send
and File
choice lets
you save a
copy of your
outgoing
message in
your own
mail
database.

Working in Your Mail Database

Way back at the beginning of this chapter, we discussed how you can compose a new mail memo anytime, anywhere. That's nice, of course, but you'll probably find yourself working with mail most often while you're right in your mail database. In fact, there's a couple of reasons why you'd want to open your mail database:

✔ To read the messages that have been sent to you

✔ To reply to messages you have received

✔ To forward documents to other interested parties

✔ To search for old messages

✔ To manage, organize, and delete messages

Replying

We discussed how you read your messages in Chapter 2, so let's jump right in and see what this replying business is all about. By way of setting the stage, imagine that you've opened your mail database and you're reading an incoming message in which a colleague has asked you for directions to your house. Being the responsive and social sort of person that you are, you're going to reply to her straight away. You have two options:

✔ You can reply to her directly by choosing Create⇨Reply or by clicking the Action bar's Reply button.

✔ You can forward her document back to her via Create⇨Reply with history, or the Reply With History button.

In either case, Notes starts you off with a new memo, and automatically fills in the mail address of the person who sent you the request in the first place.

When you reply with history, Notes includes a copy of the original memo in the memo you're sending back, which is a nice way to remind the person what you're talking about. All too often, you'll receive memos in which the author expounds on some topic, leaving you without the faintest idea of what they're talking about or why they're talking about it. (Or consider the e-mail that arrives, containing just the word "No." No *what*? No bananas? No to your request for a raise? No way to know what they're talking about?) To prevent this situation, and to keep your technological reputation on the up and up, choose Reply with history, so that your readers know of which you speak. Figure 4-8 shows a sample reply with history.

After clicking either of the Reply buttons, you are free to alter the address fields. Perhaps you want to invite someone else over? Type whatever you want in the Body field and then Send or Save the message as you would any other outgoing memo.

Every time you create a reply, Notes includes a DocLink to the original document.

cc: address   DocLink

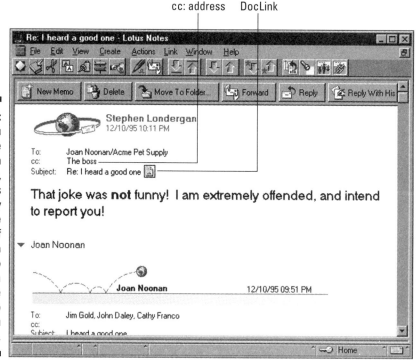

Figure 4-8:
When you choose Reply With History, Notes automatically fills in the address of the person and also includes a copy of the memo to which you are replying.

Forward, ho!

In addition to replying to a message, you can also forward a particular message. Perhaps you get a message asking about some company policy, but you're not the right person to ask. Just forward the misdirected document to the right person by using Actions⬦Forward or the Forward button. Forwarding documents is also a common way for your manager to get you to do things: Someone asks your boss a question, and all of a sudden it's your problem. Or, if you get a message (or see a document in a database), and you think that your pal should know about it, Actions⬦Forward it!

If you're forwarding a document to someone, it's usually considered proper (thank you, Emily Post) to include a cc: to the person who sent the document in the first place. That way the original author will know that you're not going to reply directly.

Other kinds of mail documents

If you check out the Create menu in your mail database, you'll see that Notes has a few other mail forms available to you. Let's face it, an e-mail message is an e-mail message, but these other, extra-special forms have been created with a few special purposes in mind:

- ✔ **Task:** Use this form for yourself as a reminder for something you need to do, or to assign a task (via e-mail) to somebody else. Task documents that you create or receive have check marks next to them in the View pane of your mail database. (Of course, just because you send a Task form to somebody doesn't mean that said person is going to do the task!)

- ✔ **Bookmark:** Use this form to send a DocLink to a person. Specifically, open the document you want to reference and then choose Create⬦Mail⬦Workflow⬦Bookmark.

- ✔ **Phone Message:** Use this form to take down information when you get a phone call for somebody else.

- ✔ **Serial Route memo:** Use this one to send a document to a bunch of people, one person at a time. This is useful if you need "sign off" on something, and you want to make sure that everybody sees the document, in order.

- ✔ **Memo to database manager:** Use this to send a message to the guru behind your database.

Figure 4-9 shows just one example of the special forms in your mail database: the Phone Message form. As you can see, it's just a mail message with some extra graphics and buttons — which is true of all the custom forms, no matter what their purpose.

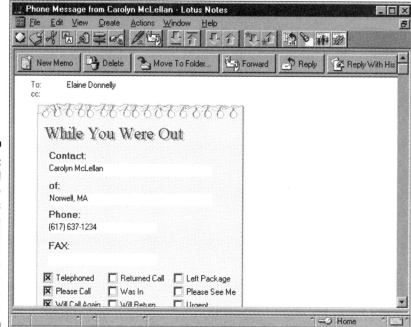

Figure 4-9:
Your mail database comes ready-made with several special forms, like this Phone Message form.

Chapter 5

Managing Your Mess(ages)

· ·

In This Chapter

▶ Deleting unwanted messages

▶ Creating and using folders

▶ Searching for messages

▶ Printing Notes documents

· ·

*A*fter you read your messages, then what? Do you have to do anything with them? Can you keep them, or do they disappear after you read them?

No, yes, and no. Any other questions? End of chapter.

The truth is, you really don't have to do anything with memos after you've read them. They just continue to pile up in your e-mail database the same way that stuff accumulates on your desk. They don't automatically disappear after you read them. It would be awfully irresponsible of Notes to delete messages that you may need later.

This chapter deals with the various things that you can do with a message or a group of messages after you read them.

The Scrap Heap of History

To keep a message, you need to do absolutely nothing. Unless you actually punch the proper keys to delete a message, Notes saves it in your mail database forever and ever. But every message you keep is that much more disk space you're using up on your Notes server, so you should seriously consider deleting most of your messages.

If everyone in your organization kept three-year-old memos from Fred saying "Meet me for lunch," then your company would have to keep buying more hard disks for your e-mail server, and those who share your Notes server would run out of disk space, and everyone would notice that the database was getting slower and s-l-o-w-e-r. This may explain why someone in your office is constantly sending out messages asking people to clean out their e-mail databases.

Selecting messages

Of course, before you choose any command that does something to a document, you have to tell Notes which document (or documents) are going to be affected by the command you're about to choose. If you want to do something to just one document, well, then, selecting it is easy. You either click the document in question with the mouse, or you use the up-arrow and down-arrow keys to select it in the View pane. Either way, when the selection bar is highlighting the document you want, you're in business.

If you need to select more than one document, highlight the first document and press the spacebar. (Watch for a little check mark to appear next to the document in the View pane). Then you highlight the next document and press the spacebar again. Then you highlight the next document in the View pane, and press the.... Oh well, you get the idea.

If you want to select multiple documents with the mouse, click right where the check mark will appear — in the column immediately to the left of the message(s).

If you change your mind, you can use either technique (the mouse or the spacebar) to *de*select a message.

You should find out what the policy is in your organization about the maximum size of mail databases. You can also check out Chapter 7 for some tips on how to archive messages that you don't need anymore.

How can you find out how large your mail database is? Open your mail database and then select File⇨Database⇨Properties. When you click the Info tab (the one with the small letter i in a circle) in the Database InfoBox, you see something remarkably like Figure 5-1. Note that this irresponsible blot on society has an e-mail database that is almost 6 megabytes and has over a thousand documents!

Figure 5-1:
The
Database
InfoBox tells
how big the
database is:
in this case,
5536 KB.

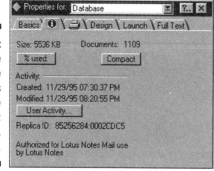

The most sensible course of action, of course, is to delete all memos that you won't ever need again as soon as you've read them. If you don't delete memos right away, you will have to go back through your database every so often and delete the old messages.

To delete a message, do any of the following:

✔ While the memo is open on-screen, press Delete. This marks the memo for deletion, puts the memo in the Trash folder, and opens the next memo in the list. Doing this doesn't actually delete the message; it only marks it for deletion. If you open the memo again, you will see word [Deleted] in the title bar.

✔ In the View pane, highlight the document you want to delete and either press Delete or click the Delete button on the Action bar. This also marks the message for deletion. You can tell that the message has been marked for deletion because a little trash can appears next to it in the View pane.

✔ Highlight a memo and press the spacebar or click in the far left column. A check mark appears next to the highlighted memo. This is the best way to select a bunch of memos for eventual deletion. After you check all the memos that you want to delete, press Delete or click the Delete button in the Action bar. Again, you know that the messages have been queued for deletion, because the little trash can appears next to them in the View pane.

✔ Select the message(s) you want to delete, and then choose <u>A</u>ctions⇨Move To Folder. Select the Trash folder from the Move To Folder dialog box and then click the <u>M</u>ove button.

✔ Drag the message from the View pane and drop it on the Trash folder in the Navigation pane.

If you change your mind and decide that you don't want to delete a message, now is the time to act! All you need do is

1. **Open the Trash folder (by clicking the folder's name in the Navigation pane).**

2. **Highlight the message (or use the spacebar to select a bunch of them, if you want to rescue more than one).**

3. **Choose <u>A</u>ctions⇨Remove from Trash, or click the Remove From Trash button.**

   Presto! The messages return to their original folders.

If you change your mind about deleting a message, you can always open the Trash folder to get it back. A message that's been marked for deletion doesn't get removed from the database until you do one of the following:

  ✔ Press F9 to update the database.

  ✔ Close the database.

  ✔ Choose <u>A</u>ctions⇨<u>E</u>mpty Trash.

No matter which of these three methods you choose to empty your Trash folder, you'll always get one last chance to change your mind, via the dialog box in Figure 5-2. If you want to keep the messages that you've marked for deletion, choose <u>N</u>o, and you'll be happy to find the messages still saved in the database.

Figure 5-2:
When you finally decide to empty your Trash folder, you get one last chance to change your mind.

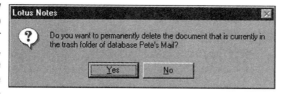

Another way to save server disk space is to *archive* messages. This is a way to take old messages and move them from your mail database on the server into a special database on your computer. Check out Chapter 7 to find out how to archive.

The easiest and fastest way to delete a document is to highlight it in the View pane, press Delete, and then press F9.

Fun with Folders

Of course, you aren't going to delete *all* of your messages; therefore, those that you keep ought to be arranged in some sort of system. Depending on the folder you're using, all your memos may be arranged by date or by the person who sent them, but those arrangements may not be particularly useful for your day-to-day work. If you're not happy with the folders that are already in your database, you're just going to have to create your own.

Creating a new folder

When you want to add a new folder to your mail database, follow these steps:

1. **Choose Create⇨Folder.**
2. **Name your new folder in the Create Folder dialog box (shown in Figure 5-3).**
3. **Click OK.**

If that seems easy, it's because, well, creating a folder *is* pretty easy. As soon as you click the OK button, your new folder is visible in the Navigation pane.

Figure 5-3:
Use the
Create
Folder
dialog box
to put a new
folder in
your mail
database.

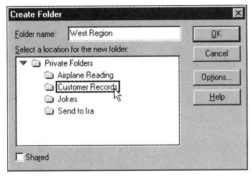

You can put folders inside of other folders. If you want your new folder to be inside another folder, select that folder in the Create Folder dialog box. In Figure 5-3, the new folder (named West Region) will go inside the Customer Records folder.

Putting a document in a folder

To put a message (or a bunch of messages) in a folder, select the message(s) and choose Actions⇨Move To Folder. Select the folder name from the Move to Folder dialog box and click Move.

You can use your mouse to put a document into a folder. Just drag and drop the message from the View pane to the desired folder in the Navigation pane.

Opening a folder to see what's in it

To open a folder with the mouse, just click the folder you want in the Navigation pane. You can also choose View⇨Go To and choose the folder from the Go To dialog box.

Deleting a folder

If you no longer need a certain folder in your mail database, select the folder in the Navigation pane and choose Actions➪Folder Options➪Delete Folder. Bye-bye!

Deleting a folder also deletes all the documents in that folder, so be careful! If you want to delete a folder without removing the documents in that folder, you first have to move the documents to a different folder.

Oh Where, Oh Where?

Folders are a great way for you to make some sense of the piles and piles of e-mail you'll be receiving every day, and folders certainly will help you find a particular message when you need it. But what about when the boss calls and asks you to find some memo she sent you last month about one of your company's clients? You look in all the likely folders and don't find anything on that client, but you know that you *never* delete messages about clients.

Rest assured that, if you didn't delete the message, it's still there, somewhere.

Hunting down a particular message can be a chore, unless you know who sent you the message. If you do, just switch to the folder that is most likely to contain the message you're trying to find (if all else fails, use the *All Documents* folder) and then sort the messages in the folder by name. Just click the little Sort arrow in the Who column heading. (We talk about this sorting business in Chapter 3.)

When you sort the folder based on the Who column, all of the messages from a particular person are listed together, which makes a document easier to find. Use the arrow keys and PgUp/PgDn to move through the documents in the View pane.

If you want to jump right to the messages from a particular person, rather than having to scroll down through the alphabet, use Quick Search. With the Message selector in the View pane, just type the name of the person you're looking for. As soon as you start typing a name in the View pane, the Quick Search dialog box appears, as you can see in Figure 5-4. Enter the name you're trying to find and click OK. Notes quickly takes you to the first message from that person.

You have to sort the messages in the View pane before you can use Quick Search.

Figure 5-4:
Use the
Quick
Search
dialog box
to quickly
find a
message.

If you don't know the name of the person who sent the message you're trying to find, you'll just have to hunt a little harder, and look through a lot more messages.

You can create a Full Text Index for your mail database so that you will be able to very quickly search the contents of the documents. This book has a whole chapter that discusses indexing a database — Chapter 18.

All the News That's Fit to Print

Notes is supposed to allow the world to enter the information age and eliminate the use of paper. The world hasn't reached that goal yet — we're still using enough paper to bury the Empire State Building every year. So it stands to reason that, sooner or later, you will want to print one of your e-mail messages from Notes.

You can print a single document, such as the one that you happen to be looking at on your screen or the one currently highlighted in the View pane, or you can select a bunch of documents in a view and print them all.

If you want to print the document that's visible on-screen, click the Print SmartIcon or choose File⌐Print and watch for the dialog box in Figure 5-5.

Despite all the buttons and fields on the File Print dialog box, you don't really have too many decisions to make. In fact, you're probably only interested in entering the Print range (whether you want to print the entire document or just some of the pages), and View options (whether you want to print the document you have selected or, instead, print the contents of the View pane). If you choose Print selected documents, you get the *contents* of the selected messages printed. If you choose Print View, Notes prints exactly what you see in the View pane — only the columns are printed.

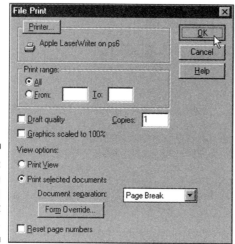

Figure 5-5:
Use the File
Print dialog
box to print
your e-mail.

Assuming that you choose to `Print selected documents`, and assuming
that you are printing more than one message, you have to decide how Notes
should separate one printed message from the next. Your choices for Document
separation are

> ✔ **Page Break:** Each document will start a new page.
>
> ✔ **Extra Line:** Between each document, Notes will print a line.
>
> ✔ **No Separation:** Each document follows the one before it, with
>   no separation.

If you choose Page Break, you may also decide how to number the pages,
assuming that you are numbering the pages (see Chapter 13 if you are). Select
the `Reset page numbers` check box, and each new document will start with a
page number of 1. Otherwise, the first page of each new document will just get
the next consecutive page number. Check out Chapter 13 for more information
about printing documents.

Chapter 6

Making the Most of Your Memos

In This Chapter

▷ Including other files in your memos

▷ Creating and hiding sections

▷ Using custom forms

*I*n the age of power ties, power lunches, and power lifting, it just stands to reason that there should be power memos. After you receive your tenth meet-me-for-coffee-at-10:00 memo, you may find yourself saying: "There must be more to memo writing than this. I'm getting wired from all this caffeine."

Well, you can do *plenty* more with memos than just arrange meetings. With your dazzling memos, you can be the talk of the office, a legend among your coworkers.

Enclosed Please Find

One reason for writing a memo is to discuss some information that already exists. For instance, you might want to get some feedback on a report that you're writing in Microsoft Word. Do you have to retype the whole report into your Notes memo? No way, José! This is the '90s! Notes, being the high-tech marvel that it is, comes to the rescue. You have several options for getting around the chore of typing the whole report again.

Why, I oughta paste you

If you've spent any time copying and pasting in other programs, you're familiar with the Clipboard. When you use the Edit⇨Copy command, your computer holds the information you've selected in the Clipboard so that you can Edit⇨Paste it into other files, documents, or applications. The simplest way to get information from a separate program into Notes is to use the Clipboard.

Say you are preparing a memo about a section of a report written in Microsoft Word. Copy and paste that section from the report right into your memo and then add your own comments in and around the pasted text. Of course, you can also paste an entire file, unless it's too big to fit in the Clipboard. For more information about copying and pasting, see Chapter 17.

Attaching attachments

If you write a paper memo that explains a report, you might decide to paper clip the report itself to the memo so that the recipient can see what you're writing about. That's what a Notes *attachment* is: a file attached to a memo. Figure 6-1 shows an e-mail message that includes a file attachment. If you're a keen observer, you'll notice that the attachment takes the form of an icon that usually tells the recipient what program the attached file was created in.

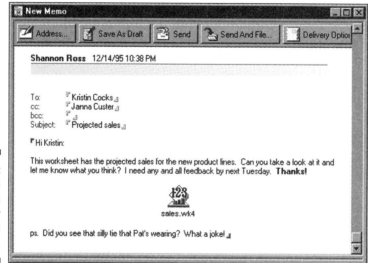

Figure 6-1:
You can attach files to your e-mail messages.

Feel free to attach virtually any type of file to any Notes document — binary files, compressed files, executable files, graphics files, and any other file created in any another program. Keep in mind that attaching a large file makes a large memo and increases the size of your database.

 To attach a file to a memo, put the cursor where you want to place the attachment and select File⇨Attach or click the file attachment SmartIcon. The Create Attachment(s) dialog box that you see in Figure 6-2 appears; use this dialog box to pick the files to attach.

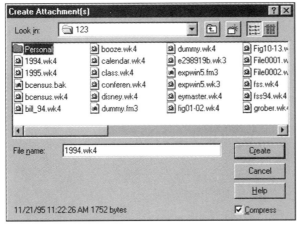

Figure 6-2:
Use the
Create
Attachment(s)
dialog box
to add a file
from your
computer to
a Notes
document.

In the File name box, highlight the proper filename and press Enter or click Create. You can even attach more than one file (at once, no less!) if the files are all in the same directory. Highlight the first file and then hold down Ctrl while you select the other files that you want to attach. To select several consecutive files, highlight the first and then press Shift as you click on the last one; Notes selects all the files in between.

Imagine getting a memo with an attachment — and nothing else. What is it? What program did it come from? What are you supposed to do with it? Sensible questions all, and ones that you ought to answer for the recipient when you send an attachment with your memo. Don't leave the person guessing.

What should you do if you receive a message with an attachment? Well, you can

- ✔ *View* it, to take a little peek inside and see (or even print) the file's contents

- ✔ *Launch* it, to open the document with the program that was used to create it in the first place (assuming that you have said program installed on *your* computer)

- ✔ *Detach* it to put a copy of the file on your computer, to have for your very own

When you double-click an attachment icon, you're presented with the Attachment InfoBox, like the one in Figure 6-3. Click the View, Launch, or Detach button, depending on what you want to do with the file.

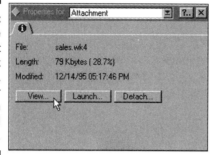

Figure 6-3:
Use the
Attachment
InfoBox
to view,
launch, or
detach an
attached
file.

What a view!

If you click the View button, Notes shows you as much of the file as it can through the *File Viewer*. Figure 6-4 shows a spreadsheet attachment that's being viewed. Notice that there's a new choice on the menu: Spreadsheet; this is the menu where you'll find the Print command that you can use to get a paper copy of the attachment's contents. Of course, when you view a word processing document, the new menu choice is Document instead of Spreadsheet, and so on. You will be able to view files from most popular computer programs.

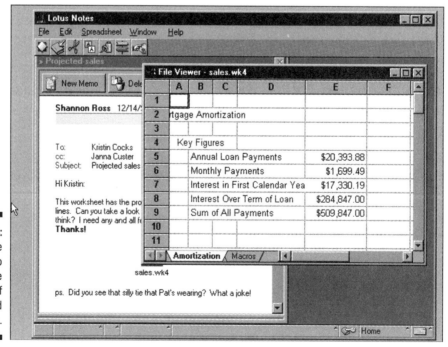

Figure 6-4:
Use the File
Viewer to
see the
contents of
an attached
file.

You do *not* need to have the computer program that was used to create an attachment to View the attachment.

Choose File⇨Close to close the File Viewer and return to the document you were reading in the first place.

The File Viewer only works in the Windows version of Notes. If you use OS/2, Macintosh, or UNIX, you're out of luck. You can only detach and launch attachments.

Let's do launch

If you choose Launch rather than View, Notes starts the program that was used to create the attachment and automatically opens the attachment in that program.

To launch an attached file, you *must* have that file's program installed on your hard disk. If you don't have the program, you'll have to rely on the File Viewer to see what's in the file.

Detaching yourself

You may choose not to view or launch the attached file. For any of the following reasons, you may, instead, decide to detach the file:

- ✔ You want to use it later.
- ✔ You don't have the software required to launch it.
- ✔ You want to put it on a floppy disk to take to another computer.

If you choose Detach from the Attachment InfoBox, you get the Save Attachment dialog box shown in Figure 6-5. Use this dialog box to tell Notes where on your hard disk you want to save the file and what name you want the file to have.

Figure 6-5: When you detach an attachment, use this dialog box to tell Notes where to put the file.

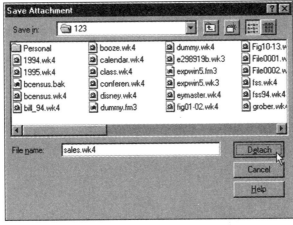

Because Windows relies on a file's *extension* (those three characters after the period) to know what kind of file it is, you shouldn't change the file's last name.

Don't mention this to the folks at Lotus (we don't want to hurt their feelings), but it would be clearer if they had used the word *Save* rather than *Detach*, because the word "detach" creates the impression that the file is actually removed from the memo, which it isn't. A copy of the file is saved to a disk, but the attachment still remains attached to the memo.

Importing files

If you want the recipients of your message to actually see the contents of a file when they open your memo, rather than just a symbol, then attaching the file isn't such a hot idea. Rather, Import is the command to use, because it brings the contents of a file right into your message in readable form. *Importing* converts a file that was created in another program into a format that is readable in a Notes document.

You may not be surprised that the files you import have to be some sort of data file, with real words or numbers or graphics that people can look at. You can't, for instance, import executable files (files ending with the extension EXE) because they are program files, not data files.

Place the cursor in the spot where you want the imported document to appear and then choose File⇨Import. The dialog box in Figure 6-6 appears.

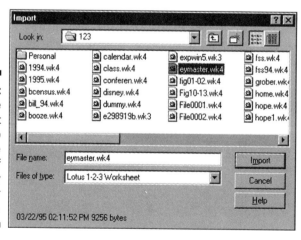

Figure 6-6:
Use the
Import
dialog box to
put the
contents of
a file directly
inside your
memo.

Use the Drives and Directories boxes to tell Notes where to find your file. Then, in the Files of type: list box, select a file type (in Figure 6-6, we selected Lotus 1-2-3 Worksheet). Highlight the file you want to import, select Import, and, as quickly as your hard disk can spin, and you have the file in your Notes document.

Deciding what to do

Feeling a bit confused? Don't know whether to import or attach or use the clipboard? Maybe the following list will help clear up the confusion:

- ✔ Use the Clipboard when you want to put only part of a file in a Notes document.

- ✔ Use the Clipboard if the recipient doesn't have the software necessary to open an attached file.

- ✔ Use the Clipboard if the recipient of your memo doesn't use Notes.

- ✔ Use File⇨Import when the readers don't need to have a copy of the file itself on their local disk.

- ✔ Use File⇨Import when you aren't sure whether the recipients have the software necessary to open the file you want them to see, and you can't use the Clipboard.

- ✔ Use File⇨Import when you need to include a file that's too large for the Clipboard, and you know that your memo's recipient doesn't use Notes.

- ✔ Use File⇨Attach when the file can't be imported, such as for executable files.

- ✔ Use File⇨Attach when you want the recipient to have an actual copy of the file to keep on a local disk.

Find out more about importing and exporting files in Chapter 17.

Creating Sections

Nothing's worse than receiving (or sending, for that matter) an e-mail that's too long. In this age of information overload, how many times have you been forced to wade through pages and pages of text, only to find that about half of it is totally irrelevant?

Well, we won't have any of that in Notes! By using a *section*, you make your messages easier to read. Sections let you make parts of your document *collapsible;* that is to say, your readers don't have to read a particular part if they don't want to.

Don't underestimate the power of readability. If you routinely send messages that are too long or too boring or have ugly fonts and colors, people won't read them. Some companies even offer classes in how to create interesting and readable e-mail!

To create a section, select the paragraph(s) that you want to be able to hide and then choose Create⇨Section. Faster than a New York minute, the paragraph disappears, and you see only the first line of the paragraph, as is displayed in Figure 6-7.

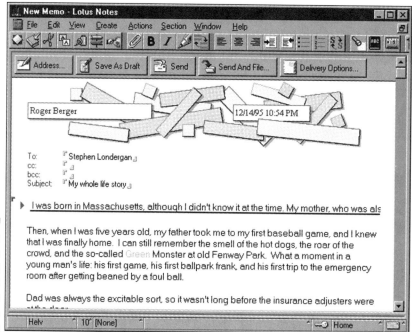

Figure 6-7: Click the triangle next to a section to see its contents.

Notice the little triangle to the left of that first line? That triangle is the reader's cue that there is more here than meets the eye. When you click the triangle, the section will expand to display all of the text; when you click it again, the section collapses and hides the words again.

Consider adding a title to your hidden section to make your document even more readable. Just type a heading before the section you want to hide and then highlight both before choosing Create⇨Section. See Figure 6-8 for an example of a document with several sections, each with a title.

That's it! Sections are easy to make and use, and are invaluable for keeping messages readable and concise. Use the Section command whenever you want to make your documents more reader friendly. And remember that you can create a section in any database, not just your e-mail!

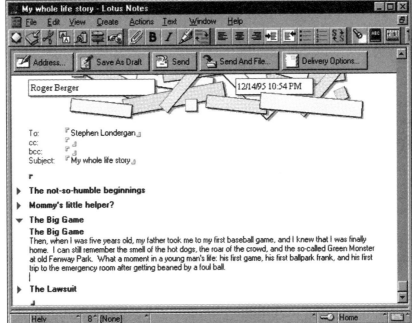

Figure 6-8:
Section
titles make
your
documents
even more
readable.

Mail Is More Than Just Memos

Most of the time when you use your e-mail database, you use the Create menu to write a memo. In some organizations, however, someone behind the scenes may have created special forms for everyone to use. For instance, suppose that you need to order some more staples. Or suppose that you need to reserve the conference room for your Monday morning poker game. Some genius may have already created a Staple Order Form or a Conference Room Reservation Form. Your company may also have forms for special announcements, special requests, status reports, or information sheets.

When you choose Create➪Mail➪Other, Notes presents you with a list of the custom forms that you can use for special occasions. They may even be already addressed, so you don't have to run around trying to find out who is in charge of ordering staples or reserving conference rooms or scheduling vacations.

This chapter presented some, but not all of the things you can put in your e-mail messages. Because e-mail messages are really just documents in a database, check out Chapter 10 for more information about composing them.

Chapter 7

Mastering Your Mail

· ·

In This Chapter

▶ Sending mail to people who don't use Notes

▶ Getting the most from your Name and Address Book

▶ Cleaning up your mail database

▶ Creating reusable stationery

▶ Some special delivery options

· ·

*L*ook at you! How you've grown! Why, it seems like it was only yesterday that you were just learning how to create a memo or use the Trash folder, and now here you are! In this chapter, we present some pretty advanced mail options; in fact, you may never need to use any of them. But, if you've got the time to read about them, we've got the time to explain them. So, without further ado. . . .

You Know, Not Everyone Uses Notes . . .

As much as Lotus hates to hear it, not every person who uses e-mail uses Notes. (Not yet, anyway.) The day is going to come when you need to exchange e-mail with someone who works at a different company or who doesn't use Notes at all. You've got to make a few special considerations in preparation for that day.

Your administrator has to take the first step

First off, your administrator has some work to do. If you and other people at your company need to exchange mail with another company that also uses Notes, your administrator has to set up a schedule of connections between your servers and theirs. If you need to exchange messages with a company that does *not* use Notes, or if you need to exchange mail with people over the Internet, that just means more work for your administrator.

In this case, your mail server needs a special program, called a *gateway*, that's used to translate messages from Notes format into a format that the other mail system can deliver. And, usually, gateways work the other way, too. A gateway can usually take a message that someone has sent from another e-mail system, convert it into a Notes mail message, and then deliver it to you.

Per usual, check with your administrator before trying to send a message to some far-flung person.

Addressing a foreign-bound message

When sending Notes mail to people at your company, you don't have to think about their e-mail name, because it's usually pretty close to what their mother calls them. Other people don't have it so easy because not all mail systems use such easily-remembered names. In fact, on some systems, people don't even use names, they use numbers!

So how are you going to know the exact names of the people to whom you're trying to send a message? You're not — at least not until you call those people on the telephone and *ask them for their e-mail addresses*. Write the address down and be careful to get it exactly right; every comma, period, and letter is important.

When you have the recipient's e-mail name, you're only half done, because you still have to figure out how you tell Notes that the address you're typing is intended for a different mail system. Time for another phone call, this time to your administrator. This lucky person will know exactly what you need to type to get the message outbound. Again, have a pencil ready before you call, because you're going to write down *exactly* what your administrator tells you.

Figure 7-1 shows a sample address for someone who works at a different company and uses a different e-mail system. The first part of the address (`7212344,899@cserve.com`) is what our friend told us was her e-mail address. The second part (`@Internet`) is what our administrator told us to use to get the mail sent outside of the company. The cc: field has the address of a person who uses Notes, but works at a different company.

Does all this seem like a pain in the neck? Well, quite simply, it is. You do have a little investigative work before you'll get the first message successfully addressed to a person — but once you learn someone's address, it's smooth sailing for all subsequent messages.

Make the other person do all the work! If your friend can figure out how to get a message *to you*, you'll be able to choose Create⇨Reply to respond to the message, and let Notes automatically determine your friend's address.

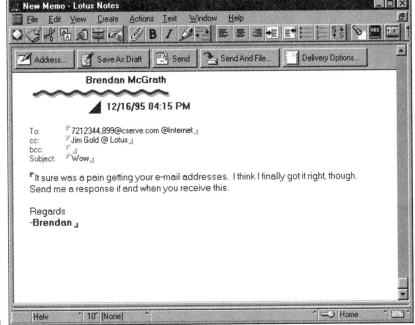

Figure 7-1:
When you
send
messages to
non-Notes
users, their
addresses
may look a
little funny.

In your message

Obviously, before you send your message off to someone in another building or another mail system, you need to think about what you're going to say. In general, other mail systems can't handle things like attachments, DocLinks, and embedded objects. Some won't even translate properties under the Text menu, such as **bold** and *italics*. You have no easy way of predicting exactly what will make it through and what won't, so your best bet is to try it, and just see what happens.

Sending attachments can be especially sticky. Sometimes they work great, sometimes they don't work at all; it all depends on the mail system that the other person is using. If someone sends you an e-mail from the Internet or some other mail system that contains an attachment, it may not arrive as an icon, but as a bunch of encoded text right in the body of their e-mail.

Bad news: If Notes has converted an incoming attachment into text, it isn't smart enough to *decode* the attachment back into a file. That's a bummer. Many public bulletin board systems (BBSs) and other online services have programs that can do this for you. Once you get your hands on one of these programs, converting a Notes message back into a file involves File⇨Exporting the message to an ASCII file, and then using another program to do the conversion. This is definitely something to ask a friend or your administrator about.

Your Personal N&A Book

Your personal Name and Address Book is a special database that you already have, whether you realize it or not. You've probably noticed the icon on your workspace, but you probably haven't had a reason to open it. Not until now, that is. Figure 7-2 shows the icon for a sample personal N&A Book.

Figure 7-2:
A sample
personal
N&A Book.

Pete's Address
Book

Your personal N&A Book is just a miniature version of the large public N&A Book that's on your Home server. Your personal N&A Book can make your life easier in two ways:

- ✔ You can create Person documents in it, which make addressing mail to certain people easy. This is especially helpful for people who have complicated addresses from other e-mail systems.

- ✔ You can also create Groups, which are used to easily send a message to a bunch of people all at the same time.

Adding a person to your N&A Book

To add a person to your N&A Book, open the database, choose Create⇨Person, and watch for the form shown in Figure 7-3.

As you can see in this figure, you can use the Person form to store such information as your friend's home address, zip code, and the like. That's all well and good, but if you're creating a Person document for e-mailing, just concern yourself with the following fields:

- ✔ **First name / Last name:** These two fields aren't for Notes, they're for you. This is where you type the person's real, spoken name.

- ✔ **Full user name:** This field is where you enter the text you want to use in To: fields in e-mail messages for this person. Remember, this does not have to be the same as what you type in the First name and Last name fields. For example, if your friend is named Stephen Londergan, but calls himself Steverino, enter Stephen Londergan in the First name/Last Name field, and enter Steverino (and any other nicknames) in the Full user name field. You'll be able to address mail to (you guessed it) Steverino.

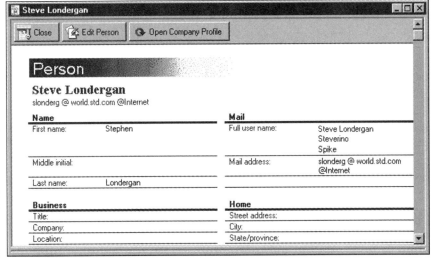

Figure 7-3:
Composing
a Person
document
in your
personal
N&A Book.

> ✔ **Mail address:** This is the most important field of all. In this field, type the
> exact e-mail address for the person you'll be sending mail to. If you're not
> sure about a person's e-mail address, see the section in this chapter called,
> "Addressing a foreign-bound message."

After you've filled out the preceding fields, save the document by choosing
File⇨Close⇨Yes.

If you're reading a message from somebody, and you want to add the person's
e-mail address to your N&A Book, use Actions⇨Mail Tools⇨Add Sender to
Address Book. If that other person has done all the investigative work to get a
message delivered to you, this is a fast and easy way to have Notes "remember"
the address.

Creating a group in your N&A Book

Friend, do you find yourself often sending a message to the same group of
people? Are you getting sick of typing each recipient's name every time you
want to send them all a memo? Well then step right up, because we've got a
trick that's guaranteed to make your life easier.

When you create a *group* in your N&A Book, you can use the name of the group
to easily send a message to that bunch of people. To add a group to your N&A
Book, open the database, choose Create⇨Group, and then fill in the form shown
in Figure 7-4.

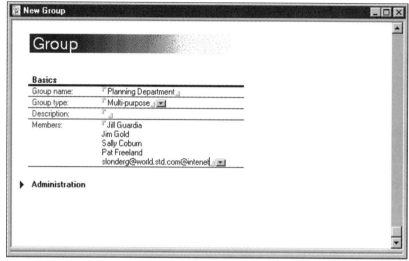

Figure 7-4:
Composing
a Group
document
in your
personal
N&A Book.

The most important (and only required) fields on this form are the Group name and Members fields. In the Group name field, you enter the name of the group, which can be any combination of letters and numbers. Since the Members field is a keyword field, you can click that little triangle next to the field to use the Names dialog box, as shown in Figure 7-5. This is a great way to make sure you spell all the names correctly!

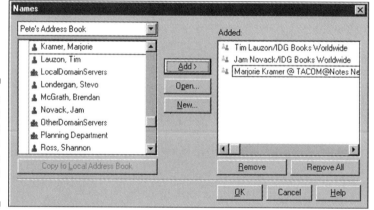

Figure 7-5:
Use the
Names
dialog box to
pick names
from the
N&A Book.

Keep your group names short, so that they're easy to type and easier to remember.

In the Members field, you enter the names of the people who will receive messages you send to the group. You can put in as many names as you want, and you can include addresses of people who don't use Notes (as we discussed in the previous sections of this chapter).

After filling out the fields listed above, save the document (File➪Close➪Yes). Then you can use the name of the group in any To:, cc:, or bcc: field. That's all there is to it!

The Person and Group documents in your personal N&A Book only work on your computer; your friend next-door can't send a message to a group if it's defined in *your* N&A Book. If everyone at your company needs to send mail to a certain group name, ask your administrator to add the group to the *public* N&A Book.

Clean Up That Mess!

The more you use Notes, the more e-mail you will receive. And the more e-mail you receive, the bigger and bigger your mail database will grow. As we discuss in Chapter 5, big mail databases take up a lot of space on your company's server (which you probably don't worry about), and also slow things down (which you will most definitely worry about). So, from time to time, you should clean up your mail, or, more specifically, you should look through your mail database to see whether it contains messages that you no longer need. You find 'em, read 'em, and delete 'em.

But what about the messages that you don't need, but can't bring yourself to delete, either? That's where *archiving* comes in. When you archive a message, you take it out of your mail database and put it in another, separate mail database. Moving documents from your "real" mail database into the archive means that your mail database will be smaller, and, as we all know, smaller databases make happier administrators. Archiving also makes your mail database lean, mean, and fast — and you'll enjoy how quickly you are able to change views and perform searches.

Do you *have to* archive mail? Absolutely not. But if your mail database is getting big and cumbersome, archiving is a way to increase your mail database's performance without having to delete a lot of messages.

When you delete a document, it's gone forever. When you archive a document, you'll be able to find it later.

Setting up an archive

Assuming you're sold on archiving, you first have to tell Notes how you want your archive to work by means of a special document in your mail database, called an *Archive Profile*.

1. **In the Navigation pane of your mail database, select the Archiving folder, as we've done in Figure 7-6.**

   This is the folder that you'll use in the future to see which documents have been archived.

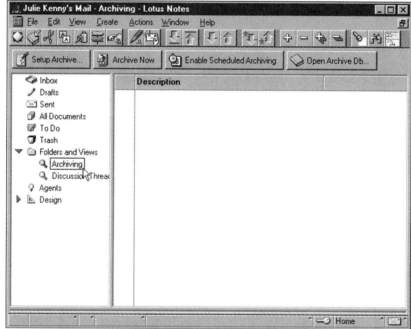

Figure 7-6:
Select the Archiving folder in your mail database to set up your Archive Profile.

2. **If this is the first time you've used an archive, click the Setup Archive . . . button in the Action bar.**

   When you do, you see the form from Figure 7-7.

3. **Select the appropriate check boxes.**

   • As you will see in the section called "Special Options for a Message," later in this chapter, some documents come ready-made with an expiration date. If you want Notes to automatically archive such documents, click the first button, `Archive Expired documents`.

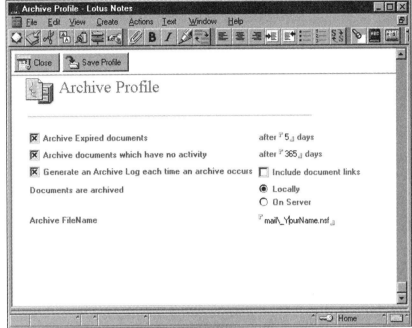

Figure 7-7:
The Archive
Profile is
used to
configure
your mail
archive.

- Use the second button, Archive documents which have no activity to decide how old a document can get before Notes moves it out of your mail database and into the archive database. You can usually safely archive documents that are untouched after a year; but you can change the after [ ] days field to allow for more or less time.

- Check Generate an Archive Log each time an archive occurs, and every time you archive documents, Notes will produce a report telling you which documents got moved.

- Check Include document links if you want this report to have DocLinks to the documents themselves. That's a neat way to be able to get to the archived documents very quickly. (More about Archive Logs later in this chapter.)

4. **Choose Locally or On Server to tell Notes the location of the archive database.**

   In most cases, the archive database belongs on your hard disk; half the reason you use archiving in the first place is so that you can free up space on your company's mail server. Check with your administrator if you're not sure where your archive database belongs.

5. **Use the Archive FileName field to tell Notes the name of the database that you want to hold the archived messages.**

6. **When you're finished filling out the form, click the Action bar's Close button and choose Yes to save the profile.**

In most cases, your Archive Profile will look like the one in Figure 7-7. If you're not sure how to answer any of the questions on the form, just do what we did in the example.

If you change your mind and want to edit the Archive Profile later, you can always use the Setup Archive... button in the Action bar. Make sure you switch to the Archiving folder first.

Archiving documents

After you set up your database's Archive Profile, you're ready to archive messages. Messages get moved from your mail database in any one of the three following ways:

- Manually, by you
- Manually, according to the age criteria you entered in the Archive Profile
- According to a schedule

The idea behind manually archiving messages is that you are going to select a bunch of messages in the View pane and move them from your mail database to your archive database. You can archive any message in this manner, even if it doesn't meet the age and expiration criteria you set in your Archive Profile.

Doing it by hand

To manually archive messages, select the messages in the View pane and choose Actions➪Mail Tools➪Archive Selected Documents. Choose Yes from the ensuing are-you-sure dialog box, and then watch and wait while Notes does the work. When Notes finishes, you'll see that the messages are no longer in your mail database, and that there's a new document, called Archive Log, at the bottom of your Inbox or in your Archiving folder. Open the Archive Log document to see what happened to the documents. Check out Figure 7-8 for a sample Archive Log.

As you can see in the figure, Notes produces a report of exactly how many messages were moved, when they were moved, and most important, where they were stored. Assuming you selected to include document links in the Archive Profile, the Archive Log also has a DocLink to each of the documents that got archived.

Telling Notes to do it for you

If you'd rather not select the documents yourself — if you want Notes to automatically decide which documents to move based on the criteria in your

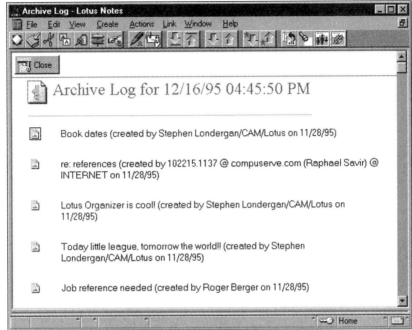

Figure 7-8:
An example
of an
Archive Log.

Archive Profile — click the Archiving folder in the Navigation pane and then click the Archive Now button on the Action bar. Notes checks all of the documents in your mail to see whether they meet the age requirements, and then moves the ones that qualify. Don't worry, Notes always produces an Archive Log when it finishes looking for documents to move.

Use the Archive button from the Archiving folder once a month to keep your mail database neat, trim, and fast.

Archiving on auto-pilot

The last way to archive documents is according to a schedule. Check with your administrator if you want archiving to occur automatically each week — without you having to do anything at all.

I Need a Vacation . . .

You work hard, and you certainly deserve a little break. A week of fun and sun? Heading to Jamaica, or the Bahamas? Great! Make sure you change the message on your office answering machine, so that callers know that you're away from the office. You've gotta keep up that reputation you have for responsiveness, after all.

And while you're at it, set up your mail database so that Notes will automatically reply to any mail you get while you're on the beach. If you create an *Out of the Office Profile*, people will know why you're not responding to their e-mail.

1. **Open your mail database.**

2. **Choose Actions⇨Mail Tools⇨Out of Office.**

    Up pops the form displayed in Figure 7-9, so you can tell Notes how you want to handle your mail while you're away.

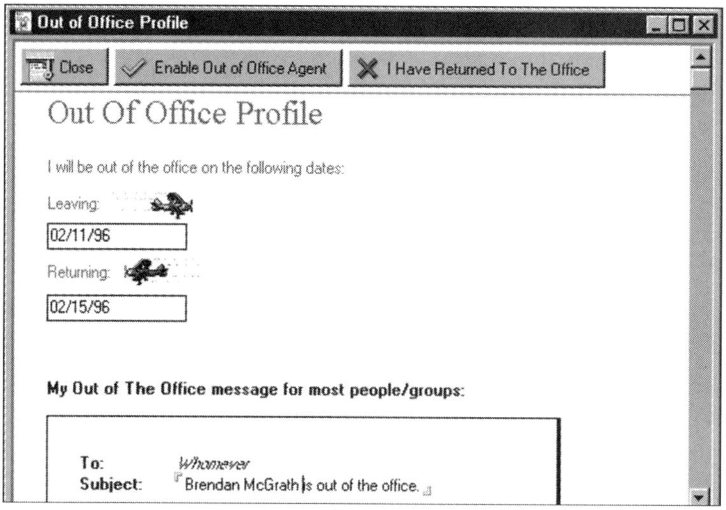

Figure 7-9:
Create an Out of Office Profile so Notes will automatically respond to the e-mail you receive while you're on vacation.

Out of Office Profile

Close | Enable Out of Office Agent | I Have Returned To The Office

Out Of Office Profile

I will be out of the office on the following dates:

Leaving:
02/11/96

Returning:
02/15/96

My Out of The Office message for most people/groups:

To: *Whomever*
Subject: Brendan McGrath is out of the office.

3. **Enter the dates you'll be gone in the Leaving and Returning fields.**

    Notes automatically replies to any mail you receive during this period.

4. **Enter your profile.**

    See the rest of this section for all that this step entails.

5. **Click the Enable Out of Office Agent button in the Action bar.**

6. **Select the name of your Home server from the Server name dialog box.**

Entering your profile involves answering three questions:

✔ What message should Notes send to most people?

✔ Which message should go to some special people?

✔ Which people shouldn't get an automatic reply?

In the `My Out of The Office message for most people/groups:` box, simply type the subject and body of the message that you want Notes to automatically send to the majority of the messages you receive. Figure 7-10 shows a sample response you can use, but feel free to say anything you want.

Figure 7-10: This is the reply we'll be sending to most people.

You may decide to send a different, special, reply to certain people. Maybe you want a unique message for your boss or you coworkers? In the Out of Office Profile, enter the names of such people in the `People/groups who should receive a special message:` field. Use the `My Out of The Office message for special people/groups:` field to enter the subject and body of the message for these people.

Click the arrow next to the `People/groups who should receive a special message:` field to choose people and group names from the N&A Book.

Some people may not deserve any response at all. Use the `People/groups who should not receive any messages:` field to enter their names. This field is useful if, for example, you regularly receive company-wide announcements or department bulletins that don't merit a reply.

If you subscribe to any Internet-based mailing lists, be sure to include their names in the `People/groups who should not receive any messages:` field. If you don't, every message you receive from the mailing list will trigger one of your automatic responses, which may very well end up being sent to the whole list, over and over again.

When you finish entering your profile, click the Enable Out of Office Agent button on the Action bar. Select the name of your Home server from the Server Name dialog box.

Don't forget to turn off your automatic replies after you return from your little vacation. When you're back at the office and ready to start replying to e-mail yourself, choose Actions➪Mail Tools➪Out of Office and use the I Have Returned To The Office button so that Notes stops sending messages for you.

Using the Same Memo Again and Again

If you find yourself regularly sending essentially the same memo to essentially the same people, you'll want to create *stationery*. Then next week, when it's time to send your regular message again, you won't need to create a new message; instead, you'll edit the stationery, which will have the names, subject, and so on already filled in. And the week after that, you do the same thing. And the week after that, and the week after that. . . . You get the idea.

Creating stationery

Creating stationery is really just a matter of filling out the address fields (To:, cc:, bcc:) and the Subject: field, typing the part of the memo that's the same each time you send it, and then saving the document. Here are the nitty-gritty steps:

1. **Choose Actions➪Mail Tools➪Create Stationery.**

2. **Choose Memo from the Create Stationery dialog box.**

3. **Enter the appropriate names in the To:, cc:, and bcc: fields and a topic in the Subject: field.**

   Don't worry if this information may vary, you'll be able to change these fields each time you use this stationery to send a message.

4. **In the Body field of the stationery, enter the parts of the message that you want to send each week.**

5. **When you're done, click the Close button in the Action bar and enter a name for your Stationery document in the Save as Stationery dialog box.**

   Notes tells you exactly what it did with your stationery, as you can see in Figure 7-11.

Don't get confused by the memo form you see when you create new stationery. Despite all appearances to the contrary, you are not entering the text of a real e-mail. Rather, you are entering the parts of the message that you'll be sending on a regular basis *later*.

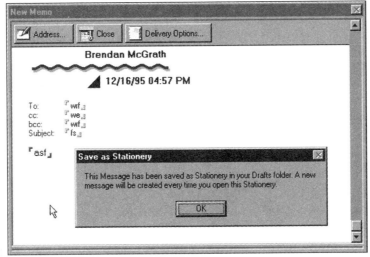

Using stationery

When the time comes to send an e-mail based on your stationery, open your mail database and click the Drafts folder in the Navigation pane. Any and all of the Stationery documents you have will appear, as shown in Figure 7-12.

Open the stationery that you want to send and then add whatever you want to the To:, cc:, bcc:, and Subject: fields as well as to the body of the message. When you send your e-mail, Notes saves a *new* document in your mail database, and leaves the Stationery document just the way it was when you started — so you can use it again next time.

Special Options for a Message

Chapter 4 discusses such delivery options as Importance, Mood stamps, Delivery reports, and Delivery priority. You can find the more advanced options for message delivery in the Special Options dialog box (see Figure 7-13), which you can reach by choosing Actions⇨Special Options.

As Figure 7-13 shows, you can do the person you're sending your message to a favor and indicate that your message has an expiration date. This helps the reader determine which messages to delete if she (or he) is cleaning up her (or his) mail database. Her (or his) mail archive will also use this date, as we discuss earlier in this chapter.

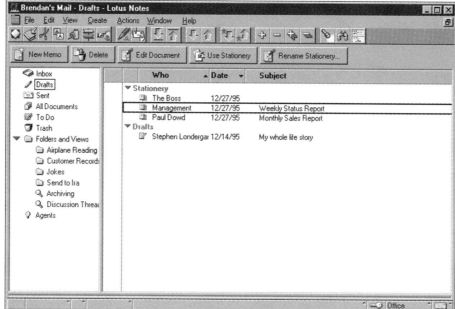

Figure 7-12:
Double-click
a Stationery
message to
send a new
e-mail
based
on that
document.

If you need a response by a particular date, use the `Stamp message with a "Please reply by" date:` field to warn your recipient of same. The date you enter in this field will appear at the top of your e-mail.

When you use your mail database to create a reply to a message, Notes automatically puts the name of the person who sent you the e-mail in the first place in the To: field. If you're sending a message, but want replies to come back to someone other than you, use the `Replies to this memo should be addressed to:` field to enter the name of the person who should receive replies to your message.

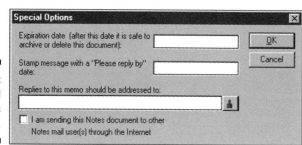

Figure 7-13:
The Special
Options
dialog box.

Part III
The Brave New World of Notes Databases

The 5th Wave   By Rich Tennant

And finally, do you feel your client/server environment keeps you well connected to your department?

In this part...

1mportant as it is, mail is only one part of the miracle that is Notes. The other work you'll do in Notes involves Notes databases. Your mail is contained in a database, so you already know a fair amount about how databases work in Notes (if you read Part II, that is). The purpose of Part III is to let you peer into the heart of a database and discover what makes it tick.

The next chapters guide you through the maze of database features, then show you how you can add some touches of your own. You'll be able to use each database you encounter more efficiently, to tinker with some parts of a database, and to gain the skills that propel many database designers on to fame and fortune.

Chapter 8

Back to Databasics

*Y*ou've heard it before; Notes is a database program. But what does that mean? In the simplest terms, a Notes database is nothing more than a collection of documents. But, in not-the-simplest terms, Notes databases represent a way for you to share information with other Notes users who may be just down the hall or scattered all over the world. In this chapter, we'll look under the hood of the average database and be sure that you recognize what you see there, and we'll show you how to find and start databases.

A Notes database could be a directory of the people in your company, a series of hot sales leads, or a discussion forum in which people overcome their reluctance to express their opinions on any number of topics and respond to each others' opinions. One way or the other, you'll find that Notes databases allow you to interact with people in ways you've never thought of — and with people you've never thought of, either.

How to Speak Database like a Native

You're much more comfortable in a country when you speak the language. When you enter the world of databases, the same is true. So here's a list of the sorts of words you routinely hear from people who are fluent in the database language:

✔ A *database* is a collection of information. Most of the Notes databases you'll use aren't on your computer but rather on a Notes server somewhere.

✔ A *document* is what's in a Notes database. Notes documents are composed and saved by people, at least one of whom looks just like you. You can read and sometimes edit other people's documents. Or, depending on the type of database you're using, you can also create your own documents.

✔ A *form* is a part of a database that you use to view, compose, and edit documents.

✔ A *view* is a summary of the documents in a database. A view displays documents in a database, but not necessarily all of them. Because a database can have many views, you may have one view that shows just your customers in California and another view that lists your customers by shoe size. Yet another view may display completely different documents, such as a list of companies that may be hot sales prospects.

✔ A *field* is a place where you grow turnips. In a database, a field is a place where you enter data. When you're composing or editing a document, each field is marked by little L-shaped brackets. Notes boasts eight kinds of fields. You can consult the following list if anyone ever asks you what they are:

Text	Rich text
Time	Authors
Number	Names
Keywords	Readers

✔ The *data* is whatever information an author entered into a field when composing or editing a document in a database.

So, putting it all together, someone may open the Company Personnel *database,* compose a new *document* using the Personnel Information *form,* type **Liz Watters** in the Full Name *field,* and then enter some other data and save the whole thing in the database as a new document that will be listed in the All Employees by Name *view.* Then they'll all go out and plant a turnip.

Finding a New Notes Database

Your boss — communicating with you through Notes e-mail, of course — tells you to start using a particular Notes database to respond to customer inquiries. Although you've heard other people in the department talking about this database, you've never used it before. What do you do?

Get the specifics. As an employee, you aren't expected to know about the existence of every database in use in the organization or where each one is located. Don't expect to find the database in question on your hard disk; databases are usually placed on a server somewhere so everyone can use them. After all, databases aren't *yours;* they're *ours.*

Ask your boss or a coworker for both the database's name *and* the server's name before you try to find it. Knowing its filename may be helpful, too; often several databases have very similar names — Customer Tracking, Customer Data, Customer Leads. Knowing the filename guarantees that you are accessing the right database.

Whenever you need to open a database that you haven't used before, just follow these steps:

1. **Choose File⇨Database⇨Open.**

   Selecting this command gives you the dialog box displayed in Figure 8-1.

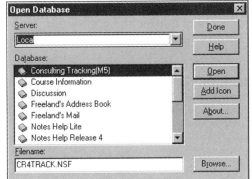

Figure 8-1:
The Open
Database
dialog box.

2. **Look in the text box under the word Server.**

   In Figure 8-1, this text box says Local. If you're using a Mac, that space says Notes Data Folder instead of Local. Either way, this is where you want to look if the database you're seeking is on your own hard disk. If it isn't, go on to Step 3.

3. **Click on the down arrow across from the word Local.**

   You now see the names of one, a few, or lots of Notes servers, depending on how your administrator has set up Notes at your company. If you don't see the name of the server you're after, use the scroll bar to move down the list.

4. **Select the server you want by double-clicking its name.**

Your company may have other Notes servers that are in different groups; however, their names won't appear in the Open Database dialog box. If you're trying to find a server that's not on your list, try typing the server's name and clicking Open. If that doesn't work, contact your administrator.

When you double-click the name of a server in the Server: list box, a list of the databases on that server appears in the Database: list box. Double-click the server you want or highlight it and click the Open button. If you aren't sure which of several databases with similar titles you want, check the file name in the Filename: text box.

Sometimes, for all sorts of reasons, database designers flip a switch in a database so that database won't appear on the Database list. Because, in this case, you have no way of seeing the name on your computer, you'll have to ask a living, breathing person for the filename. Then you can type that filename in the Filename: text box to open that document.

Servers, servers, everywhere

You're on a quest to find a Notes database and you know that it's on a server. But which server? Most companies have more than one. Your company may have one server with databases belonging to the marketing department, and another with databases for sales, and so on. You get the idea. Some companies have hundreds of Notes servers, some have a few, and some may only have one server (for now).

When you're trying to find a new Notes database, knowing where to start looking can be tough. If your boss didn't tell you which server to use, be adventurous: Just start looking on the various servers until you find the database in question. And, hey, you just might come across some other Notes databases that interest you, too.

The server names you see in the Open Database dialog box are the whim of your administrator. The names may be very functional (and grown-up) like "Marketing," "Sales," and so on. Or the names may be more imaginative like "Sleepy," "Bashful," "Doc," or "Grumpy" (bet you can't name all seven). When push comes to shove, though, you should ask someone which server you're supposed to use. It's easy to get sidetracked while searching for a particular database, and you often feel like you're looking for hay in a needle stack.

I hear you knocking, but . . . (certification problems)

As you may imagine, your administrator has all kinds of tricks to determine which people get to use which servers. If you ever double-click a server name in the Open Database dialog box and get an error message that says either Your ID has not been certified to access the server or You are not authorized to use the server, it probably means that your administrator has to do something to allow you to use that server. You can't do anything to fix this problem, so send your administrator an e-mail to ask for access.

Be sure to cc: your boss so that your administrator knows that you're not kidding around here.

To be able to use a server, both your User ID and the server's User ID have to have a common certificate. Giving out these certificates is one of the many jobs your (no doubt highly-paid and well-trained) administrator does all day. So, if Notes ever tells you that you don't have the right certificate to use a particular server, contact your administrator, who should be able to fix the problem. For more information about certificates, see Chapter 14.

Digging into directories

Just as you have sudirectories on your hard disk to help you organize your files, your administrator may have set up subdirectories on the server to help organize the databases. As you pike around on your Notes servers, you will eventually encounter one of these subdirectories. If your server has subdirectories, they will appear at the bottom of the list of database titles, as the directory names ADMIN does in Figure 8-2. An additional hint that something is a subdirectory and not a database is that its icon is a folder instead of a book.

Figure 8-2:
At the
bottom of
the list of
databases
may be
some sub-
directories
containing
more
databases.

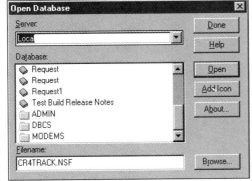

To see a list of the databases in that subdirectory, double-click the directory's name. You can use the item on the list that looks like an up arrow with two periods to return to the parent directory on the server.

To Open or to Add, That Is the Question

When you've located the correct server and database in the Open Database dialog box, you have two choices:

✔ **Open the database right away.**

If you click Open (or double-click a database's title, which has the same effect), Notes does three things. First, it adds that database's icon to your desktop for future reference. Second, it closes the Open Database dialog box. Finally, it opens the database you chose.

✔ **Add the icon to your desktop so you can easily open the database later.**

If you click Add Icon, Notes adds that database's icon to your desktop but does not open the database. Instead, it leaves you in the Open Database dialog box so that you can add some other icons to your desktop. This button is useful if you need to collect a few databases and you want to get them all in the same trip to the Open Database dialog box. Opening each database individually and then returning to the dialog box to open another one can be quite time consuming and cuts into the things for which you were really hired — having meetings and doing power lunches. Or is it *doing* meetings and *having* power lunches?

Whichever method you choose, opening the database or adding the icon, the next time you want to get into this database, you won't have to go searching for it in the Open Database dialog box. You'll be able to just double-click the database's icon right from your desktop.

In a word processing program, you simply open a document and start reading. Before you open a document in Notes, however, you must open the database in which that document is contained.

The Database Door Creaks Open

What's inside a database? That depends.

If you're opening a database for the first time ever, you'll see the database's Policy document, written with great care and attention to detail by the database designer to anticipate questions about the database, its use and purpose, and its designer. Remember the old expression: "When all else fails, read the instructions"? Responsible, mature, meticulous users read the Policy document very, very carefully. The other 99 percent of the population immediately presses Esc to close it and gets right to work in the database.

The person who creates the database writes the Policy document. Of course, some database designers are more conscientious than others, so some Policy documents will be more instructive than others. In fact, a lazy database designer might not create one at all, so don't be surprised if you occasionally see a blank screen when you open a new database.

After carefully reading and dismissing the Policy document screen, you see one of the views in the database, as shown in Figure 8-3. It may be only one of several tables of contents of the database, but it's the view that the designer of the database decided that you should see first.

A database may have several views, and many views don't contain all the documents in a database. Under Folders and Views, in the upper-left pane of the screen, you see a list of other folders and views you can use. (We unveil the mysteries of folders and views in the next chapter.)

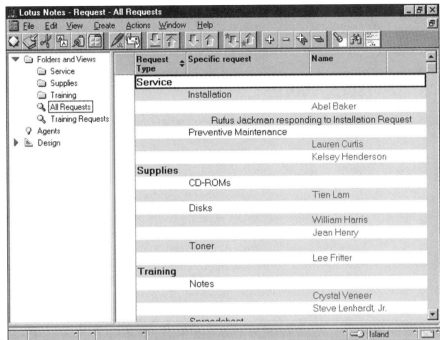

Figure 8-3:
A typical
view in a
typical
database.

Each time you open a database (after the first time, that is), you see the view or folder you were using the last time you were in that database. Notes is pretty good about remembering what you were doing the last time you were there, even if you aren't.

When You Need Help

Sometimes you try to do something and get caught halfway through the procedure, unsure of the next step. Or maybe you're trying to figure out how to do something that you've never done before. Look to any of these places for a helping hand:

- ✔ Notes' built-in Help feature
- ✔ The Using document that's in every database
- ✔ Your Notes manual
- ✔ This book
- ✔ Your friends
- ✔ The documentation databases

 ✔ The Koran/Talmud/Bible (Admittedly, these books aren't exactly chock-full of Notes tips, but they may be a good source of comfort for your non-Notes related problems.)

Help, Notes!

Notes has a help system that you can use in two different ways: you can ask for help about the particular activity you're stuck with, or you can peruse the entire Notes Help database.

Using context-sensitive help

Press F1 anytime, anywhere, for help with what you are currently doing.

Good news: Like most software these days, context-sensitive help is always just a keystroke away in Notes. Whenever you get stuck, you can always press F1 (or the help key on a Mac), and Notes will do its best to show you a help screen that's related to whatever you're doing at the time. As always, you press Esc to close the Help document.

Bad news: The context-sensitive help in Notes may be less useful than the help that's available in other programs. That's because the help that comes with the program only deals with how to use the Notes program, not with how to use any particular database. When you have a question about the particulars of an application you're using, you'll have to get to the database's own help screen. Getting database-specific help is covered later in this chapter, under "Turning to a database's Using document."

Reading the Help database

Got a few minutes before your next meeting? All the screens that you see when you press F1 come from a Notes database called, appropriately enough, "Notes Help." You can rifle through the documents in the Help database the way you read any other database. They have lots of information that you might never even think to ask about with the F1 key.

Out of sight, out of mind: How do I find the Policy document later?

After you use a database for a couple of months, you'll probably forget all about the Policy document. After all, you only saw it once — the first day you used the database. Because the Policy document may have lots of useful information, it's possible you'll want to refer to it in the future, especially if you dismissed it quickly the first time you saw it. Don't worry, the Policy document is always close at hand. Just choose Help⇨About This Database, and — bingo — there it is.

The icon for the Help database is probably already on your desktop, so you can just double-click it and go to town. If the Help database's icon isn't on your desktop, use the Open Database dialog box to find it. If, to save disk space, the Help database wasn't installed on your own computer (local), you can use the Help database that's on any one of your Notes servers.

Turning to a database's Using document

Every database has a *Using document,* which is similar to the Policy document described earlier in this chapter. Like the Policy document, the Using document is created by the person who designed the database and is intended to help you figure out how use the database. To see a database's Using document, you have to open the database in question and then choose Help⇨Using This Database. Check out Figure 8-4 to see a sample Using document.

Some application developers (but not the good ones) are lazy, so don't be surprised if you occasionally see a dialog box that says `No help is available for this database` when you try to see a database's Using document. If this happens to you, call the database designers with your questions. When these folks get sick of answering the same questions over and over again, they may decide to go ahead and create a Using document.

Dusting off your Notes manuals

Of course, we can't ignore the Notes manuals, which contain everything you ever wanted to know about Notes. Come to think of it, they probably contain *more* than you ever wanted to know about Notes. If you didn't receive a set of Notes manuals when you got the program, give a call to your administrator.

When all else fails, read the manual.

Using this book

Despite the title of the book, we think you were positively brilliant for buying this book. We hope that you'll use it as a reference all through your career with Notes, and our intent was to organize it so that you can quickly find the information you need.

You should tell your friends, your coworkers. and your boss about this book. Shouldn't everyone in your company have a copy? *Lotus Notes for Dummies* makes a great gift, too. Imagine the squeals of delight when your children see their own copies of this book decoratrively wrapped next to their birthday cakes. Maybe you should buy a couple of extra copies, just to be safe.

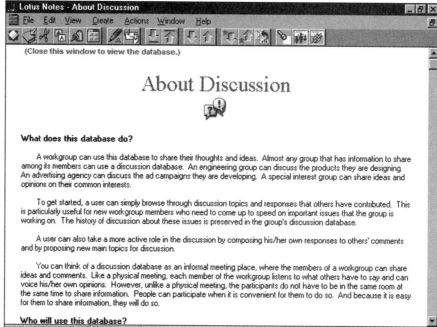

Figure 8-4:
The Using document *should* tell users how to use the database. That's the designer's responsibility. Get it?

Calling on your friends

Given the fact that Notes is *group*ware, it's safe to say that there's a whole group of people using Notes at your company, and any one of them (or at least the friendly ones) can be a great resource for help and tips about using the program. Don't discount their importance! You can call them, e-mail them, or ask them in the cafeteria line.

Lots of companies even have a special Notes database just so people can ask each other how to use Notes. If your company doesn't have one of these, maybe you should suggest to your administrator. If you tell your administrator that one of these databases would keep you from calling the help desk as often, we'll bet that the database will appear within the hour!

Using the documentation databases

Last but not least, you can always look for help in the Notes documentation databases. You'll find them on just about any Notes server, in the DOC directory.

Don't overwhelm yourself — these documentation databases are *not* for the faint of heart. Unless you're destined to be a power-user of Notes, and un-less you'll be doing stuff like creating your own databases and installing Notes servers, you probably don't have to bother with documentation databases.

Chapter 9

Come on in, the Database Is Fine

. . . .

. . . .

*W*hen you open a database (and dismiss the Policy document, if this is the first time you've opened this database), you get your first glimpse of the contents of the database itself. (Check out Chapter 8 for more information about opening databases and Policy documents.)

Very probably, the opening screen looks like Figure 9-1 and is the starting point from which you will do the work in the database. This chapter gives you an idea of what you are seeing, how to change the appearance of the screen, and how to burrow even deeper into the database.

What a Pane

When you're looking at an open database, you may see the screen divided into several sections, called *panes*. Each pane has a name and a *default* (prepackaged) location. We say "default" because you can change the location of a pane.

Depending on your mood, your religious preference, or your current needs, you can resize any or all panes. Click and drag any border separating two panes to change the amount of space each takes up on the screen.

The Navigation pane

In the upper-left corner of the screen in Figure 9-1 is the Navigation pane. This pane lists all the folders and views that you can use. Sometimes, a database designer makes life a little easier for users by putting labeled shapes or buttons

Document   View

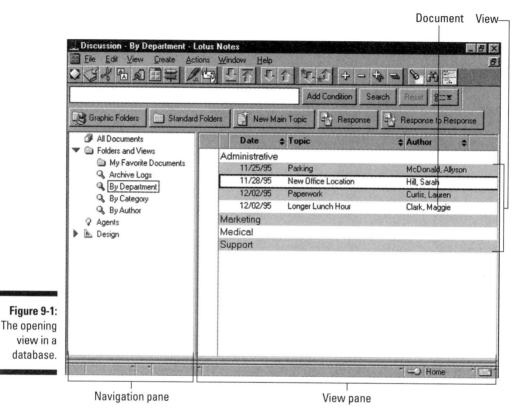

Figure 9-1:
The opening
view in a
database.

Navigation pane   View pane

or colored areas in the Navigation pane. Those shapes are called *navigators* and usually represent other items you can look at or actions you can take. In Figure 9-2, the Navigation pane contains a navigator that presents options to see other views or folders and a button that allows you to close the current window.

To see the list of views and folders instead of a navigator, choose <u>V</u>iew⇨<u>S</u>how⇨ <u>F</u>olders. To see a graphical navigator (assuming that at least one exists), choose <u>V</u>iew and then the name of the navigator you want to see. Generally, though, your best bet is to leave the screen the way the designer left it.

The View pane

The View pane contains a list of the documents, possibly listed under categories. These documents are the ones which were placed there by the user (if a folder name is highlighted in the Navigation pane) or chosen by formula (if it's a view name which is highlighted).

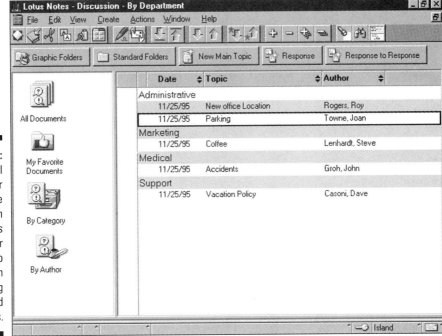

Figure 9-2:
A graphical
navigator
in the
Navigation
pane makes
it easier for
you to
switch
among
folders and
views.

The Preview pane

The Preview pane, at the bottom of the screen, allows you to see the contents of the currently selected document. This pane may not be visible when you open a view; you need to click and drag the bottom of the View pane up to expose the Preview pane or choose View⇨Document Preview. In Figure 9-3, we've opened the Preview pane so that we can see the contents of the document highlighted in the View pane.

In this world of bewildering choices, it's even possible for you to change the place where the Preview pane appears. Choose View⇨Arrange Preview... and then select the screen location where you want to see the Preview pane. We've displayed your choices for you in living black and white in Figure 9-4.

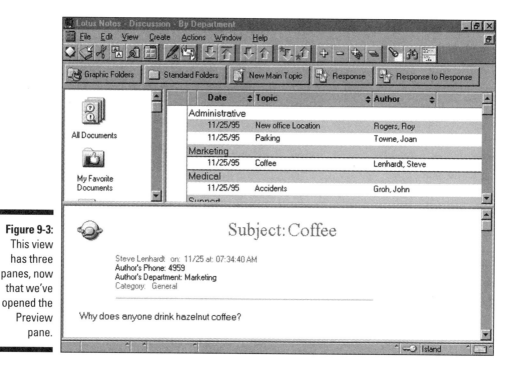

Figure 9-3:
This view has three panes, now that we've opened the Preview pane.

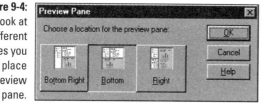

Figure 9-4:
Just look at the different places you can place the Preview pane.

I Was Just Thinking of View

Every database has at least one view — most databases have several. A database view does three things:

- It *summarizes* the documents that are in the database.
- It *sorts* the documents in the database.
- It *selects* documents in the database.

Figure 9-5 shows a view within a database that's used to list various requests. This view is showing (or *selecting*) only requests for training. Requests for supplies or service are not included in this view. This view sorts the documents by the course category and then by the name of the specific course the person is requesting. This view also summarizes the documents by showing the additional information (requester's name and the date of the course). It's probably a safe bet that each of the documents selected here has more information than this particular view actually displays in its columns; the designer of the view decided that this selected information best summarized each document.

What's in a view, anyway?

Each line (row) in a view represents an individual document, and each column represents information contained in that particular document. (We discuss the nitty-gritty details of documents and fields in Chapter 10.) Some views may show alternate lines in a different color, as in Figure 9-5, because the view designer took pity on the users of the view, fearing that it's hard to see what data is on what line.

Each column in a view displays the value of a particular field in the document. For example, in Figure 9-5, the first column displays the type of course that employees wants to take, the second column lists the specific course title, the third column has the name of the person requesting the course, and so on.

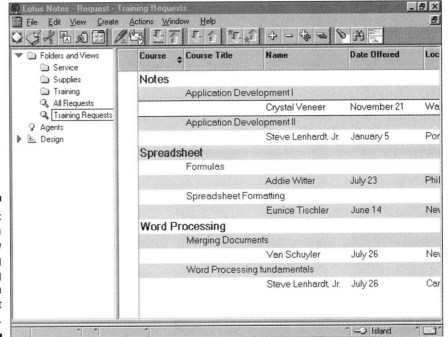

Figure 9-5:
This is a view showing only training requests in a request database.

Often, the database designer makes it possible for users to change the width of a column. Click and drag the right-hand border of a column head to the left to narrow the column or to the right to widen it.

When the stars come out

In many databases, Notes tracks which documents you have read and which ones you haven't. This distinction is particularly helpful in a discussion database, where you don't want to waste time on the documents that you've already read. You can *usually* tell that a document is new (or at least that you haven't read it) because it will be a different color than the rest of the documents. A document that you haven't read before will *always* have a little star next to it, in the left-most column of the view.

Usually, unread documents are red. But don't be surprised if, in some databases, they're some other color. The database designer gets to decide what color they'll be.

Response documents are documents that are composed by users to, you guessed it, respond to another document in a database. Most databases, like the one shown in Figure 9-6, display response documents indented under the document they are responding to.

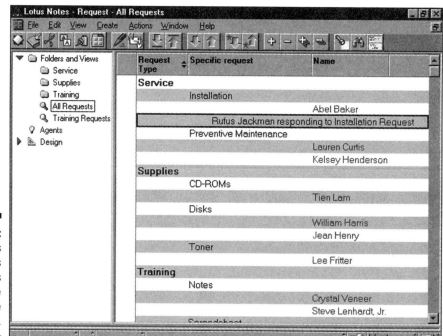

Figure 9-6:
Rufus
Jackman's
document is
a response
to a service
request.

A Sort of Category

As we mentioned at the beginning of our discussion on views, one of the things a view does is sort the documents; that is to say, it lists the documents in some particular order. A view in our request database might list the documents sorted by the course type, and another view might list the documents sorted by the employees' names.

Some views, though, are not only sorted but also *categorized*.

When a view *sorts* its documents, it lists them in alphabetical order according to what they have in a particular column, and it shows what each document has in that column even if it's the same as what the document above has. On the other hand, when a view *categorizes* its documents, it still sorts the documents, but it lists a particular field value only once, followed by all the documents that have the same value in that field.

Confused? It's easier to see than it is to read. Take a look at Figure 9-6, in which you can see all requests entered in the database. There are three requests for Service: one for Installation and two for Preventive Maintenance. In this view, all service requests are listed together, as are specific types of service. If it weren't for categories, the word "Service" and the specific requests would appear in every row. That's one for the Department of Redundancy Department.

Put on your glasses or squint and then look carefully at the heading of the first column in Figure 9-6. See the little double arrowhead? When you see one or two arrowheads, it means that the thoughtful database designer has given you the ability to re-sort the column. In other words, if the column is arranged in ascending alphabetical order, clicking anywhere in that column heading will change the sort order from ascending to descending (Z to A).

One of the reasons that views have categories is to make the view a little neater and easier to look at. You can further neaten up a view by *collapsing* and *expanding* categories.

In Figure 9-6, the entire view is expanded. In Figure 9-7, the Service Category is completely expanded, the Supplies category is completely collapsed, and the Training category is expanded, but its subcategories are collapsed. The documents are still there, and they'll appear like magic when a category is expanded.

Okay, how do you do it? Easy, but it depends on what you want to expand or collapse.

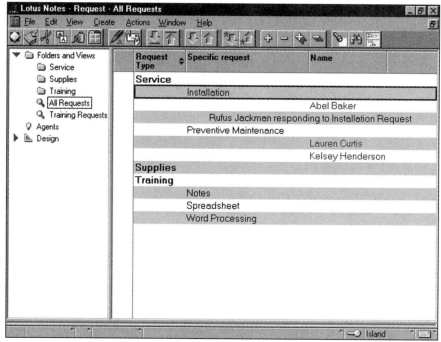

Figure 9-7:
This view
has one
category
completely
collapsed,
one partially
collapsed,
and one not
collapsed
at all.

Here are the ways to expand or collapse *a single category:*

✔ Use the arrow keys to select the category in question and choose
View⇨Expand/Collapse. Then choose either Expand Selected Level or
Expand Selected & Children or Collapse Selected Level. (If you have
visions of little flat children running around your neighborhood, you
missed the point about Expand Selected and Children. It means expand the
current category and its subcategories.)

✔ It's even easier to press the + (plus key) to expand a selected section, or
the – (minus key) to collapse a selected section.

✔ Best yet, rather than trying to remember all that, just double-click the
category you want to expand or collapse, or highlight the category and
press Enter.

Here are the ways to expand or collapse *the whole view:*

✔ Choose <u>V</u>iew⇨<u>E</u>xpand All or <u>V</u>iew⇨<u>C</u>ollapse All.

✔ Press Shift + + (that's Shift and the plus sign) to expand the whole view or
Shift +– (Shift and the minus sign) to collapse the whole view.

Using Folders as Holders

No doubt about it, views are great, and you won't hear us criticizing them. But they do have a disadvantage. You, Mr. or Ms. User, can't determine what is in a view. Oh sure, if you know how, you can create a view selection formula and use that to determine what is and isn't included. But what if you want to store a bunch of documents of your own choosing together in one place? What if, for example, you want to put together all the documents that need your immediate attention or documents on a vague subject (like industry trends) that may be hard to put in a formula in a view?

The answer to this plaintive cry is . . . folders. Like views, *folders* are ways to display some contents of a database. In the upper-left corner of the screen in Figure 9-8 is a list of folders and views under the creatively named heading "Folders and Views." For those who like a challenge, can you tell which are views and which are folders? (Hint: The symbols next to the names of the folders and views are folders and magnifying glasses.)

The designer of the database may have created one or more folders for you to put stuff in. Despite its name, you can use the folder for anything you like. After reading Chapter 10, you'll know how to create and modify your own folders.

Figure 9-8:
This Navigation pane lists folders and views and shows that someone is dragging a document into the Service folder.

Keep the following important facts in mind as you use folders:

- ✔ You put documents in a folder by clicking and dragging a document from a view or folder into a folder. In Figure 9-8, the document which is highlighted in the view is being dragged, kicking and screaming, into the Service folder. You may also find a button somewhere on-screen that allows you to assign the selected document(s) to a folder.

- ✔ Putting a document in a folder does not create a new copy of the document, it just lists the document in a new place.

- ✔ You can remove one or more selected documents from a folder by choosing Actions➪Remove from Folder. You may also have a button somewhere that allows you to remove a document from a folder.

- ✔ Removing a document using the preceding method does not delete it from the database. It simply removes it from the folder.

- ✔ Don't press the Delete key to delete a document from a folder; that will delete it from the database permanently.

- ✔ There is no selection formula for a folder; what is in the folder is determined by you, the user.

- ✔ Folders have columns just as views do. Each column shows the contents of various fields in the documents. If you add a document to a folder, and that document doesn't contain any of the fields listed in the columns, then there won't be any data to display in the column, so you won't see the document listed there.

It's very likely that you'll sometimes want to see the documents in a database listed in a different way. In other words, you will want to switch to a different view or folder. As long as you can see the Navigation pane, you can click on any folder or view. Give Notes a second or two, and the new choice opens.

So, What Can You Do with the Documents?

Among the things you can do with the documents in a view are

- ✔ Select them
- ✔ Read them
- ✔ Forward them
- ✔ Add them to a folder
- ✔ Print them
- ✔ Delete them

Selecting documents

You can do all kinds of things with documents — print them, delete them, forward them as an e-mail — but first you need to select them.

How to select them one at a time

In a word processing program, if you want to make a word bold, you first select the word somehow and then use some command to make the word bold. This same concept applies to selecting documents in a view. If a view has a couple of documents and you want to do something to one of them — print it, delete it, or recategorize it — you have to select it first.

By now, you've probably noticed that a box surrounds a single document in a view or folder. It's called the *selection bar,* and you use it to highlight an individual document. Whatever document is in that box is hereby *selected.*

But what if I want more than one?

Funny you should ask. Say that you want to print five documents in a view. Sure, you'll use the selection bar to select them, but how do you tell Notes that you want more than one? The easiest way to select multiple documents is to select the first document in question and then press the spacebar. When you do, you'll notice that the document gets checked off in the far-left column of the view, as you can see in Figure 9-9.

If you need to select a few documents, select each one and press the spacebar. If the documents you want are one after the other, just hold down Shift while you press the arrow keys to move the selection bar over the documents. Notes checks them off.

Better yet, if you use a mouse, you can select a bunch of documents all at once by clicking and dragging over in the left column where you saw the check marks appear.

Finally, you can deselect a document that you mistakenly selected (oops!) by using any of the methods that you used to select it in the first place. In other words, if you have already checked off the document, then selecting it again unchecks it.

Reading documents

If you have the Preview pane visible, you can read a document simply by highlighting its line in the View pane. If you only see a tiny sliver of the document in the Preview, increase the size of the Preview pane by clicking and dragging its border.

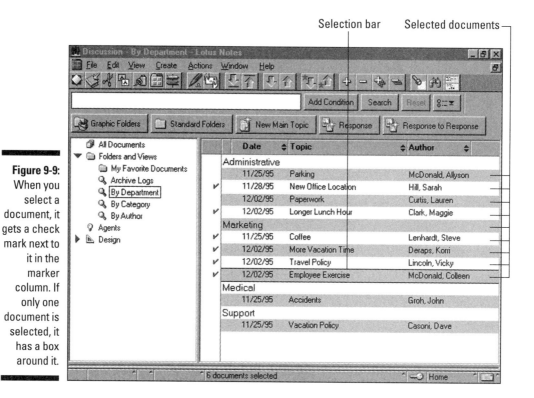

Figure 9-9:
When you select a document, it gets a check mark next to it in the marker column. If only one document is selected, it has a box around it.

Or, if you want the document to fill the screen, open the document by pressing Enter. If you have a mouse, you can just double-click to open the document for reading. You can then press Esc to close the document and return to the view.

Forwarding a bunch of documents

Every now and then, you want someone else to see a document that you're reading. You can call them and tell them to open the Sales Database on the Marketing Server, use the Hot Prospects View, and check out the doc with the title, "This Guy Has A Million Dollars to Spend." But why not save the call and a lot of time and just send the document to that person? Highlight one document, or select several documents, and then choose Actions⇨Forward. Enter the name of everyone who should see the documents and then send the memo. The selected documents become the body of the memo.

Adding documents to a folder

In the section "Using Folders as Holders," we describe the process for adding documents to a folder. Be sure that the documents you add to a folder are visible in that folder. If the documents don't contain fields listed in the columns, you may not see them listed in the folder.

Printing from a view

When you have a view or a folder open (as opposed to a document), and you choose File⇨Print, you get the dialog box shown in Figure 9-10.

This dialog box has a lot of stuff in it — and you may have even *more* options because what you see depends on the kind of printer you have.

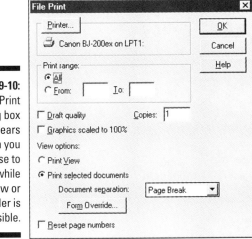

Figure 9-10:
The Print dialog box appears when you choose to print while a view or folder is visible.

The most important buttons in the dialog box are the ones under the line View options: Print View and Print selected documents. Use these buttons to specify whether you want to print the view as it appears on-screen or, instead, print the actual documents that you have selected.

Use the other buttons to determine what the headers and footers should look like, whether Notes should reset the page numbers for each document it prints, and so on. Check out Chapter 5 for more information about printing.

Deleting documents

To delete documents, select the document (or documents) that you want to get rid of and press Delete. The documents don't actually disappear, but each document gets marked with a little recycling bin, as shown in Figure 9-11.

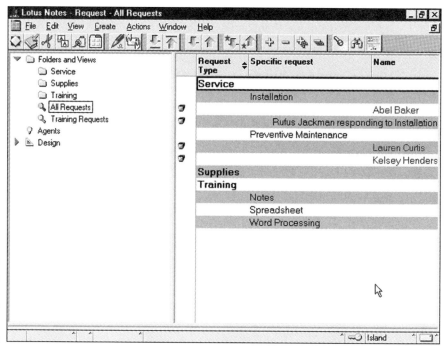

To actually dispose of the marked document, do one of the following:

- Press F9.
- Choose View⇔Refresh.
- Close the database.

If you try to take any of the preceding actions, Notes makes you confirm that you want to delete some documents with a Yes/No dialog box. That's good, because you can choose No (if you goofed) and Notes won't delete the documents after all.

If you've marked a document to be deleted (but haven't yet taken any steps to finalize the deletion) and you decide that you don't want to delete it after all, select the document and press Delete again. The trash can disappears. You can stop worrying, because that document's not going anywhere.

Of course, you can't necessarily delete a document just because you know how to use the Delete key. In fact, in most databases, you can only delete a document if you are the person who composed it in the first place. So that means that you can't delete anybody else's documents, and you don't have to worry about anyone else deleting your documents, either.

Chapter 10
What's up, Doc(uments)?

The heart of any Notes database is the documents that are in it. (If you're familiar with a program like Paradox or Lotus 1-2-3, documents are like records.) A *document* is all the information about a particular — well, a particular whatever. Here are some examples:

✔ If the database you're using is a purchase-tracking system, you may have one document for each customer and one document for each order they've placed.

✔ In your e-mail database, each document is a message.

✔ If you're using a discussion database, each document made by each person is a separate comment on the topic at hand.

✔ In a database full of pages from the World Wide Web, each page is a document.

We should also say right up front that we intend this chapter to be more of a reference than anything, so you may not want (or need) to read it all in one sitting. Just take it off the shelf as questions arise.

A Document with All the Fixin's

When you open a document, you see all kinds of things: words, pictures, icons, even objects. If you're going to be a Notes big shot, you'd better know what all these things are about. Here's what you'll see in your travels:

✔ Static text

✔ Fields

- ✔ Buttons
- ✔ Hotspots
- ✔ Icons

Static text

No, static text doesn't have anything to do with rubbing your feet on a rug in the winter time. *Static text* just means words that are a permanent part of certain forms. It's called "static" because you can't change it.

The kind soul who created the forms in the databases you use no doubt included some static text. Static text can be the title of the form, field names, or maybe some instructions about how to use the form. Take a look at Figure 10-1 to see some examples of static text.

Static text

Figure 10-1: Static text helps you to figure out what to do with the parts of a document.

Fields

Fields

Fields are where the action is in a document. They contain the information that matters, the information that you *can* add and change when you're composing or editing a document. And fields come in a number of different flavors (not quite 31). Here are some of the basic types of fields you're likely to encounter:

- ✔ Text
- ✔ Rich text
- ✔ Date
- ✔ Numbers
- ✔ Names

You may be able to put away your calculator: editable versus computed fields

In most cases, when you compose a new document, the fields are empty, and it's your job to enter the new name, address, and so on. However, you may occasionally encounter a computed field. A *computed field* is a field for which the program automatically calculates the contents.

For example, say you're using a database that tracks customer orders, and it has three number fields: a Quantity field, a Price field, and a field named Extended Cost. The database manager would probably set up this Extended Cost field as a computed field. This means that, when you enter a value in the Quantity field and then enter a value in the Price field, Notes automatically multiplies the two together and puts the answer into the Extended Cost field. Pretty neat, huh?

Computed fields are often noneditable. In the preceding example, if your computer is already automatically calculating the Extended Cost field, why would you want to change it?

It's really true — computers can't make mistakes. Only people can.

If you have a Ph.D in Notes, you probably know about other fancy fields and speak official field-name-ese. As for the rest of us, these field names will do just fine.

When you're entering a new document, it really is hard to know what the fields' data types are. In other words, it's hard to tell just by looking whether a field is a date field or a number field or even a text field. Just use common sense; if the field's name is something like Quantity or Price, it's a safe bet that Notes expects you to enter a number. If the field is Address, you can bet it's a text field.

Text fields

A *text field* is just what it sounds like. A text field can contain any combination of characters: letters of the alphabet, digits, punctuation, you name it. A text field might contain a customer's name, your colleague's street address, or a description of property that's for sale.

A text field can contain a maximum of about seven thousand characters. That's more than you'll ever need to put in a text field, so don't worry about it!

You may encounter a special kind of text field, called a *section,* which hides certain information in a document. On-screen, a section appears as a bolded title (sometimes a name) with a triangle to the left of it. To see the information in a hidden (or *collapsed*) section, you must click the little triangle right next to the section title. (See Chapter 6 for more on how to use sections in your e-mail messages.) Sometimes, despite your clicking the little triangle next to a section's title, you just can't get into it. This means that the section you're trying to view is *protected.* You can't get into this section, but you can double-click the section title to see who can.

Another special kind of text field is the *keyword* field. A keyword field is just a text field in which the possible entries have been "pre-ordained" by the person who created the database. That's good news, because it means that (A) you don't have to type a keyword field's contents, because you get to pick from a list of the possible values, and (2) you don't have to worry that you'll make a mistake in the field. Figure 10-2 shows an example of three kinds of keyword fields:

- ✔ **Radio buttons:** In a *radio button field,* you can only choose one of the options in the list. You select the value you want by clicking it or using the arrow keys to highlight the option you want and then pressing the spacebar to select it.

- ✔ **Check boxes:** In a *check box field,* you can make more than one selection. Click as many of the values as you want, or highlight them with the arrow keys and then use the spacebar to select them.

- ✔ **Dialog list:** Last but not least, there's the *dialog list field.* This field looks an awful lot like a regular text field, but you can tell that it's a dialog list field by the little arrow next to it, as shown in Figure 10-2. When you click that little arrow (or press Enter in the field), you get a dialog box listing the possible values.

If you're using a dialog list field, you can also press the spacebar to cycle through the options that are available. (Using the spacebar is a little faster than using the dialog box.) You can also type the first letter of any of the options to choose it, which is even *faster.*

It's default of de field

The person who created your database may save you some time (and typing) by including *default* values in some fields.

Say that most of your customers are from California (hey, dude!). If you're lucky, someone has set up a default so that every time you compose a new Customer Profile, the State field already says California. You can change the State field if you want to — after all, not *all* your customers are from San Francisco — but think of all the typing you *don't* have to do for the people who are in California. Think of default values as being suggestions.

Lots of Notes databases have default values in fields that hold things like area codes, state names, and author names. That's good, because these defaults can save you mucho time and typing.

Dialog list box field

Regular text field

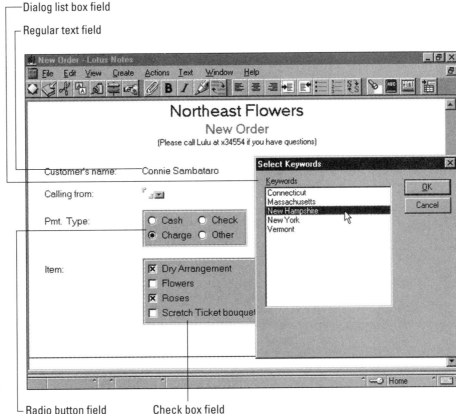

Radio button field   Check box field

Figure 10-2:
Keyword
fields save
you time
because
you just pick
a value from
the list.

Rich text fields

Rich text fields are what separate Notes from all the rest of the database programs in the world. *Rich text fields* are like regular text fields in that they often contain plain words and numbers. So, what's so "rich" about them, you ask? Well, in a rich text field (unlike a regular text field) you can use the Text menu to make words bold or italicized or a larger font. Just try that in a program like dBASE or Paradox — or in a regular Notes text field, for that matter. It's also only in rich text fields that you can create the magic of embedded objects, file attachments, and pictures.

So how do you tell the difference between a rich text field and a regular text field? You probably can't, or at least you can't by just looking at it. When you're creating a document, text fields don't *look* any different from rich text fields. If you really want to tell the difference, you'll have to be adventurous. Type a few characters in the field you're trying to identify and then try to make them bold. If you can boldface the characters you just typed, it must be a rich text field. If Notes won't let you make the characters bold, italicized, or anything fancy, the field you're in must be a plain text field.

What's even more intriguing (well, moderately intriguing, anyway) is that a rich text field can also contain information from other programs. Using the powers of *object linking and embedding*, you can use a rich text field to store the contents of a Lotus 1-2-3 spreadsheet or perhaps an MS-Word document right in the middle of your Notes document. (See Chapter 17 if you're hungry for more on this topic.)

One of the latest computer buzzwords is *compound document*. A compound document is a document that includes several objects. For example, you might put a document in a database to show your colleagues the progress you've made on a project you've been working on. In the body of the message, you include a Lotus 1-2-3 spreadsheet, a Freelance chart, and an audio recording of the new jingle. That's a compound document. Notes can include all that fancy stuff in one rich text field.

Rich text fields can also contain attachments. You use attachments to include a computer file in a Notes document. In the old days, you would do your expenses in Lotus 1-2-3, print the spreadsheet, and then give the piece of paper to your boss for approval. Now, because you're using Notes, you can actually *attach* the spreadsheet to an e-mail message and get it to your boss electronically. We're one step closer to the paperless office! (Do you think people will use floppy disks instead of napkins to wipe their mouths in the paperless office cafeteria of the future?)

Any rich text field can hold many, many megabytes of information — you can send someone an e-mail and include in it a Lotus 1-2-3 worksheet, *and* a Microsoft Word document, *and* a copy of your CONFIG.SYS, *and* a scanned picture of your new baby.

Date fields

Date fields hold (you guessed it!) dates. You may be surprised to learn that you can also enter times in a date field. If you're using a database that tracks customer calls, for example, you may need to enter a date or time.

The format you use to enter a date or time depends on the way your computer was set up. If, upon trying to save a document, you get the error message `Unable to interpret time or date,` you probably used dashes when you should have you used slashes. Or maybe you used slashes when you should have used dashes! Try one way or the other to see which your computer accepts.

Number fields

Number fields hold numbers, pure and simple. Don't try to enter any non-number characters — like slashes, dashes, letters, or smiley faces — in a number field.

Name Fields

Name fields are special because they hold a person's name for some kind of security reason. For example, most Notes documents have a computed field that automatically records the name of the person who composed the document. This feature allows people who read the document to know who wrote it, and it reminds Notes itself who should be able to edit the document later. (In most databases, you can only edit a document if you composed it yourself.)

You may occasionally encounter *editable name fields.* A database may have a field where you must enter the name of the person who should receive your purchase requisition, for example. If you do someday find your cursor in a name field, just type the person's name as it would appear on their business card: **Pat Freeland** or **Elaine Donnelly**.

Buttons

In addition to static text, fields, and sections, you can count on running across *buttons* during your adventures with Notes. Buttons help you do things quickly. You've probably already used the buttons on the Action bar while you were in your mail database. Well, you may also encounter such buttons right on the forms in some databases, like the one in Figure 10-3.

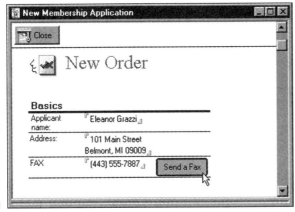

Figure 10-3:
Click a
button once
to use it.

If you see a button and you want to use it, click it. (That's pretty easy, right?) You can also use the arrows to select it and then press the spacebar to "push" the button.

Of course, what happens when you click a button depends on what the database designer has programmed that button to do.

Hotspots

A *Hotspot* is a special part of a document that does something. Clicking on a Hotspot may display some little tidbit of information or open a different document in a different database. If you could click the Hotspot in Figure 10-4, it would display the new PC supplier's name.

Figure 10-4:
When you
see a word
enclosed in
a little green
box, you
know it's a
Hotspot.

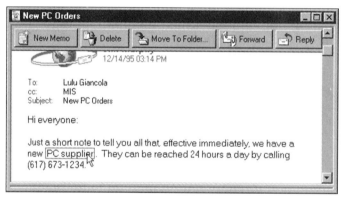

To use a Hotspot, you click it or select it with the arrow keys and press the spacebar.

Pop-ups

The most common kind of Hotspot you'll encounter is called a *Pop-up*. Pop-ups usually appear as text enclosed in a green box which you can click to display a reminder, a hint, or more information about a particular word or sentence. Figure 10-5 shows a Hotspot containing a Pop-up. Press and hold down the mouse button anywhere in the green box to see the Pop-up. (In Chapter 13, we explain how to create your own Pop-up.)

Some Pop-ups aren't intended to show you information but rather to take you somewhere. When you click inside a green Hotspot box and get a Pop-up message with a view or document title (like the one shown in Figure 10-6), you know that you can double-click the Pop-up to go to that document or view.

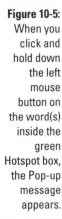

Figure 10-5:
When you click and hold down the left mouse button on the word(s) inside the green Hotspot box, the Pop-up message appears.

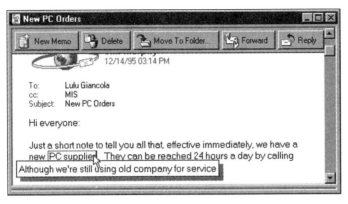

Figure 10-6:
When a Pop-up message has a View or Document title in it, you can double-click it to go to that database.

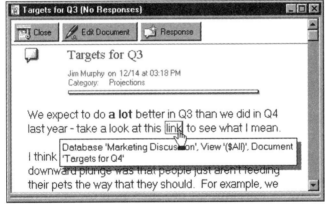

The second kind of Pop-up doesn't show you anything and doesn't take you anywhere, either. This kind of Pop-up works very much like a button. When you click it, something happens. What exactly happens depends on a little computer program that somebody writes to work with the Pop-up. Some text in the document itself should tell you what's going to happen, as you can see in Figure 10-7.

Links

A *link* is just a quick cross-reference to some other Notes database. Say you're using your company's Q&A database to ask someone in Human Resources about whether you get to take Veteran's Day as a holiday. Unbeknownst to you, though, someone else asked the very same question last week. Rather than answering your question (and duplicating the answer given last week), your H.R. representative may decide to compose a response document and include in it a link to the document with the original answer. You can see an example of such a link in Figure 10-8.

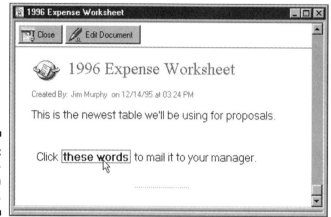

Figure 10-7: Some Popups perform actions.

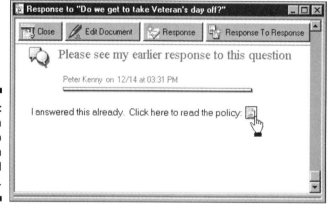

Figure 10-8: Links are a way to quickly open a related document.

Links take you to a particular document, to a particular view, or just to a particular database. Figure 10-9 shows a document with each type of link. The first one opens a document in the Sales database; the second whisks you off to the Performance view in some other database, and the third takes you to a discussion database.

You click a link once to see where it's going to take you; you double-click a link to actually go and see the linked information. When you're done, press Esc to return to the document that you were reading in the first place. Skip to Chapter 13 if you want to create your own links.

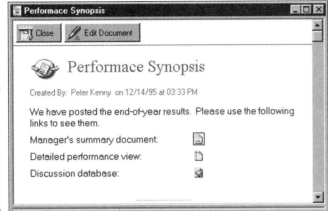

Figure 10-9:
Here, you
encounter
Document,
View, and
Database
links.

Objects

You may notice, as you're reading a document, that it contains an *embedded object* (which is usually just called an *object*). More specifically, the document contains data from some other program; it may be a Lotus 1-2-3 worksheet, a couple of pages from an MS-Word document, or a QuickTime movie. Figure 10-10 shows a document that has one of these fancy-shmancy embedded objects.

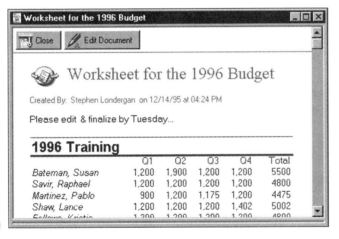

Figure 10-10:
This
document
has an
embedded
Excel
spreadsheet,
which is
called an
object.

There are two cool things about objects:

- ✔ First, Notes displays the object in its original format. In other words, if someone has included an Excel spreadsheet in an e-mail, it looks like an Excel spreadsheet.

- ✔ Second, through the wonders of Object Linking and Embedding (also known as OLE), when you double-click the object itself, Notes starts the program that created the original object and lets you review it (and maybe edit it) there. And, when you finish your edits, you can save the object back into the Notes database, not on your computer. That way, other people can read (and, if you want them to, edit) your work. Sound awesome? Check out Chapter 17 for more on embedding objects.

You must have the originating program installed on your computer to activate and edit an embedded object. In other words, you can't double-click a Lotus 1-2-3 spreadsheet to open it if you don't have Lotus 1-2-3 installed on your computer. If you don't have the original program, you'll be able to only look at the object without being able to edit it.

Icons

Another way to include data from other programs in Notes documents is to use an *attachment*. If you're reading a Notes document and stumble upon an icon like the one in Figure 10-11, you've found an attachment.

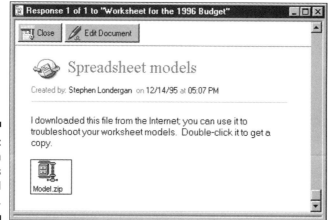

Figure 10-11: This icon represents an attached file.

Double-click the icon to open the Attachment InfoBox, where you can decide to view, launch, or detach and save an attached file. Chapter 6 covers attached files in your mail database. Chapter 17 covers attached files in general.

Come on in and Join the Party!

You've read a bunch of documents in a Notes database, and now you want to jump into the fray and make your own contribution — you're going to add your own new document.

You have to open the database in which you want to compose a new document before you start messing with the Create menu. More often than not, you'll already have a database open when you decide to create a new document — just make sure that you do, and that it's the database in which you want to create your document. If you don't need to open the database in which you'll be creating a new document, then at least be sure that you select the database's icon on the workspace before choosing Create⇨whatever.

Using the Create menu

When you choose Create, Notes gives you a list of the documents that you can create in that database, as shown in Figure 10-12.

Figure 10-12:
Use the
Create
menu to
compose
new
documents
in a
database.

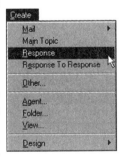

It just stands to reason that the list of documents you can compose from the Create menu will vary from one database to the next. In your mail database, you can compose a Memo or a Reply; in a different database, you can compose different kinds of documents. We can't give you examples of their names, because the names of the documents depend on the databases you use.

Writer's block

Just finding the Create menu doesn't mean that you can actually compose documents in a given database. Some databases only allow you to read documents without allowing you to compose your own. (Don't take it personally.)

 If you're not sure whether you're allowed to compose documents, open the database in question and look in the Status bar. If you see a little picture of eyeglasses, you can forget about the Compose menu — you only have *Reader* access to that database and consequently can only read the documents that other people have composed.

 Call your administrator if you want to add documents to a database in which you only have Reader access.

Getting your inheritance from the right document

Does it matter which document is open when you compose a new one? The answer to that question is a definite "maybe." Many databases have documents that rely on a feature called *inheritance*. Inheritance is a way for Notes to pass information from a document that's already in the database to the new one you're about to compose.

We'll use our hackneyed Customer Service database example again. In it, you can compose two types of documents: a Customer Profile and a Customer Order. The database is already set up so that, when you compose a new Customer Order, Notes automatically fills in the name of the customer and other information about them. Notes accomplishes this feat of wonder by inheriting the values from the address fields of the Profile document that you had selected when you composed your new order. So you'd better have the right Profile open (or highlighted in the View pane) before you try to compose a new order. If you have the wrong Profile open, you'll get the wrong address in your order.

 The moral of this story is that, if you're using a database that relies on inheritance to compute some fields when you make a new document, you must have the right document open when you compose your own.

Moving around in your new document

This part is easy. As you enter values in your new document, press Tab to move from one field to the next. You can also use the arrow keys and the mouse to get from one field to the next.

 You can't use Tab to move from a rich text field to the next field. You have to use the arrow keys or the mouse instead.

Saving your new document

When you're done filling out the fields in your new document, press Esc. In the dialog box that appears, choose Yes to save your document in the database.

It's also a good idea to save the document often as you're composing it, in case you screw up, there's a power failure, or your computer crashes (although we don't recommend letting your computer drive, anyway). You can save a document any time by choosing File⇨Save.

Abandoning your new document

What's that? You say you blew it? You started composing a new document and now you've changed your mind and don't want to save it? Just press Esc and choose No from the Save dialog box. Presto — it's gone!

Play by the rules

The person who created the database may have set some rules for the fields: Perhaps you can't leave certain fields empty, or perhaps there's a rule to ensure that you enter one of the "approved" two-character state abbreviations. When you save a document, Notes validates what you have entered in the various fields against the rules (if there are any) that the database designer has set up.

Don't be surprised if you get a dialog box (like the one in Figure 10-13) when you try to save a document. This dialog box tells you what rule you've broken and insists that it's not going to let you save the document until you fix the problem. No big deal; click OK, fix your mistake, and then try to save the document again.

Figure 10-13:
Some databases have rules that you'll have to satisfy before you can save a document.

A Document Catches Your Eye

Besides reading documents and entering new ones, you can also print a document, edit it, delete it, mail it, or put it in a Personal folder.

Print it . . .

 To print the document that you have open, click the Print SmartIcon (or choose File⇨Print). You'll get the File Print dialog box, as you see in Figure 10-14. You can decide which printer to use, how many copies to print, which pages you want to print, and whether to print in *draft quality* (a faster but uglier choice). After you've made up your mind, click OK. And out it comes!

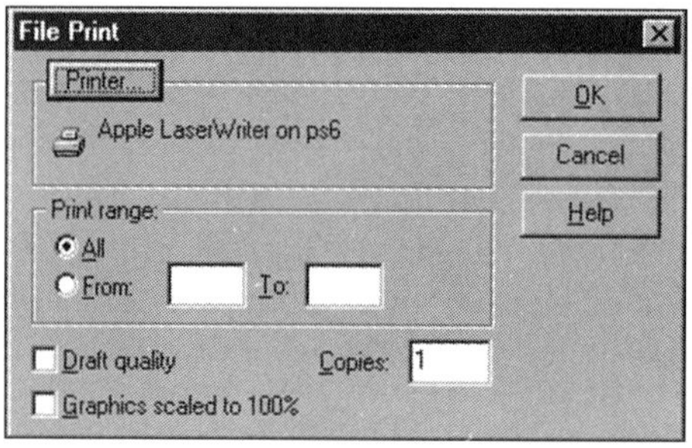

Figure 10-14:
Use the File
Print dialog
box to
print your
masterpiece.

Edit it, maybe . . .

 If you want to edit a document, you must first either open it or at least highlight it in the View pane. Then click the Edit SmartIcon (or choose Actions⇨Edit document). Assuming that you are, in fact, allowed to edit the document, Notes puts you in *edit mode,* and you can change any of the field values. When you're done making your changes, save the document just as if you were saving it for the first time. (Press Esc and then choose Yes.)

If you already have a document open, you can double-click it (anywhere) to get into Edit mode.

Of course, being able to read a document doesn't mean that you can also edit it. In fact, most databases only allow you to edit a document if you are the document's original author. (You wouldn't want somebody else to edit your document and take all the credit for your great ideas, would you?) If Notes won't let you edit a document, it's probably because you aren't the person who composed the document in the first place.

Delete it, maybe . . .

Press Delete to delete the document you have open or highlighted in the View pane. If you have a document open when you press Delete, Notes closes the document you were reading, marks it as deleted, and then takes you to the next document in the database. Notes won't actually delete the document until you update the view (by pressing F9) or exit the database, so you do have a chance to change your mind and not delete the document if you decide you've made a mistake. Refer to Chapter 4 to learn more about deleting and undeleting documents.

In most databases, after you compose a document, you (and you alone) control its destiny. You're the only person who can edit it and/or delete it. (That's good — otherwise, your rivals would be deleting your documents all day long. And that would make you look bad.)

Hey Bob, did you see this?!

You can turn any Notes document you see into an e-mail message — anytime, anywhere. If you're reading a document and decide that you want to forward it to your friend, choose Actions⇨Forward. Notes takes the document and stuffs it into a new e-mail message that you can send to your buddies. You address the e-mail as you would any other message and send it off. Refer to Chapter 4 if you need help using Notes e-mail.

Put it in a personal folder . . .

Some databases are set up with personal folders. *Personal folders* let you collect the documents in a database that interest you and gather them all in one place — which makes them easy to find later.

A good example of when you might want to use a personal folder is in the Lotus Notes Help database. This database is chock-full of documents explaining every possible thing you could ever want to know about Lotus Notes. In other words, it has way, way, more information than you need! Say you spend an hour in the Help database, trying to find out how to use the Status bar. You don't want to waste an hour the *next time* you want to check help on this topic, so you decide to put the document in your personal folder in the Help database. That way, when you need to read the Status bar help again, you can go right to your own personal folder in the Help database.

Only you will see the contents of your personal folders.

Figure 10-15 shows a sample view from the Lotus Notes Help database. You can drag the document you want to put in your personal folder from the View pane over into that little folder in the Navigator pane. You know when you can let go of the mouse, because the mouse pointer will change into a little cross (as shown in the figure).

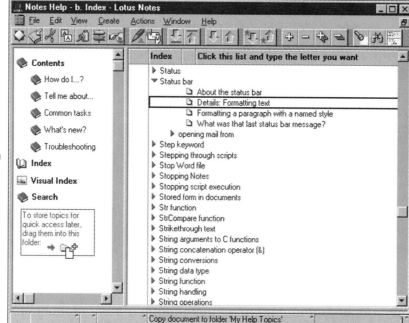

Figure 10-15:
You can drag documents from the View pane into folders in the Navigation pane.

If you're reading a document, choose Actions⇨Move to Folder to put that document in a folder.

To see the documents you've stored in your personal folder, click the folder icon in the Navigation pane.

When Things Get Sensitive

We didn't exactly save the best for last in this chapter. It's not that the following two features are bad, it's just that you'll hardly ever use them, if you ever use them at all. In fact, you should only read the rest of this chapter if you absolutely have to — only if you've been told that you'll be *encrypting* fields and/or hiding documents.

Using encryption to make fields private

Notes has a feature called *field encryption* that is an extremely secure way to make certain field values private. And we mean private! If a field has been encrypted, and you aren't one of the people who is allowed to see the field's contents, there is *nothing* you can do to spy on the field.

Okay, so why would you ever use encryption? Say your company has a database that tracks information about employees. It has fields like Employee Name, Office Location, Phone Number, and Yearly Salary. The whole company uses the database as a kind of corporate directory; people use it to look up other employee names and phone numbers and stuff.

Would you want all of your colleagues to be able to see how much money you make? Your managers want the whole company to use the database, but they want to make the salary field protected, so that only you, your boss, and the Human Resources department can see the salary field. (Your salary is surely so high that it'd breed all *kinds* of discontent and resentment if everybody could see it! We can't have that, now can we?)

When a field has been encrypted, you need a special *key* to see the field's contents. If you read a document in which there is an encrypted field, and you have not been given the key to the field, you will *not* be able to see the contents of the field. Notes stores these keys in your User ID.

If you're going to be dealing with encryption and encryption keys, we recommend you glide on over to Chapter 14.

Hiding a document altogether

Last but not least, when you compose a document, you can decide that you only want certain people to be able to read the document. By creating a *Read Access List* before you save a new document, you can be very specific and particular about the people who are able to see your document. People who use the database but are not listed in your document's Read Access List will never even know that the document is in the database!

Just before you save a document that you want to make private, choose File⇨Document Properties, and then select the InfoBox tab with the key on it. By default, All readers and above is selected, meaning anyone with access to the database will be able to see the document you're creating. Right off the bat, you'll have to uncheck that box. Then you can click the names of the people whom you trust to read the document.

If there's a person whose name is not in the list, click the Names button (with Notes' version of a silhouette) to pick other names from the N&A Books.

Figure 10-16 shows a Document InfoBox that will guarantee that only Shirley Stone, Windsor Lindor, and members of the group named Planning Department will be able to read this document.

Figure 10-16:
Use the
Document
InfoBox to
add a Read
Access list
to a
document.

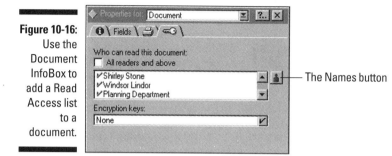

— The Names button

After identifying the names of the people who can read the document, save it as you save any other document.

If you add a Read Access List to a document, don't forget to include your name in the list; otherwise, even *you* won't be able to see the document!

Chapter 11

Building a Database with Things You Find around the House

In This Chapter

▶ Creating a new database

▶ Using a database template

▶ Modifying forms and views to make them your own

▶ Adding an icon

▶ Putting the database on a server

Notes makes it easy to create a database with things you find around the house. You don't need to have a degree in advanced programming or to start wearing a pocket protector to fashion a highly useful database. Of course, the process of database creation can become rather complex; our purpose here is just to give you a start. To tell you everything there is to know about ApDev (that's the buzz word) would take a big book. However, building on the foundation you get from this one chapter, you can go on to winning fame and fortune as a Notes database developer.

Before we go any further, we need to get one thing out of the way. If you are a Notes Desktop or Lotus Notes Mail user, sorry, you won't be able to try out the techniques in this chapter. Of course you can *read* about them, you just can't access the proper menu items on your version of Notes. (If you're not sure whether you are a Notes Mail or Desktop user instead of a full Notes user, look in the title bar of the Notes window. It'll say Lotus Notes Desktop or Lotus Notes Mail.)

Why Reinvent the Wheel?

The good news is that most of the work has been already done for you — maybe. When you installed Notes on your computer in the first place, you got a bunch of database templates.

A database template is a special kind of database that provides a design you can copy. The idea is that you use one of the templates and then modify the forms, fields, and views to suit your purposes. You still have some work to do in the customization of the database, but at least you don't have to create every single field, form, and view from scratch, right?

Lotus Notes comes with several database templates — and they're free! Refer to Appendix B for a detailed description of each. You may also find that the application designers at your company have created database templates, too. You can use and modify existing databases as easily as you can tap into the design features of a template.

In this chapter, we create a new database based on the Discussion template.

Put It on Disk

The first step to making your new database is to put on disk the shell of the database, to which you will skillfully add forms, views, and documents. Choose File➪Database➪New. You'll see a dialog box like the one in Figure 11-1. Leave the word "Local" in the server text box because that's where your new database will be stored — on your own (local) computer. Even if a bunch of people will (eventually) share the database you're creating, start out by creating it on your workstation. Wait until it's finished to put it on the server.

Figure 11-1:
This is the
New
Database
dialog box,
in which
we've
supplied
information
for the new
Discussion
database.

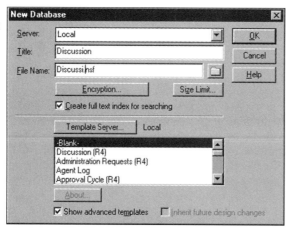

Use the Title text box to tell Notes what you want to call the database. Because the title appears in the database's icon on your workspace, you should be imaginative and descriptive in the database's title. How's "Discussion" for a title with zing? Notes automatically fills in the File Name box, although you can change the filename if you are so inclined. The *filename* is what the database is called on the disk.

The normal reasons for changing a filename are either that there's already a file on disk with that name (Notes will warn you if that is the case) or that you simply want to give the file a different name. Notes supplied DISCUSSI.NSF in Figure 11-1, but maybe you prefer DISCUSS.NSF. (Capitalization doesn't make a hog's hair of difference in naming files.) But don't change the *extension* (those three letters after the period at the end of the filename) because .NSF is the way Notes identifies one of its databases.

In the New Database dialog box, you're better off leaving Encryption and Size Limit alone, but it's a good idea to check the Create full text index for searching check box so that users can find text in documents easily.

All templates available on your computer are listed in the window below the Template Server button. You can see a few more if you check the Show advanced templates box. Click the Template Server button if you want to tell Notes which of your company's servers you want to check for templates. If you know that one of the servers has a special template on it, you can use this button to tell Notes that you want to see a list of the templates on that server.

Highlight any one of the template names and then click the About button to see some information about the highlighted template. You can also check out Appendix B of this book for a more detailed description of each of the templates.

When template names are highlighted, the Inherit future design changes box is *active* (which means that you can change it). When you're ready to create your own database, be sure that this box is not checked (just click in the box if it has a check mark in it to remove the check mark). When this box is checked, it means that the database will periodically look at the template to see whether they have the same design. If they don't, the database automatically allows the template to change it. Poof. All your changes are undone.

Highlight the template you want for your new database (or -Blank- if you want to create your own database from the ground up) and then click OK. Notes grinds its gears for a minute or two and creates the new file.

A message box appears asking if you want to index your database now. You don't, because there are no documents to index. (What does that mean? Full text indexing is covered in Chapter 16. For now, just take our word for it.)

You know you're ready to continue when you see the database's Policy document, which, in this case, says About Discussion. Press Escape to dismiss this document. Now you get your first glimpse of your shiny, new, never-been-used database — just like the one in Figure 11-2.

Under the SmartIcon palette are some *action buttons* created especially for this database, that users can click to perform common actions like creating a New Main Topic. Action buttons are unique to each database and are often unique to a particular view or document.

The *graphics* in the Navigation pane are items that users can click to open different views. A sophisticated database designer like your worthy self has no time for such toys, especially if you want to change some of the elements of the database. Fortunately, one of those toys — the Standard Folders action button — allows you to replace the graphic navigators with a real, adult menu. Click that and you see a menu in the Navigation pane, like the one in Figure 11-3.

With this less graphic menu available, you can still open any of the same folders and views associated with the graphics by clicking Folders and Views, and then clicking one of the four names. Of course, there are no documents in those views yet — this is a brand-new database.

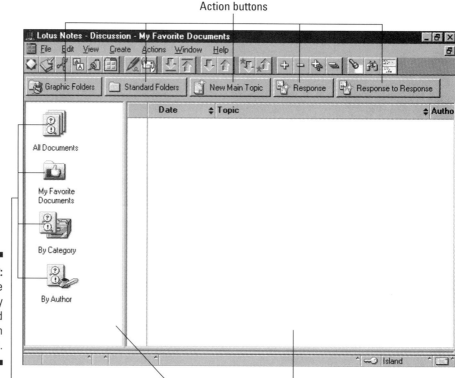

Figure 11-2:
Here's the newly created Discussion database.

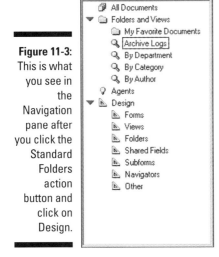

Figure 11-3:
This is what
you see in
the
Navigation
pane after
you click the
Standard
Folders
action
button and
click on
Design.

In Figure 11-3, we clicked on the word "Design" in that list to show the various elements of the database which you can design.

Customizing Your New Database

So you created the database following the instructions in the preceding section. You may not need to customize it all. In many cases, you can just use it the way it is — no assembly required.

But, because it's your database and you own it, you can make structural modifications to the new database — maybe add a new field to the forms, change some colors, or perhaps modify the way some of the views work.

Feel free to tinker to your heart's content. If you don't like what you've done, no harm; no one will know but you.

Okay, computer's running, database is open, menu's all set — take a deep breath, and then we'll show you how to make some modifications to put your personal stamp on the database and give you some tricks of the trade.

Of the many parts of a database, the forms and the views are the most important. They are what users see and most often use. In this section, we'll show you how to modify one of the forms in your database. *Forms* are the database elements containing fields and text with which users create documents in your database. In the Navigation pane, look for the word "Design" and, under it, the word "Forms." If you don't see anything listed under Design, click Design and the list of things you can modify appears. Click on Forms to see the list of all forms in the database, as visible in the View pane on your screen and in Figure 11-4. The form we're going to show you how to modify is called *Main Topic*.

The asterisk (*) next to the name indicates that the Main Topic form is the *default* form. When you read a document, you read it using the form with which it was originally composed. But what if the form that was used to compose a document somehow got lost? Then Notes automatically uses the default form to let you read the document.

Double-click on Main Topic to enter design mode for this form. Don't worry if you get the two message boxes in Figures 11-5 and 11-6 warning you of the dire consequences of modifying the form. We're not concerned in the least about these messages, so you shouldn't be either. Click OK in both boxes, because the form will not inherit changes from a template and you aren't going to do anything to the parts that deal with mail.

Some of the things you can do to a form are:

✔ Add some static text

✔ Add a field (we added one for people to enter their phone numbers and one for people to select the name of the department where they work)

✔ Change the background color of the form

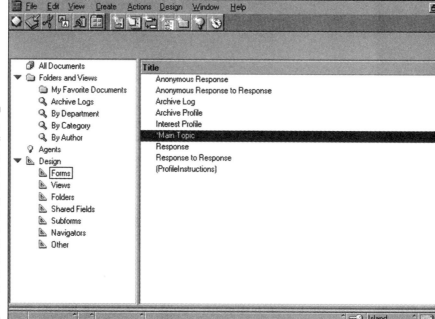

Figure 11-4:
The list of forms in this database appears in the View pane when you click on Design and then Forms in the Navigation pane.

Figures 11-5 and 11-6: Don't let these message boxes worry you — just click OK in both of them.

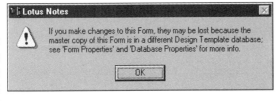

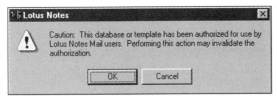

What's in a form?

Once you leap the message-box hurdles, Notes puts you in design mode for the Main Topic form. The design screen looks like Figure 11-7. You see two panes: the Design pane on top (where you add elements to the form) and the Programmer pane at the bottom (where you write formulas for parts of the form). If you want to see more of the Design pane or more of the Programmer pane, click and drag the border between the two panes up or down. In Figure 11-7, we increased the size of the Design pane and highlighted the From field.

A form usually has several possible elements; *static text*, *fields*, and *graphics* are the most important.

- ✓ **Static text:** As the name implies, this text is ever unchanging. You type it, save it with the form, and, whenever users compose a new document or read an existing one, the static text is there to help them understand the information in the fields. The title of a form or, in Figure 11-7, the text `This document and its responses will be deleted on` are examples of static text.

- ✓ **Fields:** These are slots where users enter information or where Notes does some calculations and inserts information automatically. Fields appear with a box around them in design mode; otherwise, their appearance changes depending on the type of field and whether you're in read or edit mode for a document. In Figure 11-7, Subject is a field.

- ✓ **Graphics:** These are pictures you create in another program (Paintbrush, for example) and then paste into the form. An example of a graphic that you may want to insert into your form could be the company logo. In Figure 11-7, we've inserted the two symbols to the left of the subject line.

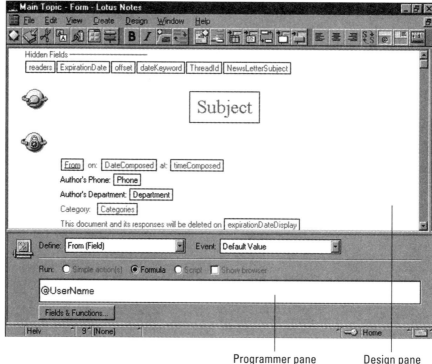

Figure 11-7:
This is the design screen for the Main Topic form showing the Design and Programmer panes.

Programmer pane   Design pane

@Why @are @we @talking @like @this?

As you highlight each existing field in a form, you see the formula written for that field in the Programmer pane. Click in the From field, for instance, and you'll see the formula @UserName in the Programmer pane.

The From field is a *calculated field*. It automatically adds the author's name to that field, thus freeing the author for more lofty pursuits, like filling in other fields. @UserName is one of many Notes functions, it returns the name of the current user.

In case you are burning with curiosity about the meaning of @UserName — a brief explanation. There are many functions in Notes which function as preprogrammed formulas. They all begin with the @ symbol, and they are called *at functions*. This one, @UserName, automatically returns the name of the person whose Notes ID is being used for the current Notes session.

In Figure 11-7, notice that the two lines at the top are hidden, or so it says on the first line. If they're hidden, how come you can see them? Notes isn't lying to you; it just means that, when users are composing a document or reading an existing one, they won't see that stuff. They don't need to; it's internal information for the form and the database to use. In our example, we're going to leave this stuff alone because we don't want to throw a wrench in the machinery of this fine database.

If you do choose to delete anything while modifying a form, use standard editing techniques; in other words, use the Backspace or Delete keys to delete one character or field at a time or highlight whatever you want to delete and then press Delete.

Give me some static

In the Main Topic form, the first field that users will see is the Subject field, but they have no way of knowing what to type there. Their phone number? Number of living relatives in Honduras? Shoe size? So we're going to give them a clue with some static text. To add static text to a form, click where you want the text to appear (in our case, just to the left of the Subject field) and type the text you want. As you can see in Figure 11-8, we typed **Subject:**

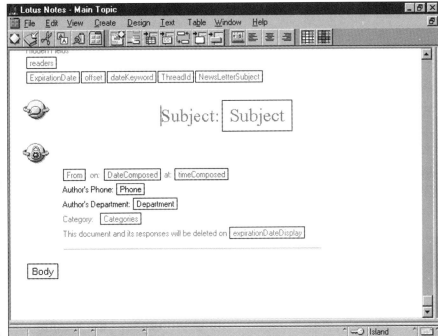

Figure 11-8: Here is the form with the word "Subject" added as static text to help the user.

When you're adding static text before a field, be sure to include a colon and a space; otherwise, readers will see something like `SubjectThe Cafeteria Menu`.

After you've entered your static text, you may decide to center it. We did. Click on the centering SmartIcon.

We did one more thing to our static text. We changed its appearance to make it look like the field right next to it. You should do the same thing to any static text you add. Just follow these steps:

1. **Highlight the static text and press the *right* mouse button.**

2. **From the menu that appears, select Text Properties.**

    Up pops an InfoBox like the one in Figure 11-9.

Figure 11-9:
InfoBoxes
are the
place to
change
characteris-
tics of just
about
everything
in a data-
base. This
one is for
static text.

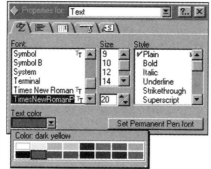

3. **If the box to the right of Properties for: doesn't say** `Text`, **click the down arrow at the end of the box and select Text.**

4. **Use whatever bells and whistles you need in the InfoBox to set your static text so that it matches the text in the field next to it.**

In Figure 11-9, we clicked the AZ tab (which activates the font page) and then chose Times New Roman and 20 points. We also clicked the arrow below Text color to show you a dazzling array of shades of gray. In real life, the color we selected resembles moldy cat food, but at least it matches the field color.

A dream of fields

In the form we're creating, we are going to allow users to enter their phone numbers and the departments for which they work. One field will require them to type information, the other will allow them to choose from a list.

To add a field

Follow these steps to add a field:

1. **Place the cursor where you want the field to be.**

2. **Type the static text to be associated with the field. Don't forget to press the spacebar or Tab to open up some space after the static text.**

3. **Click the Create Field SmartIcon or choose Create⇨Field.**

    The InfoBox, like the one in Figure 11-10, appears for the new field.

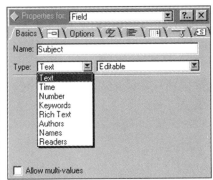

Figure 11-10: Every new field starts out its life in an InfoBox like this one.

4. **Enter the field name in the Name: text box.**

5. **Click the down arrow on the text box right next to Type: and choose the type of field.**

   We'll choose Text for both the Subject and the Phone fields, because Notes doesn't really consider a phone number to be a number.

6. **Click the down arrow on the second text box right in the Type: line and select whether the field will be editable or one of the three types of calculated fields.**

7. **Set any other properties you want, such as font or alignment, by clicking the appropriate page tab and making the choice.**

8. **Click the X button to finish.**

If Step 6 piqued your interest and you simply must know more, here are the three types of calculated fields:

- ✔ **Computed:** The field can be recalculated every time data is changed.

- ✔ **Computed for Display:** No data is saved with the document in the field; it only appears when the document is opened.

- ✔ **Computed when Composed:** The field is calculated once, when the document is first composed, and then never again.

Give 'em a choice

Now to create a field where people can select their response from a list of choices, rather than having to type it. This kind of field, called a *keyword field,* isn't just handy for people who want to avoid a bit of typing but also for those who forget from time to time the name of the department for which they work. Then, too, there's the added bonus of avoiding the heartbreak of typos and of standardizing responses so you don't wind up with "Management," "Personnel Management," and "Personnel" for the same department.

Back in Figure 11-7, we created a field where people could select their department name from a list, rather than having to type it. Here are the steps for creating such a field:

1. **Place the cursor where you want the field to be.**

   You may have to place the cursor at the beginning of an existing line and press Enter to open a new line; then move back up to the new empty line.

2. **Type some static text and a space.**

   We typed **Department:** .

3. **Click the Create Field SmartIcon.**

   The InfoBox appears, with the Basics tab selected.

4. **Type the name of the field.**

5. **Select Keywords as the type of field.**

6. **Leave the field as an Editable one.**

7. **In the box below Choices:, enter the names of the departments in the company, as we did in Figure 11-11.**

   We used three, but the list can extend downward indefinitely for very large or complex companies. You may want to consider checking Allow values not in list in case a new department is created or you think you may have forgotten a couple of the existing ones.

Figure 11-11:
We're busy
adding
keywords
to the
Department
field in this
dialog box.

 If you weren't in a mood to put the keywords in alphabetical order, click the Sort button to have it done for you.

8. Click the X in the upper-right corner when you're done (and you are).

Okay, nicely done. Now save the form by choosing File⇨Save or clicking the File Save SmartIcon. To see how the form works, choose Design⇨Test Form. Here is where you can take the new form for a test drive. Fill in the fields to see how they work.

In Figure 11-12, we show what happens when users click on the down arrow next to the Department keyword field. A list appears in which they can select their department. And, because we cleverly allowed extra values, a user can type in a name missing from the list in the New Keywords: field.

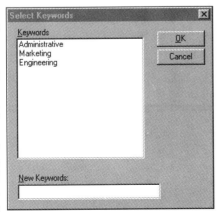

Figure 11-12:
A new form
being put
through its
paces. Here,
a user
clicked on
the arrow
next to the
keyword
field.

When you're done experimenting, dismiss the form (press Escape, unless you have a preferred method of dismissing documents) and decide whether to save the new document. If you're just experimenting, you may want to choose No.

And now, for a little color

Finally, we add a splash of color to give our form, well, dash. With the form in design mode and the cursor anywhere, click the right mouse button. From the context menu that appears, select Form Properties. An InfoBox now graces your screen with the Basics tab already selected. At the right side of the InfoBox, click on the down arrow below Background color and select something light. We aren't going to bother including a picture of the newly colored form because it would still look gray to you.

You probably know this, but what looks good in living color on your screen may be completely illegible on paper if printed in black and white. Therefore, it's a good idea to print a test document to be sure that people will be able to read it before you start selling your database printouts on street corners.

Looking at Things from a New View

Views are the lists of documents in a database. Some views can show the same documents as other views but arranged differently. For example, in the Discussion database, documents created using the Main Topic form are listed in the By Category view and in the By Author view. Other views may list documents created with a different form. For instance, a Human Resources database may have one view listing all employee information documents, open to all employees, and another listing their salary history, visible only to those who need to know such information.

In this section, we're going to show you how to create a new view. For our example, we created a view that arranges the discussion topics by the new field that we added to the Main Topic form, Department. We called this new view *By Department*.

Creating a view

To create a new view, choose Create⇨View. In a trice, or a few trices on humid days, you'll see a Create View dialog box like the one in Figure 11-13.

We made some changes to the dialog box in Figure 11-13 before taking this picture. For instance, we dubbed our new view *By Department*. We also chose to make this a *Shared view,* meaning that it's available to all users of the database.

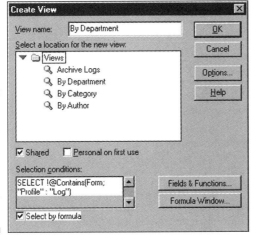

Figure 11-13:
The Create
View dialog
box appears
as soon as
you choose
Create⇨
View.

In addition to Shared views, you can choose from two other types of views:

✓ **Private:** This is the default type of view. In other words, if you don't choose one of the other two types, Notes automatically makes your new view private. Any user can create a Private view for use locally. When you create a private view, there's no way other users can see it.

✓ **Personal on first use:** Anyone can use this type of view, but the moment they do, it becomes a Personal view (like a Private view) with characteristics that make each local version slightly different from all other local versions of the same view. Only database designers can make views that are Shared or Personal on first use.

You use the Create View dialog box to make one other decision: You determine where your view will be listed. Of course, it will appear in the Navigation pane somewhere under Folders and Views, but you get to decide exactly where in the list your view goes. Under Select a location for the new view:, we decided to list our view beneath the word "Views." If we had highlighted an existing view name, the new view would have been listed under that view and indented.

The easiest way to create a new view for your database is to take one of the existing views, copy (not to say "steal") it, modify it, and save it. If you like this idea, click the Options button in the Create View dialog box to select an existing view to use as the model for the new one. A new dialog box, like the one in Figure 11-14, appears. Select the view you want and click OK in each dialog box to return to designing the view.

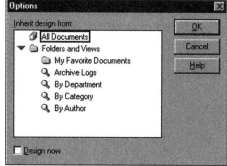

Figure 11-14:
In this dialog
box, you can
pick a view
to provide
the design
for the new
view.

If you don't follow the preceding tip and choose an existing view to be a template for your new view, your view may get its design from one which the designer selected from among its peers to be the model for all future views. If your database designer didn't take that step, you'll get a blank view that you'll have to build completely, making it the first of its kind in the modern world.

Adding a new column

After you've dealt with the Create View dialog box, chosen a view to model your own after (or opted for the hard route and are starting with a blank view), and chosen Design now in the Options box, you should find yourself in design mode, which looks like Figure 11-15. The screen looks a lot like it did when you were designing a form — there's the Design pane at the top and the Programmer pane at the bottom, where you write formulas.

Because we are in our custom By Department view, we need to add a column in the Design pane to list the department of the person who wrote the document. It's going to be the first column on the left.

To insert a new column, here's all you have to do:

1. **Select the existing column which will be to the right of your new column.**

   Notice in Figure 11-16 that the first little teeny column head (to the left of the Date column) is a bit darker than the others; it's selected.

2. **Now choose Create⇨Insert New Column or click the Create Insert New Column SmartIcon.**

   There it is!

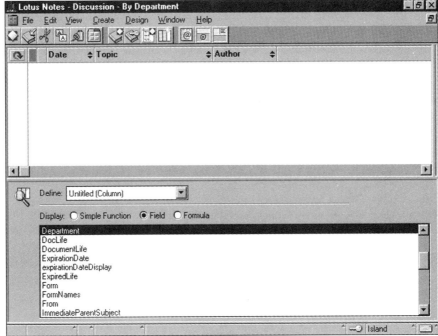

Figure 11-15:
This is how
the screen
looks while
you are
designing a
view. Of
course, you
can resize
the panes.

Dressing up your column

Your new column has no definition, no personality, no properties; that is your
next job. Below is a list of the kinds of things you can do to spruce up a column.
Before you do anything, make sure that the new column is selected and then
click the right mouse button and choose Column Properties from the menu. The
Column InfoBox appears.

Widening

The first thing you may want to do is widen your column so it shows all the
data it's supposed to. You can change a column's width in three ways:

✔ The first way is in the Column InfoBox (see Figure 11-16), which you open
by selecting a column and then clicking the right mouse button and
choosing Column Properties from the menu. Use the up and down arrows
to increase or decrease the column width, or type the number of characters wide you want the column to be. This is useful if you want to change it
just slightly, from 10 to 11 characters wide, for instance.

✔ The second way involves using your mouse to avoid the dreaded InfoBox. When you move the mouse pointer around in the tops of the columns in the view, you'll notice that the pointer occasionally changes to a vertical bar with two arrows on it. If you want to change a column's width, you can roll the mouse pointer to the right edge of the column in question until the pointer becomes a little bar. Then click and drag to the new column width. Use this to make more dramatic changes.

✔ The third way is to allow your users to set the width of the column. On the Basics page of the Column InfoBox, just check resizable. When users open the view, they'll see a border between column heads for columns they can resize with the mouse.

Title

You may decide the column needs a title to explain its contents. On the Basics page, Figure 11-16, we decided not to give the column a title because we made the column only 1 character wide, and what kind of title has only one letter? If you have a wider column and want a title, just type the column title in the Title: box on the Basics page.

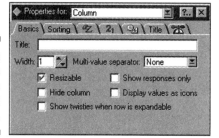

Figure 11-16:
The Basics
page of the
Column
InfoBox.

Sorting

Decide whether to sort the column. On the Sorting page, Figure 11-17, we checked Ascending next to Sort so that the Departments will be listed in alphabetical order from A to Z. We also checked Categorized. (As you can see in Figure 11-18, when you categorize a column, it lists each department only once with all the documents that have the same department name in that field listed right underneath.)

Putting something in the column

One more little detail, put something in the column. In the Programmer pane, click on Field and select the field you want listed in the column. In Figure 11-18, we selected Field and highlighted Department because that is the field we want listed in this column.

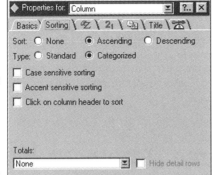

Figure 11-17:
The Sorting
page of the
Column
InfoBox.

If you're interested in seeing how the view is coming along, click on the circular arrow to the left of the first column. Until you do, you may see question marks in the column you're working on. After the click, you'll see any existing documents displayed according to your design. Of course, you need to be sure that you have some documents to show in the view. We do, because we took the time to create a few for demonstration purposes, as you can see in Figure 11-18.

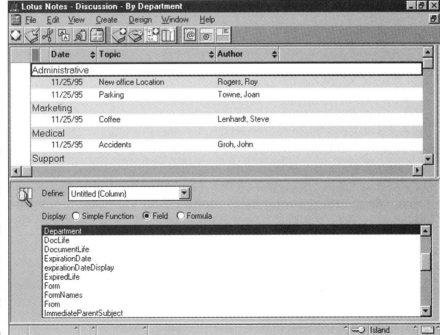

Figure 11-18:
Here, we
assigned
the
Department
field to the
first column
and tested
the view to
see how it
looks.

Saving your work

 It's a brave soul who doesn't periodically save what he's doing. Every so often, as you're creating your new view, click on the Save SmartIcon or choose File⇨Save. Then, when you're done with your modifications, press Esc and choose Yes to save the view. Your new view will proudly take its place with the other views in the Navigation pane.

Folders — Personalized Document Holders

A folder is like a view with one important difference. Views have a special formula, called a *selection formula,* that determines what documents that view will include. Folders have no such thing. You click and drag a document from a view into a folder; that's how documents get into folders. Often the crafty database designer adds an action to a view which allows you to select documents and assign them to a folder. The action may be visible in the Actions menu or as a button in the Action bar. Select the document or documents you want to include in a folder and choose Actions⇨Move to Folder.

You create and modify folders the same way you do views, so we don't need to go through all that again — except to tell you that, to create a new folder, choose Create⇨Folder. To modify an existing folder, click Folder (below Design in the Navigation pane) and then select the folder you want to modify in the View pane.

 Like views, folders have columns, and columns usually contain the contents of fields in documents. Now what if you drag a document which has no fields displayed in the folder into that folder? Right, you won't see the document at all. If that happens, you need to redesign the folder or create a new one more to your liking. The database you use may have some folders already created, and you may have been curious about why they were all empty. Now you know.

 By the way, to remove a document from a folder, don't press the Delete key — that permanently deletes the document from the database, a bit of overkill don't you think? To remove a document from a folder, highlight it and then choose Action⇨Remove from Folder.

The Icon

No database would be complete without a symbol, displayed on each user's desktop, with the name of the database. Put on your beret, grab your brushes, and then — under Design in the Navigation pane — click Other. In the View pane, you see Icon. Double-click Icon, and you get a display similar to Figure 11-19.

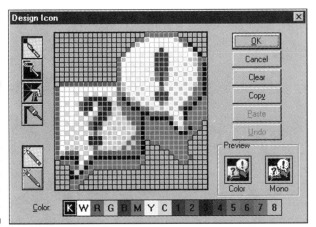

Figure 11-19:
This is the
Design Icon
screen,
showing the
icon for the
Discussion
database.

You can now use your mouse to draw or modify the picture that will represent your database. You're out of luck if you don't have a mouse; designing an icon is one of the times that you *have* to have a mouse in Notes. When you're done with your masterpiece, click OK. (For more specific instructions on creating an icon of your very own, check out Chapter 14.)

If you are artistically challenged, consider using the Copy and Paste buttons to steal an icon from another database or to paste in a picture from another program.

Help!

As your creation nears completion, you may want to consider giving your users a bit of help with your database. The best way to do that is to modify the About or Using documents. Click Design and then Other, just the way you did to design the icon. Choose either document, Using or About, and edit away. Remember that these two documents may be the only help they can get about your database, and they may need all the help they can get if they're new to Notes and not an expert like you. See Chapter 8 for more information about database Policy and Using documents.

The *About document* gives a general overview of the database, its purpose, and (if you want to include it) your name and phone number and the place where you'll be hiding in case people have questions or suggestions about the database. The *Using document* is used by users to learn how to use the database. Huh? Let's just say it provides an overview of the views, forms, and other features that people might find useful.

Deciding Who Can Do What in Your Database

If your ultimate goal is to put your database on a server so that others can use it, you'll need to define the *Access Control List*. This is how you give specific levels of access to different people. To bestow powers selectively, choose File➪Database➪Access Control, and you'll come face-to-face with the Access Control List dialog box illustrated in Figure 11-20.

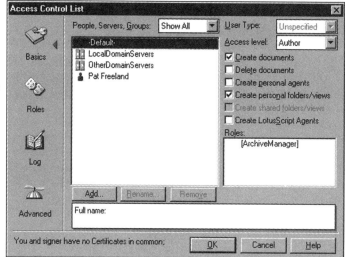

Figure 11-20:
The Access Control List dialog box where you determine who has what access to your database.

If you're the only person who will be using your database and the database will be on your computer (and not on the server), don't bother with this.

As you can see in Figure 11-20, because we clicked the down arrow next to Access level:, seven levels of access are available:

- ✔ **Manager:** Can do anything to the database, including deleting the file entirely. Most important is the ability to change the Access Control List.

- ✔ **Designer:** Can do everything the Editor can do, plus change the forms and views.

- ✔ **Editor:** Can do everything the Author can do, plus edit the documents that other people created.

✔ **Author:** Can do everything the Reader can do, plus compose new documents and edit or delete his or her own documents.

✔ **Reader:** Can read the documents in the database.

✔ **Depositor:** Can only compose documents in the database. Depositors cannot read other people's documents.

✔ **No Access:** Can do nothing, *nada*, not even open the database.

The process of creating the whole ACL (as those in the know call it — some even pronounce it "Ackle" . . . really) is rather complex. We'll make it simple: Just highlight -Default- and determine what the default level of access will be. You can be the Manager, which makes you the Big Deal. Let everyone else be Authors, which is the way Notes set things up to begin with.

Of course, if you want to get into the ACL a little deeper, click Add and then type in the name of someone else you'd like to give special access to the database. We think that a great way to celebrate April Fools' Day is to deny access to your database to some of your friends with a keen sense of humor. Be the life of the party, loads of laughs.

To keep a fellow worker from seeing the database at all, enter his or her name in the text box like the one in Figure 11-21. Click OK twice to return to the main Access Control List dialog box, highlight the person's name, and select from the Access level drop-down list the access you want to give that person — in this case: No Access.

Figure 11-21:
Enter names
or groups to
whom you
want to give
unique
access.

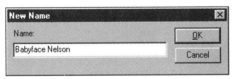

Run It up the Flagpole

If you want other people to be able to use your new database, you need to put it on a Notes server. Putting a database on a server is not something every Tom, Dick, and Mary can do; otherwise every Tom, Dick, and Mary *would* do it, and pretty soon the Notes servers would have no disk space left. So you may have to solicit special dispensation from the Notes administrator to be able to put your database on the server.

After you have the proper permission, you can put your database (in all its glory) on the server by selecting File⇨Database⇨New Copy. Use the Copy Database dialog box, like the one in Figure 11-22, to determine which server your database will be on and what the title and filename will be. You can also decide whether to put the whole database up there or just the design without the documents by choosing Database design and documents *or* Database design only.

Figure 11-22:
This is the Copy Database dialog box, used to create a copy of a new database on a server.

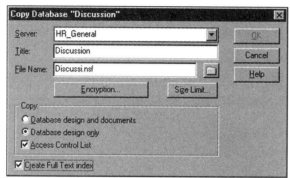

Check Access Control List to be sure that the ACL goes along with the new database. Make sure that your own name is in the database's Access Control List before you copy the database onto the server. If you forget, you may not be able to even open the database at all . . . much less make any future design changes!

Part IV

Getting the Most out of Notes

The 5th Wave   By Rich Tennant

In this part...

*R*eading and sending mail, and even puttering around in a database, are pretty much standard Notes fare. Part IV shows you how to become a power user of Notes by customizing it to your own specifications.

Up to this point in the book, we've discussed how to use Notes the way it fell out of the box and onto your computer. From this point on, it's time to take command. This part of the book should make you feel like you've stared the beast down and mastered it. No more intimidation, no more feeling as though the program is running you. You're in charge here, after all!

Chapter 12

Jazzing Up Your Text

· ·

In This Chapter

▶ Selecting text

▶ Changing the appearance of existing text

▶ Formatting text as you type it

▶ Creating nonkeyboard characters

▶ Changing margins and setting tabs

▶ Setting pagination

▶ Setting alignment and spacing

▶ Using paragraph styles

· ·

*W*hen you send a memo or create a document, don't you want people to notice it? Of course you do. Otherwise, you wouldn't have written it. If one sentence or phrase is more important than other text, don't you think that you should change it in some way so that it will stand out? Naturally.

Sure, you could make the text pink and huge — and after you read this chapter, you'll know how to do that — but perhaps something a bit more subtle will do the trick.

Changing Characters

All truly great documents are composed of individual characters; in fact, *all* documents are composed of individual characters. This section deals with changing those characters, one at a time or in groups such as words, sentences, or paragraphs. You can determine the appearance of a bunch of characters before you even type them, or you can pour out your thoughts onto the screen and then go back and make the changes when you're done typing.

You may want lots of fancy changes to your text, and that's fine with Notes as long as you play by the rule. There's only one rule — the text has to be in a rich text field.

You can find out whether a field is a *rich text field* by placing your cursor in it and then looking at the Status bar. If the font name and font size are visible in the Status bar, you're in a rich text field. It's as simple as that. *You* can't make the field a rich text field; the database designer did that in his laboratory in the dark of night.

You're it!

Lots of times, you'll type something and then decide to go back and change it. Before you can change its appearance, however, you have to let Notes know what it is you want to change. The act of selecting the text you want to change is called, well, *selecting*. What you can do to the text comes later; right now you can just work on selecting it.

Three terms you might as well get straight right now are: I-beam, cursor, and insertion point.

- ✔ The *I-beam* is the vertical line that moves around the screen as you move the mouse. Notes calls this line an I-beam because it looks like an I-beam used in building construction — a vertical line with little horizontal tails at the top and bottom. If you don't have a mouse, don't bother looking for the I-beam; it's not there.

- ✔ *Cursor* and *insertion point* are two names for the same thing: the thick vertical line that blinks at the place where something you type will appear.

The I-beam is always visible on-screen, but if you use the mouse to scroll up or down, the cursor may scroll off the screen. Then, if you move the cursor by pressing any cursor-movement key (such as an arrow key, PgUp, or PgDn), or if you type something or press the spacebar, the screen display changes to show you where the insertion point is.

The easiest way to select text is to click and drag across it with the mouse. When text has a dark box around it, that means it's selected. The dark box is called *reverse video* (light letters on a dark background, rather than vice versa). If you don't have a mouse, you can select text by moving the cursor to the beginning or the end of the text, holding down Shift, and pressing a directional arrow to move over the characters that you want to select. Press the left- or right-arrow key to stretch the highlighter one character to the left or right. Press the down- or up-arrow key to highlight to the same point in the next or previous line. The point is that pressing Shift while using any cursor-movement key combinations moves the cursor and highlights text on the way.

Here are some additional tips about selecting text:

- ✔ Use Ctrl along with Shift and the cursor-movement keys to speed up the process of highlighting. Shift+Ctrl+left- or right-arrow moves the highlight one word at a time. Shift+Ctrl+down- or up-arrow moves the highlight to the beginning or end of the next or previous line.

✔ Double-click a word to select it.

✔ If you want to select all the text in the current field, you're in luck — you can use the menu to choose Edit⇨Select All or just press Ctrl+A.

✔ If you want to select text in more than one field at a time while you're in edit mode, you're out of luck. Regardless of the method you choose to select text, you can only select text in one field at a time.

✔ When you use Edit⇨Select All in edit mode, you select everything in the current field. If you use it in read mode, you select the whole document. (In the latter case, the only thing you can do with selected text is copy it to the clipboard.)

✔ If you want to select two separate chunks of text, you're out of luck. You can only select one bit of text at a time.

✔ If you find that you selected the wrong text, simply select other text to correct the mistake.

✔ If you selected some text but meant to select more, hold down Shift and then click at the farthest end of the additional text or use a cursor-movement key combination. Notes adds to the selected text all text between the currently selected text and the place where you click.

✔ To select a big chunk of text, put the cursor at the beginning of the text you want to select and then use the mouse and scroll bars to scroll until you can see the other end of the text you want to select. Press Shift as you click at the other end of the text. Notes selects all the text in between.

✔ To select all text from the cursor to the beginning of the field, press Shift+Ctrl+Home. To select all text from the cursor to the end of the field, press Shift+Ctrl+End.

During sales, all selections will be final, all major credit cards accepted. Please wait for the next available salesperson. Have a nice day.

Now that I have your attention

After you've selected a bit of text, the time has come to change it. You can remove the text completely, change its appearance, change its location, move or copy it elsewhere, or check its spelling. Not only are there lots of things you can do with the text, there are often several ways to do each one. The Enhancing Text cheat sheet at the beginning of this book tells you what you can do and how to do it. Don't get nervous about trying to learn all the different ways to do things; learn the method that works best for you and forget the rest.

The Ctrl key on IBM-style keyboards and the Command key (⌘) on Macintosh keyboards work with other keys to streamline the things you do most often. Don't be careless about whacking at these key combinations, for one simple reason — if you pick the wrong one, you may be really sorry. For instance, suppose you made lots of changes to some text and then accidentally used Ctrl+T. You'd remove all the formats you just applied!

If you do use a key combination by accident, remember one more useful one — Ctrl+Z. That tells Notes to *undo* (reverse) the most recent action. If you added a lot of formats to a chunk of text and want to remove all of them at once, highlight the text and press Ctrl+T.

How about making your formatting life a bit simpler? Sure, you can take a couple hours to memorize the cheat sheet, or you can tear it out and carry it with you wherever you go. Or you can play it smart and use a magic box. Yup, everything mentioned in the cheat sheet — plus more — is included in what's sometimes dubbed a *Properties Box,* but is officially called the *InfoBox* (words with capitals in the middle are sooooo high tech). So, when you want to change something about a paragraph or a word or even just a character, simply select it then click the Properties SmartIcon. That will summon an InfoBox for whatever item in a database you currently have selected. Figure 12-1 shows the InfoBox for selected text.

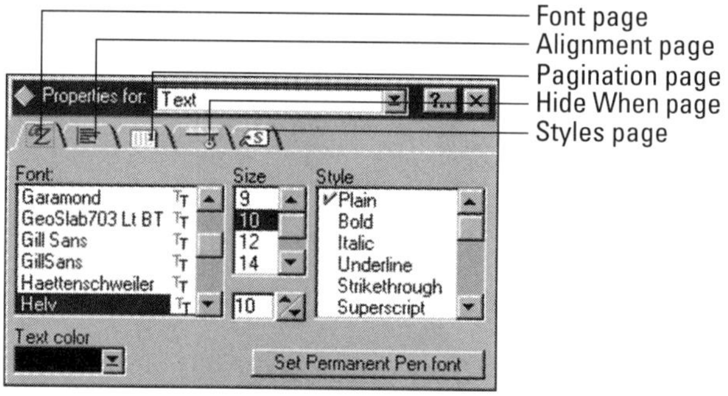

Figure 12-1:
The InfoBox
for text in a
rich text
field.

— Font page
— Alignment page
— Pagination page
— Hide When page
— Styles page

This dialog box is chock-full of ways to change selected text, including giving it a large font size and coloring it pink. The Text and Paragraph InfoBoxes, like all InfoBoxes, have tabbed pages to organize the different types of properties. Here's a brief list of the pages for text and paragraphs (we explain them in detail later in this chapter):

✓ **Font:** Set font style, font size, and text color. You also set the Permanent Pen font on this page. (See the next section for a description of the Permanent Pen.)

✔ **Alignment:** Set the alignment (left, center, right, full, or none), first line and paragraph indent, the left margin, spacing (between lines, above and below the paragraph), and add bullets or numbers.

✔ **Pagination:** Set pagination options, the right margin (this is for printing only; it has no on-screen effect), and tabs (for the whole paragraph).

✔ **Hide When:** Hide the selected paragraph(s) under all sorts of conditions. (Stay tuned if you want to know what these conditions are.)

✔ **Styles:** Assign a style to the currently selected paragraph(s). Of course, you have to create styles before you can apply them. Coming soon to a page near you — an explanation of the use of styles.

At times, it's faster to not use the Text InfoBox: when you're setting the font, font size, or style. In these cases, get in the habit of using the Status bar. Next time you're hanging around a rich text field, stop by the Status bar and click the box containing the name of the current font. In Figure 12-2, you can see the results of clicking the font box in the Status bar. The variety of fonts you have available depends upon the software and the printer you're using. Figure 12-3 shows the font sizes available from the Status bar. Figure 12-4 shows the available styles.

The same fonts, sizes, and paragraph styles are available whether you use the Status bar, the font SmartIcon, or the InfoBox. The Status bar is just a faster way of making a selection.

Figure 12-2:
Click on the
font name in
the Status
bar, and
here's what
you get.

```
Broadway-WP
BroadwayEngraved-WP
Brush Script
Brush738 BT
BrushScript
BrushScript-WP
Calisto MT
CaslonOpenFace
CaslonOpnface BT
Century-WP
Century Gothic
Century Schoolbook
ChelmsfordBook-WP
Comic Sans MS
CommercialScript-WP
CooperBlack-WP
Copperplate Gothic Bold
Copperplate Gothic Light
Courier
Courier-WP
Courier New
DomCasual
EngraversGothic BT
Eurostile-WP
Fixedsys
Frank Goth Cd
Garamond
GeoSlab703 Lt BT
Gill Sans
GillSans
Haettenschweiler
Helv
```

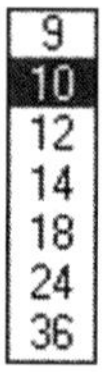

Figure 12-3:
The font size
box displays
a list of
available
font sizes.

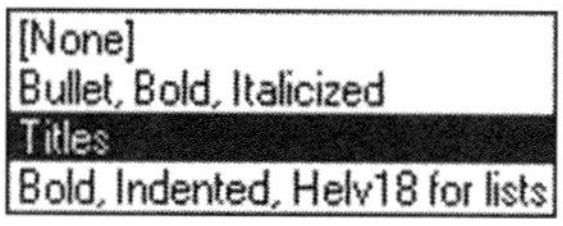

| 9 |
| 10 |
| 12 |
| 14 |
| 18 |
| 24 |
| 36 |

Figure 12-4:
The styles
box gives
you a choice
of styles.

| [None] |
| Bullet, Bold, Italicized |
| Titles |
| Bold, Indented, Helv18 for lists |

If you select a bunch of text and then look at the Status bar, you usually see the name of the font used in that selection. Sometimes, though, you may not see the name of a font. Why not? If the text that you select contains two or more fonts, there won't be a font name or size in the Status bar. But don't fret — even if the font name or size box is empty, you can still use the Status bar to choose one font for the whole selection. Click in the box where you normally see a font name and pick the font you want from the list that appears.

Putting it all together

Say you're writing a memo to the department inviting them to the annual company party on Saturday. You type the text first and then you decide to realign and enhance some of the text. You quickly learn that just putting your cursor at the beginning of a word and clicking the bold SmartIcon is not enough. Selecting the text and then choosing bold is the only way to enhance text after you've typed it.

After you get the hang of enhancing text, you can make your memos much more interesting and professional. Figure 12-5 shows an invitation/memo written by someone with no interest in improving memos, or who has a lot to learn about Notes. Nothing is wrong with the content — it's just not very interesting.

It only takes a few keystrokes to improve the appearance of the memo by using a new font, italicizing, and centering lines. The same memo with some polishing, shown in Figure 12-6, looks a lot more interesting.

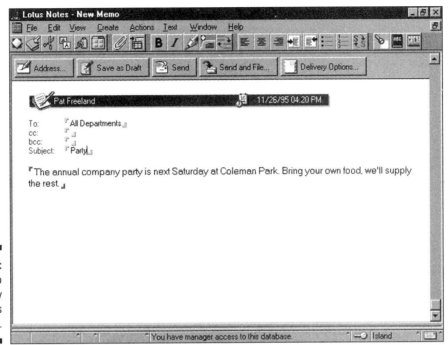

Figure 12-5:
Yawn. No
personality
to this
memo.

Figure 12-6:
That's a bit
more like it.
It is a party,
after all.

If it's a good idea to do a little interior decorating on your party memos, it's even more important to be sure that you plan just as carefully the documents that you create in the line of work. Choosing the right words is only half the battle: the other half is making a document look good.

A little enhancing goes a long way. If too many words in a document are boldface, they don't seem so important anymore. If you plaster lots of different fonts and different font colors and sizes around the page, your document may look more like a circus poster than an official announcement.

It's hard to be bold when you don't exist

Here are some of the more frequently asked questions about enhancing text:

Q: How can you select text you haven't even typed yet?

A: You can't.

Q: Can't you decide to enhance text before you type it?

A: Yes.

Q: What do you do to enhance text you haven't typed yet?

A: The keystrokes and icons described earlier work for text that you are about to type as well as for text you typed yesterday. If you are typing a sentence and know that the next few words should be bold, click the bold SmartIcon (or use one of the other techniques for bolding), type the text, and then click the bold SmartIcon to turn bold off and finish typing. If you want to center the next line you're about to type, click the center text SmartIcon and type. Voilà! (Or is it viola?)

Q: How come only one of the three Rs starts with the letter R?

A: We've wondered the same thing for years. Kind of scary isn't it?

Paragraphs with Character

Armed with the skills necessary to change bits of text here and there, we turn our attention to paragraphs. After all, there are times when you want an entire paragraph to have a unique appearance so that it stands out from the others around it or behaves the way that you want it to behave.

Here are a few things you ought to keep in mind as you work with paragraphs:

✔ You can select a whole paragraph and change the appearance of all its characters in the same way that you changed individual characters, words, or groups of words in the previous section.

✔ Summoning up the InfoBox allows you to make changes to the format of the paragraph (other than the appearance of the text).

✔ You can only apply paragraph formats to text in rich text fields.

If your keyboard doesn't have 600 keys

Our world is shrinking fast. Maybe that's why so many people are trying to lose weight. You can be in New York for lunch and France for dinner. Of course, all that eating won't do much for your weight in this shrinking world, but that's beside the point. The point, in case your mind is wandering, is that we are increasingly called upon to use words and symbols in our writing that come from other languages. You ignore the subtle differences between English and non-English alphabets at your peril.

Ignoring the fact that an O and an Ø are two different letters can bring offense, squelch a deal, or even precipitate a food fight. Referring to the Bürgermeister (the mayor) as the Burgermeister (the man in charge of the burgers at a cookout?) is not the way to ingratiate yourself to His Eminency.

You may be wondering how you're going to type a U with an umlaut, when you don't have such a key on your keyboard. It's pretty hokey to type u". Notes, recognizing that you may need to type some non-English characters, has a large number of extra characters not available on your keyboard (or in stores). The LMBCS (Lotus Multi-Byte Character Set) includes all characters available in Notes.

The LMBCS includes characters available on the keyboard as well as nonkeyboard characters — characters unique to foreign languages and such characters as © for copyright or £ for Pound Sterling. To see the list of LMBCS characters and the way to create them, check the documentation or use the Help feature (use the index and choose Characters). The way to type one of these character sets depends upon whether you are using a Macintosh or IBM-style keyboard. If you're using Macintosh, you may not be able to see the character on-screen. You'll have to print to see the character.

Mac users should use Keycaps for information on how to create nonkeyboard characters.

As an example of the way to create a character, here are the keystroke sequences used to type the Ø. On a Macintosh keyboard, press Option+Shift+O. On the IBM-style keyboard, press Alt+F1, then O, and then / (the slashmark). To find the Alt+F1 sequence (also called the *compose sequence*) for a particular character, look in help or in the documentation. If you can't find the character you're after there, you need to use the LMBCS character code. Press Alt+F1 twice, then 0 (that's a zero), then – (a dash), and then the LMBCS number for the character (like 157 for the Ø). If the LMBCS code has only two digits, 33 for instance, use 033. (This is almost as bad as dialing a long distance number with your credit card, isn't it?)

After you've created the character, you can copy and paste it if you need it again. It's faster than using the LMBCS or compose key sequences.

✔ You can change the characteristics of one paragraph at a time simply by putting the cursor in that paragraph.

✔ If you need to change several paragraphs, you must select them all.

✔ If you need to change all the paragraphs in the field, use Edit⇨Select All.

✔ If you change one paragraph, only that paragraph will contain the changes. For example, if you set tabs in one paragraph, that is the only paragraph that will have those unique tabs.

✔ If you haven't typed anything yet, use the InfoBox to set the characteristics you want all the paragraphs to have and then start typing. All the paragraphs will have those characteristics until you use the menu to set some new characteristics.

All margins great and small

You may want to change a paragraph's left or right margins. (Because the margins at the top and bottom of the page have nothing to do with paragraphs, they are in the File⇨Page Setup menu, covered later in this chapter.) You can adjust three settings in the Alignment page of the Text InfoBox:

✔ **Left Margin:** Sets the indent for all lines but the first one. The default is 1 inch, if you're using imperial measurements, or 2.54 cm, if you're using metric measurements. (You can switch from one to the other using File⇨Tools⇨User Preferences, clicking International, and choosing Imperial or Metric.)

✔ **First line:** Allows you to align the first line with the rest of the paragraph or to outdent or indent it.

✔ **Right:** In the Pagination page of the Text InfoBox. Sets the right margin for print only. This setting has nothing to do with screen display, so don't get mad when you enter a number and don't see a change on-screen. You set a right margin by clicking on the arrow next to default, choosing Other, and then typing in the size of the margin. Figure 12-7 shows a right margin set at 2 inches.

The right margin is the distance from the left edge of the paper to the right edge of the paragraph. That's the left edge of the paper. Paying attention? For a 2 inch right margin on a sheet of paper 8.5 inches wide, the right margin should be 6.5 inches. The default is 1 inch.

One paragraph, indivisible

When Notes calculates that the bottom of a page is at hand, it inserts a page break automatically so that the printer will start a new page there. The place it chooses may not always be where you had in mind; you may prefer to have a

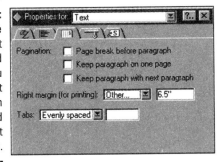

Figure 12-7:
On one convenient tabbed page, you can set pagination options and the right margin.

paragraph stay together, even if it means a bit of white space at the bottom of the page. To protect the paragraph from being split, click on the Pagination page of the Text InfoBox (see Figure 12-7). Then choose one of the following:

✔ Choose `Page break before paragraph` if you definitely want the current paragraph to start a new page. This is useful when you want to start a new section on a new page.

✔ Choose `Keep paragraph on one page` to prevent Notes from breaking up a paragraph somewhere in the middle. Notes will either keep the paragraph on the current page or shove the whole thing to the next page.

✔ Choose `Keep paragraph with next paragraph` to be sure that a paragraph is always on the same page as the paragraph following it.

Notes doesn't show text on-screen the same way it shows text when printing, so you can't always see how the document will look on the page. To get some idea of where the page breaks are, use <u>V</u>iew⇨<u>S</u>how⇨Page <u>B</u>reaks.

Keeping tabs on your paragraph

Back at the factory, paragraphs automatically have their own tabs set at every half inch. This may be fine for you, in which case you don't have to set any tabs at all. But if you're not happy with the preset tabs, you can use the Pagination page of the Text InfoBox to set new ones.

In the Tabs box, choose Evenly spaced and pick a distance between tabs, such as .75 inch. Or you can choose Individually set and then type in the location of each tab, as we did in Figure 12-8. Just type the distance (measured from the left edge of the paper) for all the tabs that you need. For that extra touch of variety, you may even enter some tabs in inches and others in centimeters. If you are using inches, you don't have to type any symbol, and if you want centimeters, just type **cm** after the number. You can't use yards, miles, quarts, or kilometers, though. Between each separate tab setting put a semicolon, not a comma. Notes complains if you use commas.

Figure 12-8:
Setting tabs
in the
Pagination
page of the
Text
InfoBox.

You may find it easier to use the on-screen ruler to set both margins and tabs. If you're rubbing your eyes trying to find a ruler on-screen, try using View⇨Ruler. A ruler like the one in Figure 12-9 should appear at the top of your screen.

Figure 12-9:
The ruler
is a
convenient
and fun way
to set
margins and
tabs. (Well,
convenient
anyway.)

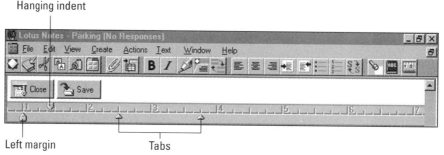

Click in the ruler where you want a tab, and a little triangle appears. To get rid of an unwanted tab, click the triangle to remove it.

The left margin looks like two houses joined at the peaks of their roofs (one is upside down) near the left end of the ruler. Move the upside down house to give the first line of the paragraph a different indent from the rest of the paragraph, which is set with the right-side-up house. (If you just joined us, that last sentence won't make a bit of sense.)

The incredible disappearing paragraph

The time may come when you need to hide a paragraph under some circumstances. You may want to hide a paragraph for several reasons:

➤ You want to save some space by hiding a paragraph when a document is being previewed.

✔ You want text to be visible only when people are editing a document, not when they are reading it, because it contains editing instructions.

✔ You want to hide it from certain readers.

✔ You have a button which executes a command in a document, and you want to hide it when you print the document so some poor chump doesn't try pushing the button on the paper.

You have seven choices for hiding a paragraph — all listed in the Hide When page of the Text InfoBox, as shown in Figure 12-10. You can tell Notes to hide a selected paragraph in any of the following ways:

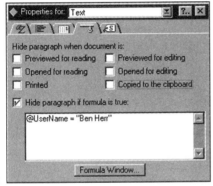

Figure 12-10: The selected paragraph will not be visible on Ben Herr's screen.

✔ **Previewed for reading:** A document highlighted in a view is visible in the Preview pane (if you make the Preview pane visible), but the paragraph set with this attribute will not be visible. Saves valuable screen real estate when space is limited.

✔ **Opened for reading:** The paragraph is only visible when you're in edit mode. It is also hidden for printing.

✔ **Printed:** As the word implies, when you print a document, paragraphs with the Hide While Printing attribute do not print. This is useful for suppressing the printing of paragraphs that you want to be visible only on-screen. You may also use this option when the paragraph contains graphics that slow down the print job.

✔ **Previewed for editing:** A paragraph set with this attribute is not visible if the document's in edit mode in the Preview pane.

✔ **Opened for editing:** The paragraph is visible when the reader is not in edit mode, but it disappears whenever someone tries to edit the document. This is a way to protect a paragraph from being changed by people who have the ability to edit documents. Be careful — after making this choice, you may never be able to edit the paragraph again.

✓ **Copied to the clipboard:** Anyone who tries to copy a paragraph with this attribute while in edit mode will find that there's nothing to paste.

✓ **Hide paragraph if formula is true:** In Figure 12-10, we wrote a formula in the formula window and checked Hide paragraph when formula is true. As the name implies, Notes looks at the formula and, if its condition is met, hides the paragraph. If the user is Ben Herr, he won't see this paragraph under any circumstances.

The preceding hide-when choices work for the *whole paragraph,* not for individually selected text. In fact, many of the text options only work on the whole paragraph — specifically spacing, list options (bullets and numbering), margins, tabs, hide when options, pagination, alignments, and styles.

We'll let you in on a way to get around being unable to edit a paragraph — you can use this trick if you goofed and chose `Hide paragraph when document is: Opened for editing`, or if you want to get around someone else's use of this feature. While you're *not* in edit mode, highlight the paragraph that is hidden when you are editing, copy it to the Clipboard, and then get into edit mode and paste the paragraph into the document. This pasted paragraph will not have the hidden attribute, so you'll be able to edit it. Of course, when you're no longer in edit mode, the paragraph will appear twice, unless you choose to hide the paragraph when the document is opened or previewed for reading.

Get in align

Alignment refers to the arrangement of text in each line, relative to the margins. You have five choices in this section of the Paragraph InfoBox:

✓ **Left:** The text lines up with the left margin and has a ragged right edge.

✓ **Right:** The text lines up with the right margin and has a ragged left edge. Surely you're thinking that there is no right margin except for printing, so what can the text line up with? The answer is simple: the text lines up with the right side of the screen for display and with the right margin for printing.

✓ **Full:** The text stretches from margin to margin so that the paragraph has no ragged edges. Full won't work if you type a really short line or if you press Enter at the end of a line.

✓ **Center:** Want to guess what this does? If you guessed that it centers the text on each line and gives lines ragged right and left edges, you may add ten points to your score and advance three spaces.

✔ **None:** Text starts at the left margin and goes to the right forever. It doesn't wrap. Often, when you import documents from other programs, you may be shocked to see that lines stretch off the screen. You have to scroll to the right until you reach the end of the paragraph and then scroll back to the left to see the next paragraph. Change the alignment to Left or Full to correct the problem.

Give me some space

Feeling cramped, squeezed, closed in? Do your memos seem to have too much stuff and not enough open space? Then you need to space out. Use the Alignment page of the Text InfoBox to s-p-r-e-a-d your paragraph(s) out over more space or to show more white space. You have three choices under each of the three types of spacing. You can use 1, $1^1/_2$, or 2 to determine the distance in each of these ways:

✔ **Interline:** between lines of the paragraph

✔ **Above:** between the current paragraph and the one above it

✔ **Below:** between the current paragraph and the one below it

Choosing all three can be a heck of a mess; you may wind up with too much spacing. Practice a bit so that your screen isn't mostly white space with a line or paragraph appearing once in a while like an oasis in a desert of white sand. If you make a selection you're not happy with, don't forget the Undo feature.

Puttin' on the style

You have to make the coffee, you have to put paper in the copier, and now you have to jump all around your documents applying the same formatting over and over again to paragraphs. It's enough to raise your blood pressure.

Calm your hackles. You may still have to make the coffee, but you don't have to go through all the keystrokes again and again to format paragraphs scattered around your document. Imagine that you wrote a report with lots of sections, and each section has its own title. You want the titles to be centered and bolded, to have one line of space after them, and to have a larger font with blue text. All you have to do is format one title, turn that format into a _style,_ and then use that style for all the other titles, thus saving lots of time and getting you home for dinner.

Applying styles also guarantees that you are consistent. After formatting 15 titles, you're bound to get bored and careless, and you might forget to add boldface along with all the other formats to a title. Using styles guarantees that the same characteristics get applied to every paragraph you select.

After you've written a title, centered it, colored it blue, bolded it, added the spacing, and changed the font, keep the cursor in the title, activate the Text InfoBox, click on the Styles tab (the last page), and click on the Create Style box. Figure 12-11 shows the Text InfoBox with the Style page visible, and — for the same low, low price — the Create Named Style dialog box that appears when you choose to create a new style.

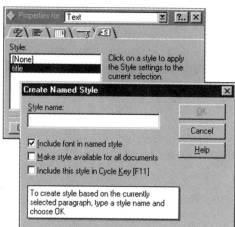

Figure 12-11: These two dialog boxes, working hand in hand, allow you to create styles.

You name your new style in, wonder of wonders, the Style name text box. You can then choose to `Include the font in the style,` to `Make style available for all documents in the database,` and to `Include this style in Cycle Key [F11]` — which means that, when someone highlights a paragraph and presses F11, the paragraph shows all available styles in succession. Click OK to get out of the dialog box and finish with the current style.

Now that you've created your styles, you can apply them to the current paragraph (the one where the cursor is) or to all selected paragraphs. Press F11 to cycle through all the styles you've created and stop when you find the one you want. Or you can apply one of the styles by clicking on the style box (immediately to the right of the font size box) in the Status bar. Click a style name and Notes automatically applies that style to the paragraph where your cursor is or in which at least part of the text is selected.

Permanent Pen — Will It Stain?

Not to worry, the Permanent Pen has nothing to do with ink that won't wash out. It has everything to do with editing, though. Have you ever read a document and wanted to add some comments of your own scattered throughout the paragraphs? Every time you do, you have to specify a new font or color or something so that readers can tell your brilliant comments from the drivel you're commenting on.

Notes' *Permanent Pen* does just that, it allows you to specify a different appearance to whatever you type. All you have to do is designate the different font as the Permanent Pen — we'll show you how in a moment — and then, whenever you want to edit a document, you activate the Permanent Pen and enter your comments.

To designate a Permanent Pen font, activate the Text InfoBox, choose a font, font size, color, and enhancement (like bold or italics), and then click the button that says Set Permanent Pen font. Done.

 Now open a document to which you have editor access, get into edit mode, and find something you want to comment on. When the muse strikes, click the Permanent Pen SmartIcon or choose Text⇨Permanent Pen and start writing.

Figure 12-12 shows a discussion document with a smarmy interjection written in Permanent Pen by a vice president.

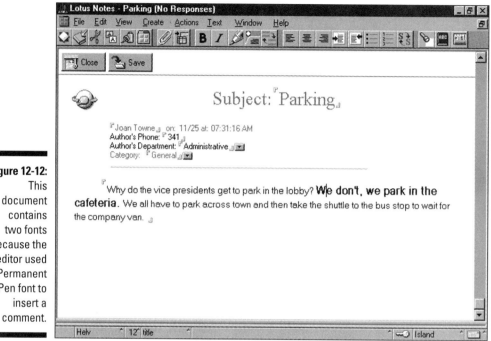

Figure 12-12:
This
document
contains
two fonts
because the
editor used
a Permanent
Pen font to
insert a
comment.

Chapter 13

Doctoring Your Documents

*I*f you took tips from Chapter 12, your characters have character, your sentences make sense, and your paragraphs have punch. Now, what about whole pages and entire documents? This chapter takes you from concentrating on the individual characters to having a global view, seeing the big picture, and making your single- or multi-page document a complete, professional, and well-crafted entity of which you can be proud.

Even as you're making nifty adjustments to individual pages and sweeping modifications to the whole document, you may not see a single change on your screen. Is it time to lose your temper? No! Individual pages are what you see when you print. You don't see separate pages on the screen unless you choose View⇨Show⇨Page Breaks. You don't see headers or footers, either. The only way to see what a page will really look like when it's printed is to print it.

Break It Up!

Notes is a very smart program; it even knows when text is at the bottom of a page. When you print a document, it automatically puts a *page break* in the proper place. That way, you don't print text into the margin or off the page and into thin air.

There comes a time in the affairs of folks, though, when they need to put a page break where Notes wouldn't. For instance, if a paragraph starts a new section and you want it to appear on a new page (even if the previous page isn't full), you can insert a page break. You can insert a page break in one of three ways:

     ✔ Via the keyboard (Press Ctrl+L)

     ✔ With the SmartIcon (click the Page Break SmartIcon)

     ✔ From the menu (choose Create⇨Page Break)

If you choose to see the page break by selecting View⇨Show⇨Page Breaks, it appears as a solid line across the screen, as you can see in Figure 13-1.

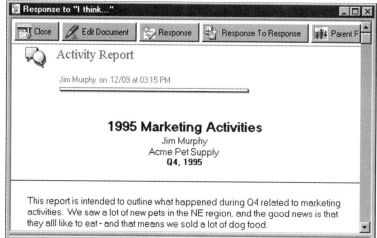

Figure 13-1:
Notes
displays
page breaks
as a
horizontal
line right
across the
middle of a
document.

To remove a page break that you don't want anymore, place the cursor on the first character after the page break and press Backspace. If you delete a page break and it appears right back again, maybe one line before or after the place where it used to be, you are trying to remove a break that Notes put there all by itself because the text is at the end of the page. That's a page break you're going to have to live with.

Putting Your Cards in a Table

If you're having dinner, a table is something on which you spill your gravy. When you're using Notes, a table is something that makes it a whole lot easier to keep rows and columns of information all lined up, without having to set up a million tabs.

A *table* is a spreadsheet you can place in your document, with rows and columns of boxes into which you type information. One of the advantages of using a table instead of tabs is that tabs normally allow wrapping of text back to the beginning of the line, whereas tables keep text aligned in the column.

Here comes a surprise — you can only put a table in a rich text field.

Setting the table

Suppose, for the sake of argument, that you need to send a message that includes a schedule. The schedule itself would be a great candidate for a table — it involves small bits of data and needs to be in tabular format.

 When you get to the place in the message where you are ready to place the schedule, select Create⇨Table. Figure 13-2 shows you the Create Table dialog box. You get to decide in advance how many rows and how many columns you want in your table. If planning ahead isn't your forte, don't panic; you can always change your mind later and add and delete rows and columns.

Figure 13-2:
The
Create Table
dialog box,
preparing
for a 3-row,
3-column
table.

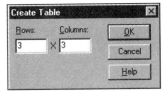

Figure 13-3 shows a table with a schedule. A schedule is just one example of a good reason to use a table; if you try hard, you can think of lots of other examples. When you add a new table, Notes automatically fits it to your screen and makes each column the same width. Needless to say, you can change the column widths, too.

Figure 13-3:
This table
has three
columns
and three
rows.

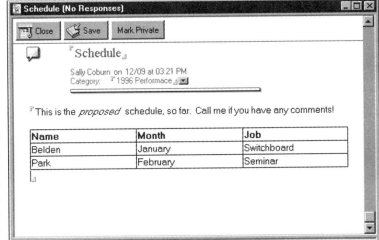

After you add a table to your document, Notes is smart enough to change the menus (did you notice?). When your cursor is in a table, you'll notice a new menu command called, appropriately enough, Ta<u>b</u>le. It's right after <u>T</u>ext, and right before <u>W</u>indow. You use this menu choice to do things like change the table's properties, add new rows, change the border style, and so on.

What if you decide to change your new table so that it is not set to *Fit to window?* Huh? By default, new tables *are* set to Fit to window, which means that the table size and column widths will change, depending on the size of the window that you are (or your reader is) using to read your document. If you make your table so that it *doesn't* Fit to window, the table (and its columns) will be the same width, no matter how big or small you make the document window. Figure 13-4 shows two tables. The first *is* set to Fit to window, so it has adjusted to the rather small window size. The other table is *not* set to Fit to window, so it stays the same size, even though the window is too small to display all of it.

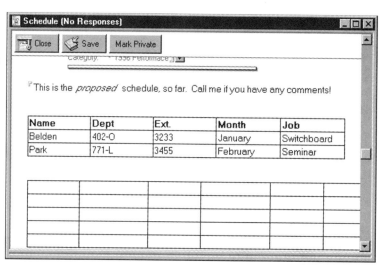

Figure 13-4: You can decide whether a table's size should change when you make a document window smaller.

If you want to make your new table the same size, no matter what, make sure that the cursor is in the table, choose Ta<u>b</u>le⇨Table <u>P</u>roperties⇨Layout (or click the Properties SmartIcon), and then click Fit to window (to turn it off). Figure 13-5 shows the Table InfoBox open with the Layout page exposed.

You also use this dialog box to set the space between rows, the space between columns, the table's left margin, and to adjust a particular column's width.

Cell borders are not people who live in jail, but are the lines that surround each cell. If you use the same Ta<u>b</u>le⇨Table <u>P</u>roperties dialog box but click the Cell Borders tab, you can choose to have a cell with a single-line border (which, incidentally, is the default), a double border, or even just a border on the top or bottom. Figure 13-6 shows the dialog box.

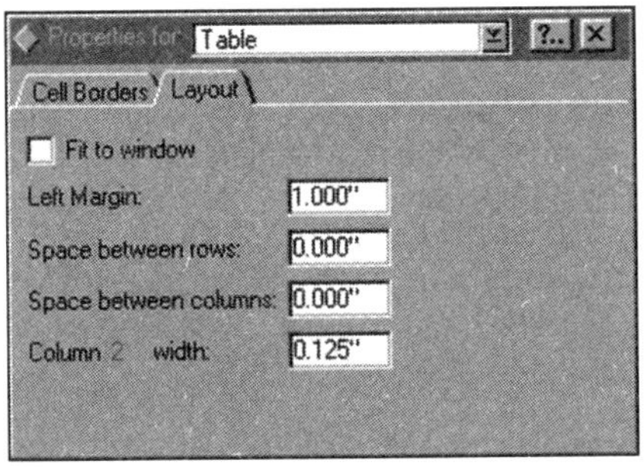

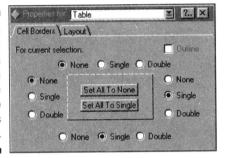

Figure 13-5:
Use the InfoBox to format a table.

Figure 13-6:
Use the Cell Borders page of the Table InfoBox to outline cells in the table.

When you've decided all the decisions and set all the settings, click OK. After a few seconds, a blank table appears where the insertion point was in the document. If (gasp of delight) your table appears exactly as you intended, then you're ready to put the cursor in a cell and start typing. When you're done with one cell, move to the cell to the right by pressing Tab, to the cell to the left by pressing Shift+Tab, to the cell below by pressing the down-arrow key, or to the cell above by pressing the up-arrow key. Of course, you can click in a cell with the mouse to move to any cell in the table.

All you have to do to change the height of a cell is type. If there's too much text to fit on one line in the cell, or if you press Enter, the height of the cell increases to accommodate the additional text. The whole row will be as tall as the cell with the most text in that row. If, however, you want to change the width of a column, you'll have to mess with the menu, the ruler, or an icon. Read on.

Open table, insert row

You're done with the table and you're about to send it, when — "Eeek!" — you cry in frustration and disbelief. You forgot to include a column for Location. Is it tragic, is it sad, are you out of luck, is it difficult to add a column? Nope! You can add a new column or row as quickly as you can choose Table➪Insert Column (or Table➪Insert Row, depending on the circumstances).

Be sure that your cursor is in the column where you would like the new blank column to be. If you want to insert a row, then put your cursor in the row where you want the new row to appear. In other words, when you insert a new column, the new column appears in the column where you have the cursor, and all other columns move to the right to make room for the new one. When you insert a new row, all other rows in the table move *down* to make room.

No more row four

We don't need Belden on the switchboard after all. In fact, we don't need that row anymore. Got your eraser? Wait a minute, this is the computer age. There has to be a better way of getting rid of a row or column.

If you want to delete an existing row, be sure to start by placing the cursor in the row you want to delete. That sounds like a simple enough suggestion, but if you aren't on your toes you'll wind up deleting the wrong row. Choose Table⇨Delete Selected Row(s) or, perhaps, Table⇨Delete Selected Column(s). When you do, you'll get the warning dialog box shown in Figure 13-7.

Figure 13-7:
Be careful;
once you
delete a row
or column,
you may
never get
it back.

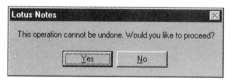

If you have the cursor in the wrong row or column, or if you chose to delete a row when you meant to delete a column, you could end up in big trouble! So *be careful*. Because an ounce of prevention is worth two in the bush, here's a piece of advice. Save the document first; then do your deleting. If you blow it, you can then close the document (without saving it) and reopen it. Now try again, and please be more careful this time!

More than one cell at a time

You may have noticed that many of the instructions in these past few pages began with some pithy instruction like "make sure you're in the right cell" or "click the cell whose border you want to change and then. . . ." So, the burning question is: What if you want to make some kind of change to *more than one* cell (or row, or column) at a time? Can you do it? Is it possible? Could it be? You bet, and it's easy. Just click and drag from the first cell to the last cell you want to change, as we've done in Figure 13-8. After you've highlighted a bunch of cells (by pressing the left mouse button, and holding it down while you highlight the cells), you can make any kind of change you want to those cells; a new font, italics, or even a new cell border are only a menu choice away.

Always make sure that you have selected the correct cell (or cells) in a table before you try to make a change to the table.

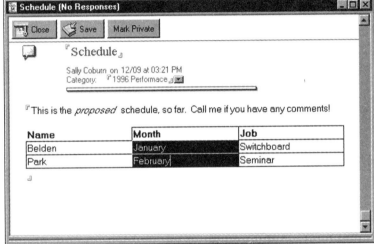

Figure 13-8:
Select cells with the mouse if you need to make any kind of "mass scale" change to a table.

Changing column widths the easy way

Way back in Figure 13-5, we showed you how to change a column's width by using the Table Properties dialog box. That's great, if you know exactly how wide you need a column to be. But what if you want to eyeball it? In other words, you're not sure of the exact column width, but it's obvious by looking that the column in question is too wide (or too narrow), and you want to make it bigger (or smaller), and you want to do it now (not later).

First, make sure that the cursor is in the column whose width you want to change. Then choose View⇨Ruler. Finally, grab that little bar shown in Figure 13-9 on the right-hand side of the column in the ruler to change the column's size. Most people find this method easier than using the aforementioned dialog box, but if you'd rather use the dialog box to manually enter a column's width, you go right ahead.

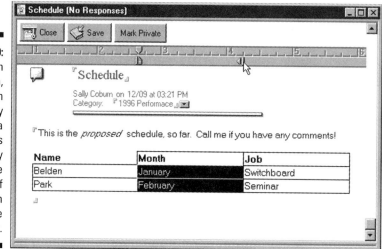

Figure 13-9:
If you turn
the ruler on,
you can
easily
change a
column's
width by
grabbing the
border of
the column
up in the
ruler.

Deleting a table altogether

Getting rid of a table once and for all is a little tricky. You *cannot* select all the cells and then just press Delete. In fact, if you do, you'll end up deleting all of the table's contents, but the empty cells will still be there. Instead, you have to select the *entire table* by putting the cursor at the end of the line just before (and outside) the table, and then pressing Shift+↓ (which will highlight the whole table). Then, and only then, can you press Delete to get rid of the whole thing.

Trying to Get a Header the Situation

Imagine this heartbreaking situation. You print a 50-page monster report. A breeze blows through the open window just as the last page comes out of the printer, and your document blows all over the place. You pick up your document and try to put it in order. You have a tough time because the pages aren't numbered. Sad, isn't it? What's a body to do? Next time, create a header and put page numbers in it; that's what.

One doc, one header

Page numbers appear in headers or footers: bits of text that appear at the top (*header*) or bottom (*footer*) of each printed page. You can choose to put other information in a header or footer, too, if you want. If a document is urgent or the kind of information spies and bad guys could really use against the company, put that information in the header. If every page says "URGENT!!" or *"Don't Show This to Bad Guys,"* the reader is likely to get the message, even if one page gets separated from all the others.

To create headers and footers, choose File⇨Document Properties, and click the tab with a little printer on it (isn't that cute). When you do, you see the InfoBox that is featured so prominently in Figure 13-10. If you want to enter the text that's destined to appear at the top of each page, click the Header button. You don't have to be Einstein to figure out that you have to click the Footer button to enter the text for the bottom of every page.

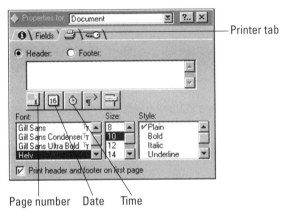

Figure 13-10:
Use the
Printer page
of the
Document
InfoBox to
create a
Header or
Footer.

Printer tab

Page number   Date   Time

Remember, you won't see headers on-screen, because they only appear on the printed page.

"What," you ask, "can the Notes user put in a header or footer?" Glad you asked:

- ✔ **Text:** Type anything you want. If you want the header (or footer) to be more than one line, press Enter at the end of the first line, second line, and so on.

- ✔ **Page Numbers:** Click the Page Number button to have a page number automatically inserted in the Header/Footer. You can even get fancy and type **Page** and then click the Page SmartIcon. The header or footer will look like this: Page &P. The &P turns into the proper page number when you print, so on page 5 you'll see Page 5. Now, if the document gets blown around, putting it in order will be much easier. Of course, you can close that drafty window and avoid the problem altogether.

- ✔ **Date:** Click the Date button to automatically insert the date in a header or footer. Printing the time or date in a header or footer is handy if the reader needs to tell which is the most recent printout among a lot of printed copies of the same memo.

- ✔ **Time:** Click the Time button, and the header or footer shows the current time (according to the computer's clock) each and every time you print your document. Notes prints the time in this format: 03:48:42PM.

✔ **A Tab:** When you click the Tab button, Notes moves the next part of the header over to the right, just as if you pressed the Tab key when typing a document. Clicking Tab allows you to make cool headers and footers with, for example, the date in the lower left corner of the page, the time right in the middle of the bottom of the page, and the Page number in the lower right corner of the page.

✔ **The Window Title:** When you click the last button, Notes puts the title of whatever document you're working on right in the header (or footer) for all to see.

You can use the Font, Size, and Style lists to determine what the Header or Footer will look like — but you can't mix and match. All text in a header is the same font, and same size, and the same style. How boring!

So, to wrap it all up, imagine that you're working in the Daily Schedule document, and you enter this in the Header box:

This is a Header | Page &P | &W

When you print the document, something like this appears at the top of page 6:

```
This is a Header              Page 6              Daily Schedule
```

Be sure to close the Properties box when you're finished.

A chicken in every pot, and a header for all docs

Creating a header or footer in the aforementioned manner is just fine and dandy, but doing so only affects *the current document.* Note the dramatic use of italics to show you that, when you open a document and create a header, that header only applies to the document that you are editing right at the moment.

You may, instead, prefer to create a header or footer for any document that is printed in a particular database. Although there are no eye-catching italics in the previous sentence, it is important to note that you can create a header or footer for every document that you print in the current database. Documents printed from other databases won't have a header unless you create one for that database, too.

 How to accomplish this technological feat? Use the InfoBox again, but this time change the Properties for: text box to the entire database, not just the current document. Click the Properties SmartIcon, and then be sure to choose Database from the Properties for: list (as you can see in Figure 13-11). Then click that little tab with the picture of the printer, and you're in business! You enter the text and other items just the same way you would for a document header or footer (as we discussed in the previous few pages).

Figure 13-11:
Use the
InfoBox to
create a
header/
footer for all
documents
in a
database,
not just the
one you're
working on.

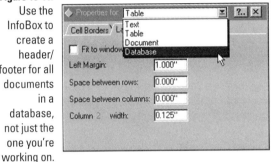

The dialog box you use when you're working with a document's header looks remarkably like the dialog box you use when working with a database's header, so be careful to pay special attention to the Properties for: list.

Set 'em Up, Boys

There's an art to setting up any printed page. So put on your beret and choose File➪Page Setup to see the dialog box shown in Figure 13-12.

Figure 13-12:
The Page
Setup
dialog box.

You'll use this dialog box most often (if you use it at all) to adjust the margins, simply by entering numbers in the appropriate fields. As we discuss in Chapter 12, you can set margins for individual paragraphs; use the Extra left and Extra right fields when you need to add even more space to your paragraph margins.

If you've included page numbers in a header or footer, tell Notes to start with a page number other than one by using the Start page numbers at field. You may find this option useful if you are printing a report from, say, Microsoft Word, and you want to include a few pages from a Notes database. You print pages one through five in Word, and then print pages six through eleven in Notes. Use the Start page numbers at field, and your reader will think all the printed pages came from the same place.

If you intend to send your printed pages to a printing service to be reproduced, you might use the Cropping features to make it easier for them. On the other hand, if you're like most people, and don't often send material to a professional printing company, you probably won't use the cropping features.

Use the Paper button to tell Notes which paper tray in your printer to use for the first page when printing and then which tray to use for all the rest of the pages. Obviously, if you don't have one of those fancy printers with more than one paper tray, you won't spend too much time with this feature! But if you do have a fancy printer (lucky you!), this is a nice way to have the first page print on that fancy company letterhead.

Search and Rescue

Everybody makes mistakes. Remember: to err is human, to forgive is divine, and to make the same mistake again is inevitable. So, in the spirit of mistake-making, you type up a long memo and then find that some text you typed was wrong. Of course, you made the mistake over and over again. You may, for example, have referred to Sue when she prefers to be called Susan.

The time has come to find all the Sues in the document and change them to Susans. Select Edit⇨Find/Replace or press Ctrl+F. Watch for the dialog box that's pictured in Figure 13-13, which we have already tailored to our specifications.

Figure 13-13:
The Find
and Replace
dialog box.

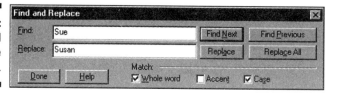

Searching for text in order to rescue your document takes a bit of planning if it's to work right. Notice, for example, these choices we've made in Figure 13-13:

- ✔ We chose <u>W</u>hole Word so that Notes doesn't go around changing "suede" into "Susande."
- ✔ We would have chosen Accen<u>t</u> if we were searching for a word that contains a diacritical mark like an accent, a circumflex, a cedilla, a freckle, or a mole. When you choose Accen<u>t</u>, Find and Replace will look specifically for that mark and will ignore any occurrences of the word without it.
- ✔ We also chose Ca<u>s</u>e so that, if the document includes the word "sue" (the legal action), we won't replace that with Susan's name.

To be sure that you find all occurrences of a word, it's best to put the cursor at the beginning of a document before you start beating the bushes for that special word.

After you've made all your decisions, typed in the text that you want to find, and the text that you want to use as a replacement, it's time to get the whole process started. You can choose one of the following:

- ✔ **Find <u>N</u>ext:** to begin at the cursor and go forward through the document to the first or next occurrence of the search text, but not do any replacing.
- ✔ **Find <u>P</u>revious:** to search from the cursor back to the beginning, but not do any replacing.
- ✔ **Rep<u>l</u>ace:** to find the first occurrence of the search text. Click Replace again to replace that text and find the next occurrence.
- ✔ **Repla<u>c</u>e All:** to get the job done quickly by replacing every occurrence of the search text with the replacement text without checking each time. Use this choice carefully, because strange and unpredictable things may happen. Imagine, for instance, if the word Sue starts a sentence: "Sue us at your peril" becomes "Susan us at your peril."
- ✔ **<u>D</u>one:** to stop the whole process dead in its tracks.

The clever little searcher may find an occurrence of the search text behind the Find and Replace dialog box, which means that you may sometimes have to move the dialog box out of the way to see the highlight. Just drag the dialog box out of the way by the scruff of its title bar.

If You're a Bad Spellar

Even if you can spell real good, you are bound for the occasional typographical error sometime in the next few years. You need to be ever vigilant for that eventuality — ready to pounce on it and correct it before it gets sent to thousands of recipients who will laugh quietly up their sleeves at you for an easily corrected oversight.

In the dialog box in Figure 13-14, you see that the person who knocked out the memo didn't notice that "corporate" was spelled wrong. Then again, maybe he didn't know how to spell it. No matter, the spell checker found the mistake.

 After you save your document (just to be safe), choose Edit⇨Check Spelling or click the Spell Check SmartIcon. Regardless of where you last saw your cursor, the spell checker starts at the beginning of the document. If it finds a word it doesn't recognize, it highlights the word (sometimes behind the dialog box) and waits for you to take some sort of action. Among the actions you can take are these:

✔ Go get a cup of coffee and let the spell checker wait until you are ready.

✔ Choose Skip the word if you want to accept the misspelling this time, but you want Notes to continue to watch for it in the rest of the document.

✔ Choose Skip All if you want to ignore this word.

✔ Choose Define to add the word to the Notes dictionary so that it will never, ever be highlighted again.

 Use the Define button carefully, because adding a misspelling to the dictionary can be very embarrassing. Forevermore, Notes will ignore that misspelling.

✔ Choose Replace to have Notes replace your mistake with the word you select in the Guess: list.

✔ Type the correct spelling in the Replace: text box.

✔ Choose Done anytime that you want to stop the spell check. Promise that you'll spell check it later?

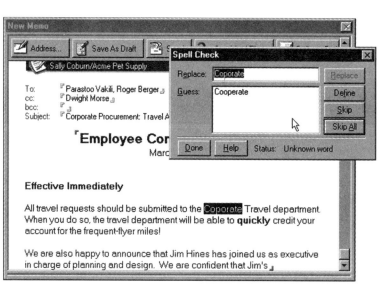

Figure 13-14:
Notes
can even
correct your
spelling —
just make
sure that its
guess is the
correct one.

Chapter 14

Notes the Way YOU Want It

· ·

In This Chapter

▶ Changing the appearance of mail memo forms

▶ Creating a new memo form

▶ Adding a folder to your mail database

▶ Changing the icon for your mail database

▶ Adding certification to your ID

▶ Creating encryption keys

▶ Adding a password to your ID

▶ Using File⇨Tools⇨User Preferences

· ·

*W*hen you get a new office or desk (or place to stand, if you're a real junior in the company), one of your first official acts is to make your new location seem familiar. Out come the pictures — your family, your significant other, your pet dog, cat, or cobra. You arrange the articles in the drawers so they're right where you need them and spread out your personal treasures across the expanse of your desk.

In similar fashion, as you snuggle into using Notes, you may find that you want to change some things about the way the program looks and works. The reasons may be cosmetic, like changing the color of the background and text of your memos, or functional, like designating your server or choosing a password for your User ID. Speaking of pictures, if you're a bit artistic, you could even change the icon for your mail database so it looks like something especially meaningful to you, like someone you love, your car, or your favorite dessert.

Mail That Has "You" Written All over It

In your company, it's very probable that everyone's mail memos look the same. They don't say the same things, of course, but they have the same appearance.

You have at your very fingertips the capability to completely change the appearance of every memo you send, so people will notice when your memos arrive at workstations around the world. Not only that, you can change several other aspects of your mail database as well. We'll cover them in this section.

When you choose Create⇨Memo, you call to the screen a blank memo form on which you write your message. This form also acts like a lens through which you read the memos that others send you. Think of this Notes form as an electronic version of the blank memo pads some companies give their employees to write memos on. Perhaps your blank memo forms have your name or a logo on them and maybe even come in a color other than white. Why not have the same qualities in your Notes memos?

Here are some reasons why you may want to change a memo form:

✔ You want to change the way memos look on your screen as you read or write them.

✔ You want people who receive your memos to see a different memo format than the one they normally see.

✔ You want some fields — for instance, the To field — to always have a certain value automatically (a *default* value).

Changing the way memos look on-screen

If we wrote about every detail of redesigning your mail memo form, this book would be twice as thick as it is now and would cost twice as much. Instead, we're just going to talk about the things you're most likely to want to change in the mail memo form. If your curiosity gets the best of you, use the Help feature to find new things to do or how to respond to an unfamiliar dialog box.

To start the whole process of customizing your mail memos, follow these steps:

1. **Open your mail database.**

2. **In the Navigation pane, choose Forms from the list under Design.**

   If you don't see items listed under the word "Design," click Design and then choose Forms.

3. **In the View pane, double-click Memo.**

   A couple of warnings appear, telling you that your changes may be lost later on. Not to worry, we'll show you how to take care of that problem later. Figure 14-1 shows the mail memo form as it looks in design mode (after you dismiss the dire warnings).

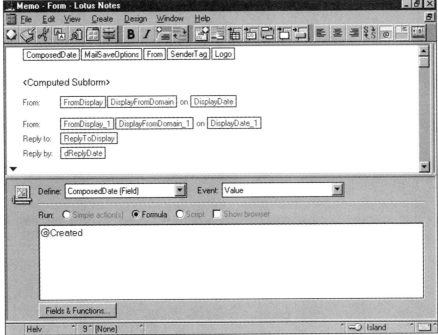

Figure 14-1:
This is the
memo form
for the mail
database
in design
mode.

4. Change the memo form to your satisfaction.

Among the quick changes you can make to your form are the following:

- Change any of the field titles (static text) such as To, From, or Subject by simply editing them.

- Change the font, font size, or color of the field titles by highlighting the text and using the Text InfoBox.

- Change the font, font size, or color of any field itself by highlighting the field definition box and then activating the field InfoBox and choosing the changes you want. You could, for instance, make one of the fields bold or make it a different font from the rest.

- Add other text or objects to the form. For instance, you could place below the body of the memo a sincere, heartfelt, and original message like "Have a nice day" to warm the cockles of the reader's heart, or you could add the company logo, or some graphic you would like associated with yourself, like an image of your motorcycle.

5. When you're done, press Esc.

6. At the prompt, choose Yes; you do want to save the form.

From now on, whenever you compose a memo, as you are writing the memo you will see your new form.

The words in boxes on your memo form represent the fields themselves. As you highlight a field, you see its formula in the Programmer pane at the bottom of the screen. Some fields have no formula associated with them, in which case that pane will be empty. Surprise. Double-click any of the fields to see the actual field definition in an InfoBox.

Mess with the formula and the more technical aspects of the field at your own risk — changing field definitions is beyond the scope of this book. When we say "field definition," we don't mean its appearance; we mean just the technical stuff like field type. If you do start to make some changes and get panicky, dismiss the InfoBox by clicking the X in the upper right-hand corner of the InfoBox, and then press Esc and choose No when the prompt asks whether you want to save the form.

One other change you might want to make to the memo is changing the background color. Once again, you use the InfoBox for that, but you need to change the word in the Properties for box from "text" to "form." Then click the down arrow in the background color box to display the dazzling choice of colors.

If this book were in living color, you could see the rainbow of hues available for your memo form's background in Figure 14-2. To select a color, click the one you like. This dialog box has other options, but they're a bit too advanced for this book.

Figure 14-2:
Here is how you choose a background color for your mail memo form.

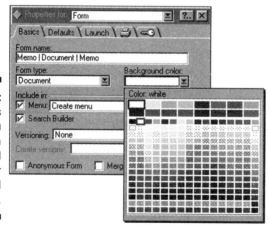

Keep in mind the colors you'll be using for your fields and static text as you pick a background color. You can create some really hard-to-read combinations if you're not careful. Imagine black letters on a brown background. If you change text colors, too, you can even get stuff like yellow letters on a pink background. It may sound springtime fresh and colorful, but the lack of contrast means that nobody will be able to read it! As a general rule, keep backgrounds light and letters dark. Light letters on a dark background are much harder to read.

One little point you ought to know: All these changes will only be visible at your end — that is, when *you* are looking at memos. So far, you've been changing forms for the first reason listed earlier in this section: to change the way the memos you read and write look on your own screen. That is, when the recipients open their copy of your memo, they see the plain old memo form they're used to seeing, because *their* form is the one used at *their* computer to read all the memos they've received.

Can you do anything to remedy this sorry situation? Yes! Read on.

Changing the way your memos look on everyone else's screen

After you've made changes to your memo form, you may want to send those changes along with your memo. Here's how:

1. **Open the InfoBox and select Properties for: Form.**
2. **Click the Defaults page.**

   It should look a lot like Figure 14-3.
3. **Click to select** `Store form in document.`

Figure 14-3:
You'll be able to find "Store form in document" in the Form InfoBox Defaults page.

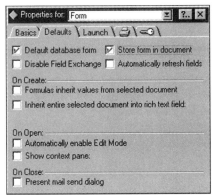

Now, when you send a message to other people, Notes will use *your* form to display your message on *their* computers. However, there is a price to pay for including a form in a memo when you send it. The memo will be much bigger, byte-wise. That means e-mail databases fill up faster and transmission over networks and modems takes longer. But that's a small price to pay for your work of art, right? Well, perhaps in the interest of being a good citizen, you should select `Store form in document` only for special forms, rather than just on a whim. Now you've changed a form for the second reason: to change the way your memos look on others' screens.

If you store the form in the documents, your form will be the one that others see when reading your memos.

Adding fields: A form is born

The third reason for changing memos is to have Notes fill in some fields for you automatically. You can create a new form for special occasions that does just that. There is no reason a person as capable as you can't create a new form completely. After all, this is *your* mail database, isn't it?

How about a form to send memos to your inner circle of coworkers and friends? You can base its design on the memo form.

Follow these steps to create a new form which is identical to the memo form:

1. In the Navigation pane, click Design and then Forms.

2. In the View pane, highlight the Memo form.

3. Click the Copy SmartIcon and then the Paste SmartIcon.

4. Dismiss the authorization warning by clicking OK.

5. Look for a message box like the one in Figure 14-4 and choose No.

We'll explain the meaning of this message box in the section "Now, to Etch It in Stone." For now, just trust us.

Figure 14-4: Protect your new form from future automatic changes.

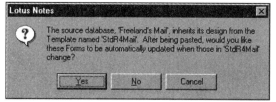

Lotus Notes

The source database, 'Freeland's Mail', inherits its design from the Template named 'StdR4Mail'. After being pasted, would you like these Forms to be automatically updated when those in 'StdR4Mail' change?

[Yes]   [No]   [Cancel]

Eventually, you'll see a new form, called "Copy of Memo," in the list of forms. That's a twin of the original Memo form. To modify this new form, double-click its name.

Remember that anytime you want to create a new view, form, or other database element based on an existing one, just copy and paste the one you want right into the same database.

You probably don't send courtesy copies or blind courtesy copies of personal memos, so you might want to delete those field titles and the field definitions. Highlight them and press Delete to remove them.

Although it's okay to delete the cc: and bcc: fields, Notes uses many of the other fields behind the scenes (such as the To: and From: fields), so it's best to avoid deleting any other fields.

If memos written on this form are always going to go to certain friends, you can permanently place their names in the To: field. If it is a departmental memo, you can put the name of the group in the To: field (assuming that the group name has been defined in either the company's or your personal Name and Address Book). To change the To: field, highlight it and, in the Programmer pane, type the new names enclosed in quotes and separated by commas (for example, you may type: **"John Smith, Sue Brown"**). It's best to copy and paste names of people and groups from the Name and Address Book so you get the whole name and spell it right.

Feel free to change the background color using the Form InfoBox. Also, Copy of Memo is not much of a name, you no doubt agree, so use the InfoBox Basics page to give your form a new name. How about "Personal Memo"? Also, be sure to use the Defaults page to select Store form in document so that your memo will look the same on other people's computers as it does on yours.

After you're done designing your form, press Esc and save the new form.

Now you have a new form to use. Choose Create, and there, in the list of things you can compose, is your new form. Won't the crew be impressed! They'll crowd around you in the lunchroom asking how you did that. Mention this book, please. You're well on your way to becoming a true Notes nerd.

A Folder to Fit Your Needs

Folders are holders for documents. You put selected documents in a folder to keep them together in one place, like memos from people giving you things to do, for instance. Of course, if you want to sound really corporate, you don't say "To Do." No sirree, you say "Action Items." Everyone, regardless of status in the organization, gets the occasional memo discussing something they have to do.

You should create a folder so that all those memos are in one place, rather than scattered around among other memos about meeting for coffee and doing lunch.

What'll it look like?

The first step in creating a folder is to look at all the views, not to see what documents are in them, but to see their design, especially the columns. Pick one you want to use as the design for your folder. Of course, you can modify the design, but if you have a similar design starting out, you can get your own folder done faster so you have more time to do your power lunch. Your choice should be easy; views in a mail database are fairly similar. The difference among views more often has to do with which documents they contain for display rather then their design.

Our suggestion is to base your new folder on the All Documents view. If it contains all documents, it should be capable of displaying any mail database documents you put in it, and if it can't, you can always try to get your money back.

1. **Choose Create⇨Folder.**

2. **In the first dialog box you see (the one in the upper left of Figure 14-5), type the name of your new folder.**

   We prefer "To Do" — thanks very much.

3. **Click the Options button.**

4. **In the second dialog box (shown in the lower right of Figure 14-5), designate the All Documents view as the view to Inherit design from.**

5. **Click the Design now box so you can get right to work.**

   Don't choose Design now if you plan to use the folder without changes.

Your To Do folder will take its rightful place as the one and only folder (until you create more), and you're ready to put documents in it. We do, however, have a modification up our sleeves.

With columns and justice for all

One of the many views in the mail database is a Tasks view. If you look at this view, you'll see that it has a column for the people to whom the task is assigned. Because this is a To Do folder, you may also want to list the names of other people (in addition to you) to whom these items are assigned. That way, you can dump all the work on them— excuse me, you can delegate and cooperate.

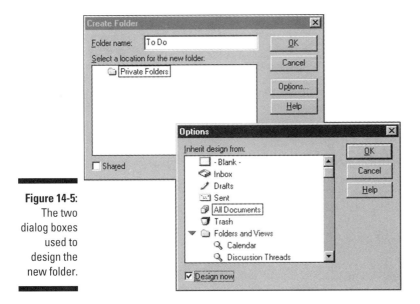

Figure 14-5:
The two
dialog boxes
used to
design the
new folder.

To copy the Assigned To column from the Tasks view into your new folder, follow these steps:

1. **Choose <u>W</u>indow to return to the main view of the mail database.**

2. **Click Design and then Views in the Navigation pane.**

3. **In the View pane, double-click the Tasks view.**

4. **Close the pesky warning.**

5. **When the view is open in design mode, click the column head of the Assigned To column.**

6. **Choose <u>E</u>dit⇨<u>C</u>opy.**

7. **Choose <u>W</u>indow from the menu and then, from the drop-down list, choose the design window for the To Do folder.**

8. **Click the Subject column and then paste the new column.**

   The new column appears to the left of the Subject column.

9. **Press Esc and choose to save the folder.**

   Within seconds, a new folder will be ready for your dining and dancing pleasure.

You can't change everyone's view of the world — just your own views of your own databases. You don't have the authority to change view designs for databases on the network . . . yet. If you become a Notes power user (read: *nerd*), you can just march into the office of the Notes administrator and demand the right to mess with any and every database you see. In the meantime, check Chapter 11 for information about how you can create views for any database.

Do folders have properties?

Yes indeed, every element of a database has its own properties; folders are no exception. Set those properties in the Folder InfoBox (see Figure 14-6). The following list describes the types of settings you can make and tells which page of the Folder InfoBox they're on.

- ✔ **Name:** (on the Basics page) If want to change the name of the folder, this is the place to do it.

- ✔ **Colors:** (on the Style page) Here you can pick from over 200 stunning colors and patterns for the background, rows containing unread documents, and column totals. In addition, you can choose a color for alternate rows of the view.

- ✔ **Lines per row:** (on the Style page) This is useful if some long winded person wrote a long name for the task or included a lot of people in the Assigned To list. If you pick more than one line per row, you can also choose to shrink a row to content so that it won't take any more room than it needs to.

Figure 14-6:
The folder's
InfoBox.

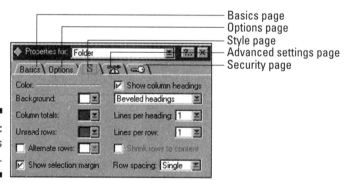

When you've finished all the changes you want to make to your folder in the Folder InfoBox, just click the box marked X in the upper-right corner. Then dismiss the folder, choose to save it, and you're done.

Icons Customized While-U-Wait

Actually, you have to do more than just wait. You have to do the work here. Your desktop has a box with an icon for each database you've added. Your e-mail database icon, which looks like everyone else's, is yours to change if you want — here's your chance to strut your stuff, be an individual, leave the pack behind, show off your creative genius . . . and waste a little time.

Start by selecting your e-mail database. Then, in the Navigation pane, choose Design⇨Other⇨Icon. A palette appears with the tools and colors you need to create an eye-catching crowd pleaser. Of course, the normal crowd seeing this icon will be just one (you), but don't let that dampen your enthusiasm.

Figure 14-7 shows the standard mail database icon with initials added to give it that warm, personal touch.

Paint Brush: Draws only straight lines
Paint Sprayer: Fills a bigger area
Paint Roller: Fills an area
Pen: Colors one pixel

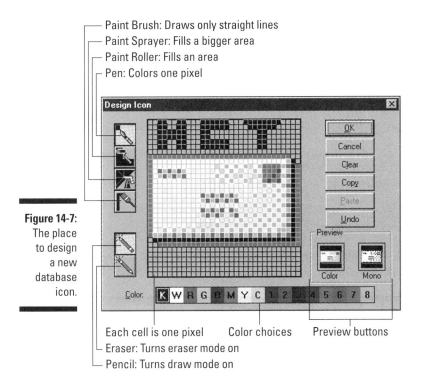

Figure 14-7:
The place
to design
a new
database
icon.

Each cell is one pixel   Color choices   Preview buttons
Eraser: Turns eraser mode on
Pencil: Turns draw mode on

The boxes to the left in Figure 14-7 seven are *tools,* allowing you to do such things as color whole areas at once, color individual squares (called *pixels*), or draw straight lines with the color you choose. The pencils in the lower-left are for drawing and erasing (should you drip a little paint in the wrong place).

If, *sacre bleu*, you've made a series of mistakes and want to start all over again, choose Clear, and the entire palette is emptied of color — you may start again. When you make a simple mistake, choose Undo, and it's as though the most recent action never took place.

As you work, you can check the Preview window to see how the icon will look on a color or monochrome monitor. Once you're satisfied, click OK and, voilà, your database has a new icon.

To copy another master's work, click the Copy button to move the icon from another database to the Clipboard and then click Paste to place it into the current palette. Or why not get into PaintBrush, create an original drawing, and then copy and paste it into the icon palette?

Now, to Etch It in Stone

To finalize the creation of your database, you should take one more step, or else tomorrow, when you open your mail database, all your work will be gone.

Remember the dire warnings about losing your work when you change something in this database? You don't? Well, a reminder here would be appropriate then. When you first tried to enter design mode for the memo form, you saw two warnings: the first was that your changes may be lost, and the second was that messing around with some fields may mess up authorization to use the database.

You're concerned about the first warning here. You didn't make any life-threatening design changes to goof up authorizations.

To prevent changes to an altered view or a changed form, follow these steps:

1. **In the Navigation pane of your mail database, click Design and then click Forms.**

2. **Next, click Memo.**

   Don't double-click, just select it.

 3. **Now activate the InfoBox by clicking the InfoBox (Properties) SmartIcon.**

4. **Select Design Document in the Properties for box.**

5. **Click the Design tab and select** `Do not allow design refresh/ replace to modify`.

6. **Close the InfoBox by clicking the X in its upper right corner.**

Now you can sleep soundly, fully confident that, when the midnight marauder comes around reversing changes made by the unsuspecting to their mail databases, your changes are safe and permanent.

Certify Me, Quick

When you go out of the country, you usually need a passport. Sometimes, you need to have your passport stamped with special permission to visit specific places. Notes uses a kind of passport and visa, too. In Notes, your passport is your *Notes ID* and the visa is a *certificate.* Your ID says that you are a Notes user, and the certificates tell which organization(s) will allow you to access its servers.

Normally, you just use Notes in your own organization. Sometimes people leave an organization — and not always for the right reasons, if you get our drift. Some of those people may become bad guys. Of course, every organization should keep an eye on comings and goings to be sure that only current members have access to Notes. But, just in case someone slips through the cracks, everyone's certification expires after a couple of years.

When your certification is about to expire, you need to get recertified; otherwise, on some dark day in the not-too-distant future, you will find that you simply can't access any Notes servers. You will usually receive a notice from the Notes administrator telling you that your number is up, and you need to get recertified soon.

TECHNICAL STUFF

What am I protecting my document from?

Some databases are associated with a *template,* a special database which provides its design to one or many real databases. Late at night, when nothing is stirring, not even a mouse, the template quietly steals into where good little databases are sleeping and removes any recent design changes, replacing them with its own design.

When you follow the steps in this section to etch your new form or view in stone, you're preventing changes to one database element. If you want to cut the cord that ties the database to its design template forever (be sure that you know what you've done and understand what you're doing), activate the InfoBox for the database, click the Design tab, and deselect `Inherit design from template`. From now on, your changes will be permanent. If some wise, distant designer makes changes to the template, those changes will not be made to your database. That means you won't be able to take advantage of improvements to the template anyone makes, because you've blocked them from being added to your database.

To see when your certificate expires, choose File⇨Tools⇨User ID and then click Certificates. Highlight each certificate (assuming you have more than one — most people don't) and information appears below telling you when that certificate expires. Figure 14-8 shows what the dialog box looks like.

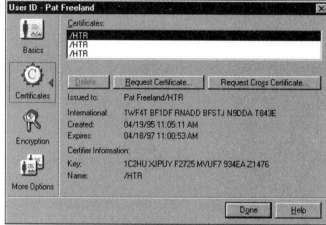

Figure 14-8:
The User ID
dialog box
shows all
sorts of
information
about your
User ID.

There's another reason to get certified — you may need to communicate with a Notes user in another company. Because that organization uses a different certificate, you can't just send a message and assume it's going to get there safe and sound.

The good news is that getting certified is easy. And it's free. And you don't need to get recertified very often (usually only once every couple of years). And the sun'll come out tomorrow. Here's what you do:

1. **Use File⇨Tools⇨User ID.**

2. **Click Certificates and then choose Request Certificate.**

3. **In the dialog box that appears on your screen (and in Figure 14-9), type the name of the person to whom you're sending your request.**

   You'll need to ask around your organization to find the name of the *certifier,* the person who issues certificates.

After the certifier receives your request, you can expect a return memo with the new certification attached. When this joyous event occurs, choose File⇨Tools⇨User ID and then click More Options. Choose to Merge a Copy, select your user ID, and then click Done. You now have a new certificate.

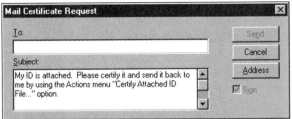

Honey, Where Are My Encryption Keys?

Cloak and dagger stuff, this encryption. You encrypt information when you want to be absolutely sure that it isn't going to be seen by the wrong eyes or even a wrong whole person. *Encrypting* means scrambling the information in a field. It takes place behind the scenes, and the only teeny, little hint that something is encrypted is that sending or opening a document containing an encrypted field takes a little longer.

You may encrypt information in two places: your mail messages and specified fields in other databases. Encryption uses *keys* to scramble and rearrange the data so that it doesn't make any sense during transmission. In the case of mail messages that you want to encrypt, you don't have to do anything about keys. Encrypted mail scrambles only the *body* field and uses the public and private encryption keys associated with the User ID for each recipient. It's all automatic. See Chapter 6 for more information about encrypting mail memos.

You do *not* use the following procedure to encrypt your mail memos, just fields in databases. Mail database is done automatically when you choose to encrypt a mail message.

If you're using a database that has an encryptable field, you may choose to encrypt the data in that field. In that case, you have to supply legitimate readers of the data with a special encryption key that you create. No key means no reading; the field will appear empty.

You can tell whether a field is encryptable because the *field markers* (the little corners showing the beginning and end of the field) will be red. Red field markers mean that users who can edit a document can choose to encrypt that field.

Suppose that you're entering data in a product planning form in which one field is for super-secret design information. Other data is information everyone in the company might need, such as product name, what it does, or why everyone needs one of these gizmos immediately. That information doesn't need to be secret, but the design information does. So you decide to encrypt the field.

Creating your key

First, you have to create the encryption key. Follow these steps:

1. **Use File⇨Tools⇨User ID and then click the Encryption button.**

2. **Choose New.**

3. **In the dialog box like the one in Figure 14-10, give the new key a name, preferably something you'll associate with its purpose.**

   Note the cleverly chosen name for the key you'll use to encrypt the design information field in the product planning form.

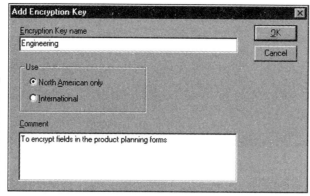

Figure 14-10:
The way
to create
a new
encryption
key.

Select `North American only` if this database will only be seen in North American installations of Notes. If you have offices around the world that might use the database, then you should choose Jnternational. Places outside North America have a different way of encrypting information. The U.S. government requires this distinction. We could tell you why, but then you'd have the CIA following *you* around, too.

Attaching your key to a document

After you create the key, you add it to the document you are writing, like this:

1. **Choose Create to start a document.**

   Of course, if you've already started the document you want to encrypt, you can ignore this step.

2. **Choose File⇨Document Properties.**

3. **In the InfoBox which appears, click the tab with the picture of a key to open the Security page as shown in Figure 14-11.**

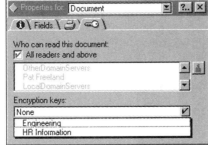

Figure 14-11:
This InfoBox is the place to pick the key to encrypt a field.

4. **Click the down arrow below Encryption keys: as we've done in Figure 14-11.**

5. **Choose the key you want to add.**

   Remember, you should already have created the key you want following the steps earlier in this section.

OK, you've added an encryption key to your document so you can encrypt the field. But who can *decrypt* it? You? Yes, but no one else . . . yet.

Sending your key

You need to send the key to anyone who needs to see the encrypted field. Choose File⇨Tools⇨User ID and then click the Encryption button and select the key you want to send. Click Mail to open the Mail Address Encryption Key dialog box (shown, for your viewing pleasure, in Figure 14-12).

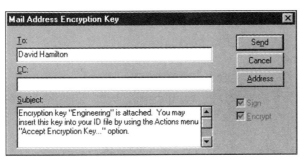

Figure 14-12:
Here we are sending a new encryption key to someone.

Enter the name, names, or group to whom you are sending the key. You can send courtesy copies (CC:) to people who ought to know you've sent the key, but those folks will not receive the key itself. The Subject: line of the memo will contain whatever text is in the Subject box, but you may change that text if you want it to say something else. Happy with everything in the dialog box? Fine; choose Send.

One more question from Notes, and the key's on its way. A question box appears, asking `Should recipients be allowed to send this key to other users?` This is your call. If the information is terribly sensitive and you want control over who sees it, choose No. People can ask you to send the key to others if necessary. If you don't want people to bother you by requesting the key all the time, then choose Yes.

Using the key

After you send the key, you're done with your part. But the recipients will have a small chore when they receive the key. They need to highlight the memo containing the key. Associated with the memo is an Accept Encryption action button. They click that, choose Accept, and the encryption key is theirs. Now, without any further ado on their part, they can read the encrypted field.

Tooling Around in Notes

The little Notes engine is throbbing quietly and efficiently somewhere inside your computer: messages are moving, secrets in encrypted fields are being kept, and you've even succeeded in customizing the look of some of your forms. There are still a few odds and ends we thought you ought to know about.

Some IDeas

Your *User ID* is the file that allows you to use Notes. If someone gets a hold of your ID, that person can use Notes pretending to be you — sending off messages, reading your mail, and peeking into encrypted fields that only the chosen few are supposed to see.

Where is your ID? Only you know that for sure, but it's probably in several places: in the Notes directory (folder) of your computer, on a floppy disk for backup storage in case something happens to your computer, and, if you have a laptop, in the Notes directory there, too. So you may have three separate Notes ID files which some ruthless person could use to his or her own advantage. Even somebody with a few ruths may take your ID and use it for dubious purposes.

Anyone with access to your computer has access to your ID. The solution is to protect your ID with a password *right now*. Choose File⇨Tools⇨User ID and then click the Basics button. Figure 14-13 shows the relatively simple dialog box into which you type your password.

Figure 14-13:
Use this
dialog box
to create
a new
password.

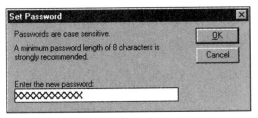

Keep the following facts in mind as you decide on a password:

- ✔ You may use a password of any length, although your administrator may have set a minimum length.

- ✔ Notes recommends a minimum of eight characters, simply because it's many times harder to figure out a long password than it is to figure out a short one.

- ✔ This may be obvious, but . . . be sure that your password is something you're going to remember. We all have to remember social security numbers, credit card codes, login names and passwords, gym locker combinations, in-laws' birthdays, and the date of our tetanus booster. Anytime we forget one of these, somebody treats us as though we're wearing a clown suit. If you set a Notes password and forget it, you are out of luck. You'll have to get a new ID and start all over — and all your old messages will be unreadable.

- ✔ This, too, may be obvious, but make sure that the password isn't something that someone else will figure out. Using your own first name is not the most secure password.

- ✔ Passwords are case sensitive, so PASSWORD is different from Password is different from password is different from pAssword is . . . well, you get the point.

- ✔ As you type in your password, only Xs appear on-screen. This is to protect your password from over-the-shoulder snoopers. Notes takes passwords *very* seriously.

- ✔ After you create your password, Notes will prompt you a second time to be sure that you didn't make a mistake.

Password-protecting the ID file on your main computer has no effect on your laptop's copy of the ID. The best way to handle this is to password-protect the ID on your main computer, then copy it to a floppy disk, and then copy it from the floppy disk to your laptop. Delete any copies of the ID file that are not password protected, or keep them under lock. (Usually, people say "lock and key," but if the key were around, why bother with the lock?)

Each of your ID files may have different certificates associated with it. If you have an ID on a floppy disk and one on your hard disk, use File⇨Tools⇨Switch ID and pick each ID, one at a time. You can see what certificates are associated with an ID file by choosing File⇨Tools⇨User ID and clicking Certificates. Add a password to the ID with the largest number of certificates and copy that ID to the floppy disk and your other computers. If each ID has different certificates, add the password to each separately.

If you leave your computer, you ought to take steps so that, if any lowlifes bent on no good walk by, they can't gain access to Notes on your computer. Press F5 or choose File⇨Tools⇨Lock ID. That command immediately disables your access to Notes until you enter your password again.

There's even a way to get Notes to lock your computer automatically if it notices that you've been away for a while. Of course, Notes doesn't know whether you've physically left the computer, but it does know how long it's been since you used it. After a certain amount of time, Notes starts missing your gentle tapping on the keyboard and disables your access until you enter your password.

To enable this time-out procedure, again select File⇨Tools⇨User Preferences, click Basics, and then enter a number of minutes in `Lock ID after [ ] minutes of inactivity`. You can see in Figure 14-14 that we are allowing 15 minutes of inactivity to pass before disabling our personal access.

Figure 14-14:
Use this
dialog box
to log out
of Notes
automatically.

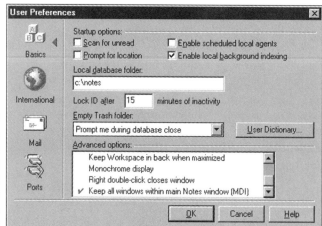

If the specified time goes by, or if you press F5, a screen prompting you for your password will appear the next time you try to do something with Notes. Type in your password, press Enter, and off you go.

If you decide to remove the password protection from your ID file, select File➪Tools➪User ID and click Basics. Click the Clear Password button, type your password, and choose OK. The password is no more.

Perhaps you just got married and have a new name, or you're in the witness protection program and need a new name, or the name you've been using in Notes isn't quite right. You can see a bunch of information about your User ID by choosing File➪Tools➪User ID and clicking Options. But don't try to change your User Name by choosing Change Name. If you do, you won't be able to use Notes anymore. Instead, click the Request New Name button and enter the name you want to use. When a mail memo like the one in Figure 14-15 appears, you need to fill in the name of the Notes administrator. Mail this request off and wait for a response. When the response arrives, open it and choose to accept the certificate.

Figure 14-15:
Identity
crisis?
Request a
new name.

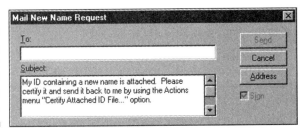

Tools that set you up

When you start your car, you fasten your seat belt, adjust the mirror, and set the volume on the radio before heading out into traffic. When you start Notes, you may also have some things you want to do or want Notes to do for you. You can set some of these things in the File➪Tools➪User Preferences dialog box.

The Basics

Figure 14-16 shows the Basics part of the User Preferences dialog box. The following list includes the most important items you can select in this figure.

✔ **Scan for unread:** automatically checks for unread memos. If you select Scan for unread, the next time you start Notes, you will see a dialog box telling you how many unread messages or documents you have. Tell Notes which databases you're interested in having it check. After all, you probably don't want to know about all the unread documents in all the databases you may have on your desktop.

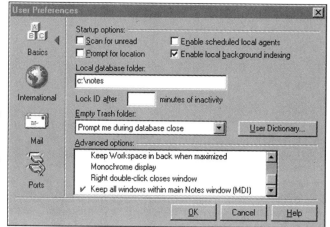

Figure 14-16:
The Basics
part of
the User
Preferences
dialog box.

✔ **Prompt for location:** tells Notes to ask you what type of location you're using in each new session. This is useful if you use your computer in different defined locations every time you start Notes.

✔ **Empty Trash folder:** offers three choices for getting rid of documents you dragged to the trash folder of a database:

• Prompt me during database close tells Notes to confirm that you want to empty the trash when you close a Notes session.

• Always during database close tells Notes to empty the trash automatically when you close a database.

• Manually means you must empty the trash yourself.

✔ **User Dictionary:** allows you to create a dictionary for words you don't want the spell checker to flag. You might want to include your name in the User Dictionary — or unusual acronyms you frequently use.

✔ **Right double-click closes window:** (under Advanced options) is a throw-back to Release 3 of Notes, when you could always close a window by double-clicking the secondary (usually the right) mouse button. Select this option if you've grown accustomed to the old method and choose not to learn any new tricks this late in your life.

Internationally speaking

Click International (below Basics in the User Preferences box), and, among other things, you'll be able to change the collation sequence (the way Notes sorts documents in views), the measurement units from Imperial (gallons, inches, miles, six packs) to Metric (meters, liters, tweeters), and the dictionary (so that when the spell checker finds errors, it will present the right alternative spellings for your context).

Checking the mail

Click on the Mail button (below International in the User Preferences box) to designate which mail program you're using: Notes, cc:Mail, or Other VIM mail (Vendor Independent Mail) program. If you select and enter a number in Check for new mail every [ ] minutes, Notes automatically checks for new mail in your mail database. Audible notification sounds a tune each time you get mail — which will quickly annoy your neighbors. Visible notification puts an envelope in your Status bar when you have new mail.

Part V
Notes in the Fast Lane

In this part...

We can't all stay in our offices, do the daily routine, and be satisfied with our basic groupware features. Some of us just have to zip into the fast lane of life. If you're one such person, you're probably aching to know how to take Notes with you on your business trips, how to turn Notes into a surfboard for the Internet, how to use Notes to interact with other programs, and how to search through all your Notes databases in the blink of an eye.

Okay, hot-shot. You asked for it. This part of the book is devoted to the Notes features for a '90s person like yourself.

Chapter 15

Notes on the Road

● ●

In This Chapter

▶ Getting ready to take Notes on a trip

▶ Replicating your mail

▶ Making your modem manipulate your messages

▶ Saving on your phone bill

● ●

*J*ust because you have to travel away from the office doesn't mean that you can't read your mail, use your databases, and generally stay plugged into what's going on back at the office. In this chapter, we'll explore what you have to do to use Notes on the road.

Say your company has one Notes server in Boston, one in New York, and one in London, and on each of these servers your administrator has placed a copy of a database that your company uses to discuss marketing strategies for the coming year. Obviously, you need the documents that have been added to the database by your English colleagues to show up in the databases in New York and Boston. And, if someone in New York edits a document, you want the changes to be distributed to Boston and London. And if someone in Boston deletes a document? You'll want that document to be deleted in both New York and London, too.

Replication is the process that Notes uses to keep the three databases synchronized with one another. Your administrator schedules calls between the servers; the Boston server may call up the New York server at 8 A.M. and then call the English server at 9 A.M. Then it would place another call to New York at 11 A.M., call England again at 1 P.M., and so on, and so on.

That's nice, but why do you care? Because, whenever you need to use Notes away from the office, you'll use the same process.

You have your laptop all set up and ready to go. Grab a cab to the airport, check your bags, and get on the plane. You're trapped in that seat for the next three hours, so why not use the time to catch up on some of your e-mail? By the end of the trip, you have 11 new e-mail messages to send, and you've composed a few documents in the databases that you brought with you, too.

Now fast forward to your arrival at the hotel. You're all checked in, you've hung your suits in the closet, checked out the treats in the honor bar, and paid off the bellhop. So now how are you going to send off that e-mail, post those documents you composed on the plane, and see whether any mail has been sent to you while you were cruising at 35,000 feet? You guessed it, you're going to replicate the databases on your laptop with the server back at the office.

Even if you aren't planning to go on any trips, you should read this chapter anyway. If you need to set up Notes on your computer at home, the steps are almost exactly the same.

Getting Your Computer Ready to Go

Needless to say, you must get prepared for your new-found career as a replicator before you even leave the office; you don't want to be stuck in the hotel room without the proper setup. Here's a checklist of the stuff you have to bring with you:

- ✔ Your computer
- ✔ Notes
- ✔ A modem
- ✔ A phone cable to connect the modem to the phone jack
- ✔ Your USER.ID file
- ✔ Your personal N&A Book
- ✔ Some databases
- ✔ Some phone numbers
- ✔ A clean pair of socks and maybe a couple of shirts, depending on the length of your stay

Taking your computer on a trip

Personal computers are certainly a great deal smaller than the computers of yesteryear. (We're resisting the temptation to launch into a story about how, when we first started in the computer business, computers were as big as a refrigerator and took three days to add up a list of numbers.) If you're lucky, you have a laptop computer. It's nice and small and probably even has a color screen. Most laptops have modems built right in, so that's one less thing to pack for your trip.

Practice setting up and using Notes from your laptop *before* you leave for your trip. That way the administrator can hear you scream (and come to help) if you can't figure out how to hook up the @#*^#$ modem.

Telling Notes about your modem

Ever wonder what a *modem* is? The short answer is that it's a piece of hardware that lets your computer (in the hotel room) and another computer (the server back at the office) talk to one another over the telephone. The long answer is boring and technical, so we'll keep the nitty-gritty details to a minimum.

Obligatory plug: IDG Books Worldwide has a great book called *Modems For Dummies* that will tell you everything you need to know about modems.

To get Notes ready to use your modem, you have to do two things:

- ✔ Tell Notes that you have a modem.
- ✔ Tell Notes what kind of modem you have.

Of course, you don't just say, "Notes, I have a modem." What you really have to do is *enable a serial port,* which sounds much worse than it really is.

A couple of words about modems

Modems are rated by their speed. Your modem may be called 28.8BPS (if you're lucky) or 2400BPS (if you're not so lucky). *BPS* stands for Bits Per Second, and it represents how fast your computer can send information over the phone. A 2400BPS (sometimes they say "2400 *baud,*" which means the same thing) modem sends 2,400 bits per second, which is pretty slow. A 9600BPS modem is four times faster, and 28.8BPS (which actually stands for 28,800 bits per second), is about the fastest modem that's commercially available right now.

You don't even have to know what a *bit* is to realize that the faster you can send them, the better! For purposes of comparison, when you use Notes at work on the network, you're probably operating at around 57,000 bits per second. The moral to this story is that, no matter how fast your modem is, it's *a lot* slower than your network.

The speed of your modem is especially important when you're dialing in to the server to replicate. The faster the modem, the faster you can replicate. And the shorter the phone call, the smaller the phone bill. (That's really important if you're calling from a hotel room, because many hotels add a *huge* surcharge to outgoing calls. A 25-minute call to the home office can end up costing a lot of money.)

Most people find that a 2400BPS modem is too slow to be practical to use with Notes. A modem that's 14.4BPS is pretty good. A modem that can go 28.8BPS is *really* fast and the best you can have.

Of course, it takes two to tango. If the modem on your laptop is 28.8, but the modem on the server you call back at the office is only 14.4, your modem is going to slow down to 14.4 to talk to the server.

Enabling your serial port

Think back to when you started Notes for the first time. Did you tell Notes then that you had a modem? If you did, you might not need to read this next section — then again, it may be worth a quick breeze-over just to make sure that everything is okay.

To enable a serial port, choose File⇨Tools⇨User Preferences, and click the Ports button. You get the User Preferences dialog box, as displayed in Figure 15-1.

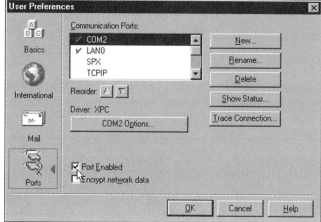

Figure 15-1:
Telling
Notes
where your
modem is
plugged in.

This part is pretty easy. Select the name of the port to which your modem is connected from the Communication Ports list box and click the Port Enabled check box.

What isn't so easy is knowing which port your modem is connected to — unless you use a Macintosh. If you *don't* use a Mac, the options in the Communications Ports will be COM1, COM2, COM3, and so on. Your modem will almost certainly be connected to either COM1 or COM2. If you're not sure which one you use, call your administrator to find out. (Some computers have their mouse plugged in to COM1, so the modem is connected to COM2.)

If you have a Mac, the port name will either be MODEM or PRINTER. The correct answer is probably obvious, unless you have some compelling reason to plug your modem into your printer port.

After you have selected the correct port name and clicked the Port Enabled box, you're almost done. Hold off on clicking OK until you read the next section, because you have to tell Notes what kind of modem you have.

Configuring your modem

While you're in the User Preferences dialog box, you should check out the COM*n* Options button. When you click it, Notes presents you with the dialog box shown in Figure 15-2.

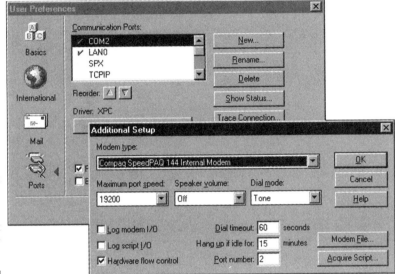

Figure 15-2:
Telling
Notes about
your
modem.

The dialog box has a bunch of options, but you only have to worry about two things. Okay, maybe three things.

The first thing you need to do is select the brand of modem you own from the list. This is important, because different modems work differently, and Notes needs to know exactly which you have.

If your modem doesn't appear in the list, choose Auto Configure (it's near the bottom of the list). And if that doesn't work out, try one of the Hayes modems, because many modems can pretend that they are Hayes modems. If all else fails, call your administrator and ask which you should choose.

The list of modems actually represents a bunch of *modem command files.* When you install Notes, you automatically get one of these command files for just about every modem under the sun. (They are really just ASCII files with the extension .MDM.) If you are short on disk space, you could delete the ones you don't need from your Notes data directory. If your modem isn't listed, and the Auto Configure option doesn't work either, call your administrator and ask for a special Modem Command file for your modem.

The other thing you need to worry about is the Maximum port speed list box. All you have to do is click the speed of your modem. Don't get your hopes up; if you only have a 14.4 modem, selecting 28.8 from the Maximum port speed list is *not* going to make it work any faster. (Nice try, though.)

The last thing you *may* want to worry about is the Speaker volume, where you can choose Off, Low, Medium, or High. When you make a call from your computer to a Notes server, you briefly hear some high-pitched whistles and squeals and pops and squeaks as the two modems figure out how fast they can talk to one another (the server's wicked-fast 28.8BPS modem may have to slow down to talk to your crummy 14.4 modem). You can decide to turn off the volume altogether, but then you won't be able to listen in to the beginning of their conversation. You might just want to listen in sometimes — especially if you are having trouble connecting — so that you can hear what's going on. On the other hand, if your modem works A-OK, you may decide to turn the speaker off so that you don't have to hear all that noise.

After selecting your modem's name from the list, setting the speed at which it communicates, and (perhaps) setting the volume, click OK twice.

Setting up your personal N&A Book

If you've been using Notes at the office, you've probably already used your personal Name and Address Book to compose a couple of group documents so that you can easily send mail to your friends. (If you haven't and you want to, refer to Chapter 7.)

Your personal N&A Book is an important thing to take with you when you're using Notes from afar, because in it you store the phone numbers for the servers you'll be calling.

Adding a connection document

Notes needs to know the telephone numbers of the servers you intend to call while you are away from the office. It stores these numbers in special *Server Connection* documents that are, in turn, stored in your personal N&A Book. You compose the documents yourself, as we explain in the next couple of paragraphs.

First things first. You have to find out the telephone numbers of the servers you're going to be calling. This is another pearl of knowledge that you'll have to solicit from your administrator. Call your administrator, explain that you are getting ready to use Notes away from the office, and ask for the appropriate server names and phone numbers.

At the very least, you'll need the phone number of your Home Server.

After you have the numbers you need, choose <u>F</u>ile⇨<u>M</u>obile⇨Server Phone Numbers, or open your N&A Book and switch to the Server Connections folder. Use this folder whenever you need to review your connection documents.

To create new connection document, choose Create⇨<u>S</u>erver Connection and enter the server's name and phone number, as we've done in Figure 15-3. When you are finished, Press Esc to close the window, and choose <u>Y</u>es to save the document.

You have to compose a separate connection document for each and every server you'll be calling while you're away from the office.

Establishing a location document

What are the three most important things in real estate? Location, location, and, you guessed it, location. And the same is true when you take your computer away from the office — Notes needs to know about your *location*. For example, when you're at the office and connected to the network, mail you send is delivered immediately. But if you're working at home, Notes should hold mail messages until you call in to the company's server with your modem. If you're in a hotel room, Notes also needs to hold your mail, and Notes has to remember to dial 9 to get an outside line. If you're using Notes in an airplane, Notes should forget all about the modem.

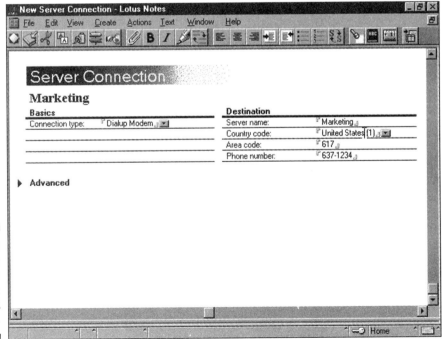

Figure 15-3:
Adding a connection document to your N&A Book.

Notes keeps all this straight via the *location documents* in your personal N&A Book. You use these location documents to tell Notes what the rules are for mail delivery, dialing the phone, and whether or not you have a replication schedule.

Notes comes ready-made with four location documents: Office, Home, Travel, and Island. When you're preparing to take your computer away from the office, you'll want to peruse these documents to make sure that they have the rules you want.

Finding your location documents

To view the location documents, open your N&A Book and choose View⇨ Locations. Notes shows you the four default Location documents in the View pane, as you can see in Figure 15-4.

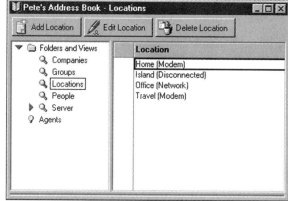

Figure 15-4:
Notes has four ready-made location documents.

Editing your location documents

Edit any one of the location documents the same way you edit any document in any database: You either select the document in the View pane and press Ctrl+E, or double-click the document to open and it and *then* press Ctrl+E. Figure 15-5 shows a sample Home location document.

In most cases, the only change you need to make to a location document is to enter the correct area code.

Make sure, in the Phone Dialing section of the location document, that you enter the correct area code; this is an important piece of information that Notes needs in order to decide whether or not to dial the area code when you place a call to the server at the office. When editing the Home location document, enter your home area code in the `Area code at this location` field. When

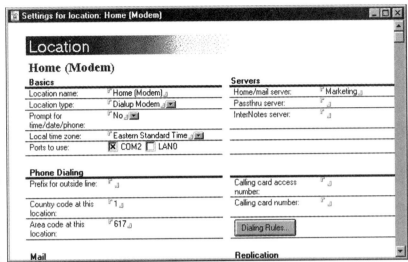

Figure 15-5:
A sample
location
document.

editing the Travel location document, be careful to double-check the area code you're calling from. If you're calling from a hotel room and need to dial a special number (usually 9) to get an outside line, be sure to edit the Travel location document and enter the number in the `Prefix for Outside line` field.

When you're done editing a location document, save it as you would any other: Press Esc to close the window, and choose Yes to save the document.

You need to edit the Travel location document each time you travel to a different city, specifying Area code and Prefix for outside line fields.

Choosing a location document

To tell Notes your current location, choose File➪Mobile➪Choose Current Location, and then select the appropriate location document from the Choose Location dialog box. When you do, Notes will know what the area code is, how to access an outside line, and whether your mail should be delivered immediately or held onto, awaiting your phone call to the server back at the office.

Every time you use your computer, be sure to chose the appropriate location document. Notes tells you which location document it's using in the lower right-hand corner of the Status bar.

Taking a Copy of Database with You

You usually want to make a copy of a database to bring with you on your trip. You can bring (disk space permitting) any database you want with you; at the very least, you need a copy of your mail database.

To make a copy of a database that you'll be replicating, select the database and choose File⇨Replication⇨New Replica. Use the dialog box shown in Figure 15-6 to tell Notes the filename for the new database — you can usually accept the default. In fact, you can probably just click OK without worrying about any of those other fancy options in the New Replica dialog box.

Figure 15-6:
Choose
File⇨
Replication⇨
New Replica
to make a
copy of a
database to
take on the
road.

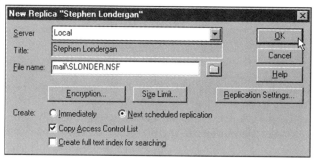

You only have to choose File⇨Replication⇨New Replica the very *first* time you're preparing a database for a trip.

When you click OK, Notes creates a replica-stub copy of the database, as you can see in Figure 15-7. A *replica stub* is a database that's totally, completely, we're not kidding around here, empty. It has no forms, no views, no documents, no nuthin'. The database won't get filled up until you perform your first replication.

Figure 15-7:
When you
first create a
copy of the
database,
the copy
has no
documents

Forget replicating — Dial in to a server live

If you have a relatively fast modem — 14.4BPS or better — you may not have to replicate at all. (Now they tell us, right?) You can choose File⇨Mobile⇨Call Server to dial in to the server directly. If you do, you'll be able to use the server databases in exactly the same way that you do when you're accessing them over the

network — it'll just be slower. When you choose File⇨Mobile⇨Call Server, all you need do is select the name of the Server you want to call and, in most cases, click Auto Dial. If you plan to dial in to a server in the aforementioned manner, leave your Location set to "office" so that your mail will be delivered immediately.

If you are creating a replica copy of your mail database, make sure that it's listed properly in each of your four location documents. This is extremely important if you will be using mail away from the office.

Before you replicate for the first time

You won't be surprised to hear that you can screw up replication, and for once we're going to advise against blind optimism. Before you try to replicate a database for the first time, you should make sure that your database's Access Control List is set appropriately. Select your database and choose File⇨Database⇨Access Control. When you do, you get the dialog box that's shown in Figure 15-8.

Figure 15-8: If the server's name isn't in this list, you'll have to add it.

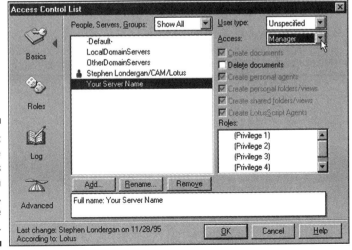

Many of the entries in this dialog box won't make any sense, but that's Okay. You're checking to make sure that the name of the server with which you'll be replicating is listed, and that its <u>A</u>ccess is set to *Manager*. If your server isn't listed, use the A<u>d</u>d button to rectify that problem.

In most cases, you'll want to list the server as Manager in the (local) database's Access Control List, but it may not be a bad idea to check with your all-knowing administrator — he or she may have a good reason to list the server differently. The right answer depends very much on the way your administrator has set up Notes at your company, so it can't hurt to ask.

Where to replicate for the first time

Now we'll have a short quiz. Please select the one and only correct answer for the following question.

You have a database on your computer that you're going to replicate with a database on a server. This will be the first time you've ever replicated the database, and you know that a whole bunch of documents have to get repli- cated into your copy of the database — several megabytes worth. Do you

> ✔ **Answer 1:** Perform the first replication over the phone from your hotel room, where long-distance phone calls cost about $1.00 per minute? Total time spent to replicate: 2.75 hours. Total cost of this one phone call: $237.50.

> ✔ **Answer 2:** Perform the first replication while you're still at work, over the network, where it will be extremely fast and won't cost anything? Total time spent to replicate: 11 minutes. Total cost: $0.00.

We hope you chose Answer 2.

To replicate a database, select the database in question, choose <u>F</u>ile↔ <u>R</u>eplication↔<u>R</u>eplicate, and click the <u>O</u>K button to start the process. You can watch the progress by switching to the Replicator Tab on the Notes workspace; if you're replicating from home, you may even hear the computer placing a telephone call.

Depending on how fast you're able to replicate (LAN or mode), and on how many documents have to be replicated, it may take a while before Notes finishes. You can go on about your work while you're waiting; Notes replicates in the *background,* which means that you can use other databases and even other programs while you're waiting for it to finish.

Well, five or six pages after you started, you're finally ready to take your computer on the road. The whole process took so long (both to do and to read about) because you were setting up for the very first time. From here on out, replicating will be a breeze — we promise.

In case you need to refer to the steps someday, here's a short-and-sweet list of what you do to prep your computer for a trip:

1. **Use File⇨Tools⇨User Preferences and select Ports to enable your modem.**

2. **Use the COM*n* button on the File⇨Tools⇨User Preferences Ports dialog box to tell Notes what kind of modem you have.**

3. **Create a Server Connection document for each of the servers you'll be calling in your personal N&A Books.**

4. **Verify that the location documents in your N&A Book are set up properly for your area code and outside-line prefix.**

5. **Use File⇨Replication⇨New Replica to make the first copies of the databases you'll need.**

6. **Select the database you're going to copy and use File⇨Database⇨Access Control to make sure that the server's Access Level is set to Manager.**

7. **Use File⇨Replication⇨Replicate to refresh your databases.**

We recommend that you do all the preceding set-up tasks while you're still at work, including replicating the databases for the first time.

Using Your Computer Away from the Office

Sure, most of the time you use Notes while you are at work and plugged into the network. Notes knows that you're connected to the network, so when you dash off an e-mail, Notes knows to whisk it off to the server through that wire snaking out of the back of your computer and into the wall.

But what if you're *not* connected to the network? What if you're working at home or you've taken your computer on a trip and you're in a hotel room? Notes has to know that when you send a mail message, it *shouldn't* try to send it through the network, 'cause you ain't got one. Instead, Notes needs to let the mail messages you compose at home pile up so that later, when you call into the server, it can send the messages then.

The most important thing to do when you first turn on your computer at home (or in the hotel room) is choose File⇨Mobile⇨Choose Current Location. This tells Notes where you are and what to do with any outgoing messages you create.

When you use the Home and Travel location documents, Notes stores any e-mail messages you create in a special database, called Outgoing mail. The icon for this database appears in Figure 15-9. Don't confuse this database with your mail database; the Outgoing mail database just holds messages until you call the server or return to the office. You *always* read your mail in your mail database — that's the database with the envelope icon.

Figure 15-9:
This database holds outgoing e-mail you compose while away from the office.

Sending mail from afar

With two small differences, composing and sending e-mail when you're remote is no different from composing and sending e-mail when you're on the network.

✔ **Difference #1:** E-mail is delivered later, when you call into the server. This can take some getting used to. When you're connected to the office network, e-mail gets delivered more or less instantaneously to the recipients. If you're working remotely, though, you won't actually dispatch the messages until you make a phone call to the server.

✔ **Difference #2:** If you're a fan of the Actions⇨Address feature, you're in for a big letdown. Using Actions⇨Address at the office lets you easily peruse your company's public N&A Book, which is located on your Home Server. If you're using Actions⇨Address at home, you can't see the company's public N&A Book; you see only the people and groups in your personal N&A Book. (If you want to send an e-mail to folks who aren't in your personal N&A Book, you'll have to type their exact e-mail addresses in your message.)

Reading your e-mail from afar

As with composing e-mail, reading your e-mail remotely isn't all that different from reading it at the office. You just have to be careful that, when you open your e-mail database, you double-click the icon for the copy of your e-mail database that's on your workstation and *not* the icon for the copy of the database that's on the server. Choose View⇨Show Server Names if you're not sure which is which. In Figure 15-10, the database on the right is the local copy.

Choose View⇨Stack Replica Icons to show only the icon for the mail database you should be using, based on your current location. In other words, when you're at the office, you'll see only the icon for your mail database on the server, but when you're at home or on the road, you'll see only the local icon.

Figure 15-10:
When you travel with your computer, you get two icons for your mail database. Use the local one.

Pete's Mail on a Sales_1   Pete's Mail on Local

Reading other documents while on the road

If you bring a copy of a database other than your e-mail database with you on the road, you just have to be careful that you use the correct (meaning *local*) icon, as we discussed with your e-mail database. Other than that consideration, you can read the documents in a local database the same way you read the documents when you're using the server's database back at the office.

Composing documents from afar

More good news: As with reading a document, composing a document in a local database isn't any different when you're on the road, either. Of course, when you compose a document in a database on a Notes server, other people can see it and read it the minute you save it. But if you're composing documents in the bush, those documents won't be accessible by your coworkers back in the office until you replicate your database with the server's database.

Enough Talk! Call That Server and Replicate!

When you're ready to replicate a database — because you've added some documents to your database, or because you want to see if any new documents have been added to the database back at the office, or perhaps because you want to dispatch the fifteen e-mail messages you just composed — choose File⇨Replication⇨Replicate and click OK.

Notes will call the server and synchronize the databases on your computer with the databases on the server. You can check the progress by switching to the Replicator tab on the workspace, as shown in Figure 15-11.

If you're calling from home or a hotel room, you may hear the modem clear its throat and dial the server. Then, when Notes finishes replicating, it tells you what happened during the call on the Replicator page. You see exactly how many documents you sent, how many you received, how many databases were replicated, and how many mail messages were sent.

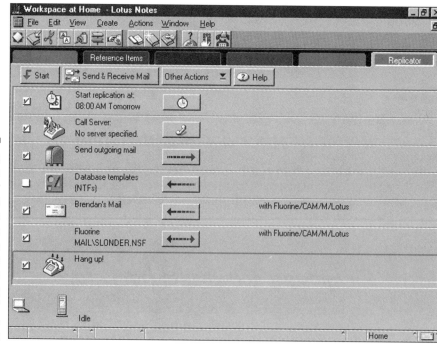

Figure 15-11: The Replicator page on the workspace shows you the progress Notes is making in replicating your databases.

Up to this point in the chapter, we've discussed replicating on demand — in other words, every time you want to replicate, you use the menus to initiate the process. But there's a better way. You can instead schedule calls between your workstation and the server. That way, you don't have to call the workstation manually. Your workstation calls automatically all day long according to a schedule that you define.

1. **Choose File➪Mobile➪Choose Current Location to switch to the Location for which you want to turn on scheduled replication.**

2. **Edit the location document for that location by choosing File➪ Mobile➪Edit Current Location.**

   You want to move to the part of the form that says Replication, as shown in Figure 15-12.

3. **Move the cursor to the Schedule: field and press the spacebar to choose Enabled (replacing Disabled).**

4. **Set the Replicate daily between: field.**

   You can either enter a range of times, such as 8:00 AM – 10:00 PM, or a series of separate times, such as 8:00 AM, 8:30 AM, 1:00 PM, 2:45 PM. A schedule of 8:00 AM – 10:00 PM with a 60-minute repeat interval is pretty common, but you can read the rest of this section to find out all your options.

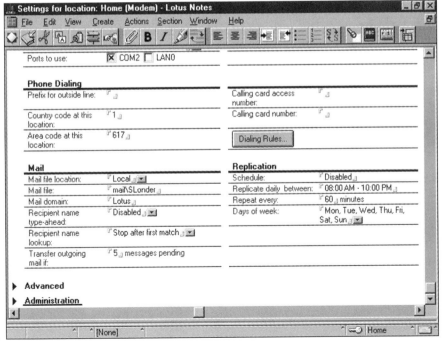

Figure 15-12: Schedule automatic replication between your computer and the servers by choosing File➪ Mobile➪ Edit Current Location.

5. **In the Days of week: field, enter the days of the week when you want to call, separating each with a comma.**

(Do you get paid overtime for working on the weekend? We hope so.)

6. **When you're finished filling out your remote connection document, press Esc and choose Yes to save the document.**

The exact times when Notes will call is determined both by the Replicate daily between: field and by what you enter in the Repeat every: field. The Repeat every: field wants a number of minutes; you enter a number such as 30, 60, 120, or 360.

Say you enter **8:00 AM – 5:00 PM** in the Replicate daily between: field, and you enter **120** in the Repeat every: field. That actually means that you want your workstation to make four calls to the server: the first call at 8:00 A.M., the second call three hours later at 11:00 A.M., the third call three hours after that at 2:00 P.M., and so on until 5:00 P.M. If you wanted to make calls more often, you reduce the Repeat every: field. For example, entering **60** would make eleven calls to the server.

If, on the other hand, you enter a series of times in the Replicate daily between: field, the Repeat every: value tells Notes how long it should keep trying to call back if the scheduled call doesn't work out because of a busy signal or something. If you enter **8:30 AM, 1:00 PM, 2:45 PM** in the Replicate daily between: field and **60** in the Repeat every: field, Notes makes its first call to the server at 8:30 A.M. Assuming that call was successful, it won't call again until 1:00 P.M. If, at 1:00 P.M., the call doesn't go through — maybe the server's phone is busy — Notes keeps trying to call back for one hour. If, after an hour, it still hasn't gotten through, Notes gives up on that call and won't try again until the schedule says so. In this case, that would be at 2:45 P.M.

Saving on Phone Bills: Selective Replication

When you master the basics of replication, you're ready to delve into some of the fancy options available to fine tune exactly what happens when you replicate a database.

Selective replication is a way for you to pick and choose exactly which documents you want to replicate. Say that, when you travel, you don't want to replicate all your e-mail, you only want to replicate messages from a certain list of people — your boss, your boss's boss, and that guy down the hall who's always sending you jokes. Selective replication is the answer. Or maybe you replicate a sales activity database, but you want to replicate only the hot leads.

The benefits of selective replication are obvious: fewer messages to replicate equals less time on the phone equals smaller phone bills. To write one of these money-saving formulas, follow these steps:

1. **Select the database in question and choose** <u>F</u>ile⇨<u>R</u>eplication⇨<u>S</u>ettings, **as we have done in Figure 15-13.**

2. **Click the** Replicate a <u>s</u>ubset of documents: **box and then click the** Select by <u>f</u>ormula **box.**

   Unless you've already modified the formula, the Select by <u>f</u>ormula box will contain the formula Select @All.

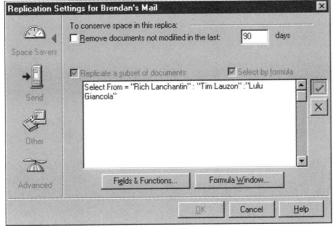

Figure 15-13:
Cut down on replication time and cost by using the Replication Settings dialog box.

3. **Enter the formula you want in the field and click** <u>O</u>K **when you're done.**

   As usual, you don't have to worry about the rest of the options in the dialog box. If your administrator tells you that you have to mess around with the other settings, your administrator will also tell you exactly what to do.

The formulas used for selective replication can get pretty fancy, but, in most cases, they're easy. The basic idea is the word *select,* followed by a field name, followed by a comparison operator (usually an equals sign), followed by a value.

In the following example of a selective replication formula, we're asking Notes to replicate only documents from a couple of people.

```
SELECT FROM = "Leslie Igoe" : "Liz Bedell" : "Mary Mooney"
```

The next example formula only replicates documents that are both "Leads" and marked as "Hot." (Notice that we now use the word "FORM," not "FROM.")

```
SELECT FORM = "Lead" & STATUS = "Hot"
```

This example replicates all the documents in the database, *except* those for the Garden State:

```
SELECT STATE != "New Jersey"
```

As you might expect, it's hard to predict exactly what formula is the right one for you. We *can* tell you that, if you want to replicate only e-mail from certain people, you use a formula very much like the first example, substituting the appropriate names for the ones used above — unless you happen to know Leslie, Liz, and Mary. If you need a complicated formula to replicate only certain documents from a database, ask the database designer and/or your administrator for help.

When you're done with your formula, click the green check-mark button and then click OK.

If one of your coworkers regularly puts documents in a folder for your attention, and you want to replicate only those documents, you don't have to write a formula. (What a relief!) Choose File➪Replication➪Settings and click the `Replicate a subset of documents:` box. Then select the folder from the box. In Figure 15-14, we're going to replicate only the documents in the Airplane Reading and Send to Ira folders.

Figure 15-14:
You can also save replication time by just replicating documents from certain folders.

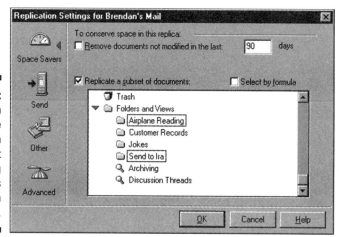

Using the Replicator Workspace Page

As you may have noticed, the last page on your workspace is called the Replicator. We have referred to it a few times in this chapter as the place to look when you're replicating with a server and want to see what's going on. You can also use the Replicator page to initiate calls, replicate databases, and do a few other things. Figure 15-15 shows the Replicator page.

As you can see in the figure, the Replicator page has a special Action bar, chock-full of buttons that are useful when you're living on the road. For example, the Send & Receive Mail button is an easy way to update your mail database.

Use the dialog box shown in Figure 15-16 to fine tune what happens when a given database replicates. You get the dialog box by clicking the arrow button next to the database that you want to fine tune.

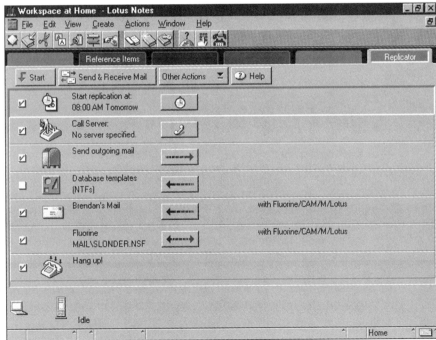

Figure 15-15:
The Replicator Workspace page.

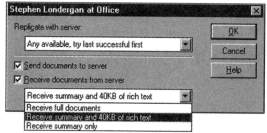

Figure 15-16:
You can
save time
and space
when you
replicate.

For example, you can make your replication only go one way, so that documents are only received by (but not sent to) the server. Or perhaps you choose to only send documents to the server — this is useful if you have a bunch of updates to post, but you don't have time right now to wait for a full database update. If you click the drop-down box, you can choose Receive full documents, Receive summary and 40KB of rich text, or Receive summary only. The last two options are a great way to save time and space, since they will allow only partial documents to be sent; you don't have to worry about tying up the phone line because someone has sent you a huge attachment or embedded object.

Most people use the Replicator workspace to work remotely; they find it easier than the menus.

Wrapping Up Replication

It's one of the cruel ironies of computer books that pages and pages are spent explaining how to set your computer up for a given task like replication, and then there's not nearly enough ink about how you use a feature like replication on a day-to-day basis. So we're going to correct that right here and now. What if you've already configured your modem port, location, and server-connection documents and gotten replica copies on your hard disk of the databases you need to take with you on your business trip to, say, San Francisco. Here are a couple of likely scenarios and how you would use Notes in each.

Our story, Part A, in which our hero shows off her laptop on the airplane and then replicates upon arrival at her hotel room

Your company has a Sales discussion database, and that's one of the databases you've brought with you on your laptop. So, while you're cruising at 35,000 feet (business class, of course), you decide to kill some time by reading the database. You turn on your computer, start Notes, and switch to the Island location profile so that Notes knows you have no way of connecting to your server back at the office.

You open the database and start reading. You see a document you want to respond to, so you use the <u>C</u>reate menu to add a document to the database. The document you just added is now saved in the copy of the database that you have with you on the plane, but it's obviously not saved in the copy of the database that's on your company's Notes server back at the office. Not yet, anyway.

So, when your plane finally arrives on the *left* coast, you'll have to:

1. **Get a cab to your hotel.**

2. **Check in at the hotel.**

3. **Plug in and turn on your computer.**

4. **Start Notes.**

5. **Choose <u>F</u>ile⇨<u>M</u>obile⇨<u>Ch</u>oose Current Location to switch to your Travel location settings.**

6. **Connect your laptop's modem to the phone jack.**

7. **Choose <u>F</u>ile⇨<u>R</u>eplication⇨<u>R</u>eplicate (or <u>A</u>ctions⇨<u>R</u>eplicate with Server from the Replicator Workspace page) to have your workstation call the server back at the office.**

When your computer finishes replicating with the server back home, two things will have happened. First, the document(s) that you <u>C</u>reated and saved while you were up, up, in the air will be in the database back at the office. Second, any documents that your colleagues posted in the database at the office will be in your copy of the database on your laptop.

Our story, Part B, in which our hero checks for new mail from her hotel room

While you were in the air, you also read and wrote some e-mail, and you've got to take care of that, too. The e-mail messages you composed while flying have been stored in the special Outgoing Mail database on your laptop.

Select <u>F</u>ile⇨<u>R</u>eplication⇨<u>R</u>eplicate (or <u>A</u>ctions⇨<u>R</u>eplicate with Server from the Replicator Workspace page) to have your workstation call the server back at the office. This time, you choose your Home Server to replicate with.

When you choose to replicate with your Home Server, Notes automatically delivers any mail that you have waiting in your laptop's Outgoing Mail database.

When your laptop finishes replicating with your Home Server, three things will have happened. First, the messages that you had queued up in the Outgoing Mail database will be gone, sent on their way to your recipients. Second, any changes you made to your mail (like deleted documents, documents in new folders, and so on) will be posted in the copy of your mail database on your Home Server back at the office. Third, any new mail messages that were received in your Home Server's copy of your e-mail database will be in the copy of your e-mail database that's on your laptop.

Our story, Part C, in which our hero heads out to see the sights and do some business

You'll be making sales calls in San Francisco for the next couple of days, so you want your laptop to take care of your replication for you — you want your Sales discussion and e-mail databases automatically kept up-to-date, without you having to be there to choose File➪Replication➪Replicate.

Here's what you do:

1. **Choose File➪Mobile➪Edit Current Location.**

2. **Switch the Schedule field to Enabled.**

3. **Leave your laptop turned on, connected to the phone line, and with Notes up and running when you leave for the day.**

When you return to your hotel room at the end of the day, you'll find that both your e-mail database and your copy of the Sales discussion database have loads of new documents and messages — hardly surprising, since your laptop has been calling your server(s) back at the office all day long. As you reply to the e-mail you have received, you do *not* have to worry about calling the server to deliver it. Notes will deliver the messages during its next scheduled phone call back home.

Our Story, Part D, in which our hero has returned from San Francisco and prepares her laptop to be used on the network again

You're home. A successful trip: ten new orders, plus treats and gifts for the kids. You plug your laptop back in to your docking station, excited at the prospect of using the oh-so-fast network instead of your ever-so-slow modem.

But first, here's what you have to do:

1. **Choose File➪Mobile➪Choose Current Location to switch to your Office profile.**

2. **Select File➪Replication➪Replicate (or Actions➪Replicate with Server from the Replicator Workspace page) one last time to have your workstation synch up any documents you added while you were on the plane flying home.**

Chapter 16

Notes 'n' the Web

*I*t won't be long before some computer pundit somewhere labels 1996 "the year of the Internet." (Hey, maybe we just did!) There has certainly been a lot of press hysteria and industry attention lately about the Internet; if you haven't seen some of it, you must have been living under a rock!

Lotus, of course, is no exception, and they've jumped on the Internet band-wagon in a big way. One of the key features of Notes Release 4 is the ability to access the Internet. Right from Notes, you can browse Word Wide Web pages, download files from FTP sites, and use custom forms. (Don't worry if that doesn't make much sense to you; after all, that's why you're reading this chapter. We'll explain each of those terms in loving detail before we're through.)

When you use Notes to navigate through the World Wide Web, you're still working right in Notes, which offers a couple of distinct advantages over other companies' World Wide Web navigators, or so Lotus thinks, anyway. These advantages include:

✔ You can get on the Web without having to learn yet another computer program.

✔ You can treat World Wide Web pages just like any other Notes document — which means that you can forward them as mail messages, print them, create DocLinks to them, and so on.

✔ Because Notes stores the pages you use in a database, you can get back to them very quickly, without having to reconnect to the Internet.

✔ You can set up your computer to access the Internet in about two seconds, without having to worry about your network and other boring stuff like TCP/IP.

Of course, we can't do the whole Internet and World Wide Web justice in one puny little chapter in this book; you'll have to get a copy of *The Internet For Dummies* or *The World Wide Web For Dummies* if you really want to learn all about the Internet. What we can do, though, is get you up and running with the Notes Internet Navigator as quickly as possible.

Obligatory Vocabulary

Any new computer concept involves a lot of techno-jargon, and the Internet is certainly no exception to that rule. We'll get this over with as quickly as possible:

- ✔ The *Internet* is a huge collection of computers that are all connected together through a vast global network. There are millions of computers on the Internet. When you use Notes to access the World Wide Web, your computer is on the Internet, too.

- ✔ The *World Wide Web,* sometimes just called "the Web" or even the "WWW," is a collection of the computers on the Internet that have special *pages* on them that you can read.

- ✔ A Web *server* is a computer somewhere in the world that is connected to the Internet and that has Web pages on it. A Web server is not a Notes server — those are two different things.

- ✔ A *page* is what's on all these Web computers. These pages contain text, pictures, multimedia files, other kinds of files, and links to *other* Web pages.

- ✔ A *navigator* is a program you use to read Web pages. Notes comes with a navigator built-in; you may have used or heard about navigator programs from other companies such as Netscape, Microsoft, America Online, and so on.

- ✔ An *InterNotes server* is a special Notes server that connects to the Internet. When you read Web pages in Notes, your computer talks to the InterNotes server, and the InterNotes server talks to the Web server that has the page you want to read.

- ✔ The term *URL* stands for *Uniform Resource Locator.* That mouthful is nothing more than the address of a particular page somewhere on the Internet. For example, `http://world.std.com/~slonderg` is the URL that you would use in the Notes Web Navigator to see a Web page about one of the authors of this book. A URL always begins with the letters *http://*.

- ✔ A *link* on a Web page is just like a link in a Notes document; it's a quick way to get to some related information. A link on a Web page might take you to another Web page, or it might connect you with a multimedia presentation, or even download a file.

✔ *TCP/IP* is the kind of network that the Internet uses. One advantage to the Notes Web Navigator over some others is that you *do not* need to have this kind of network on your computer; it does have to be installed on the Notes Web Server, though.

✔ *Browse* is the word people use to describe what they're doing when they use the Internet, as in "I just wasted about two hours browsing the Internet. Did you see that cool page for Walt Disney World?" People also use the words *cruise* and *surf* interchangeably with browse. (Can you tell that the Web is big in California?)

Setting Up

Your company has to have an InterNotes server (see the preceding vocabulary list if you have no idea what that is) hooked up to the Internet in order for you to use the Notes Web Navigator on your computer. Setting up that part of the puzzle certainly isn't your job, but you do have to know the name of this special server, and you do have to make one small change on your computer before you can start surfing. Before you can use the Web in Notes, you have to call your administrator to get the *exact* name of your company's InterNotes server.

If your InterNotes server is the same as your Home Server (that's the one that has your mail database on it), you *don't* have to modify your location document. You can skip right to the next section (called "Grab Your Surfboard").

To get rolling with the Notes Navigator, you have to add the name of your company's InterNotes server to your Location document. That sounds worse than it is. Here's what to do, step by step:

1. **Choose File➪Mobile➪Edit Current Location.**

   This opens your location document, which you may or may not have seen before. (We discuss location documents in Chapter 15.) Figure 16-1 shows a sample Location document.

2. **Enter the name of your company's InterNotes server in the InterNotes server: field on the right side of the document.**

   Spelling counts, so be sure to get it right.

3. **Choose File➪Close to exit the document, and choose Yes to save the document.**

4. **Pat yourself on the back for a job well done.**

That's all there is to it. Now, when you tell Notes that you want to view a Web page, your computer knows it has to talk to your company's InterNotes server to make that happen.

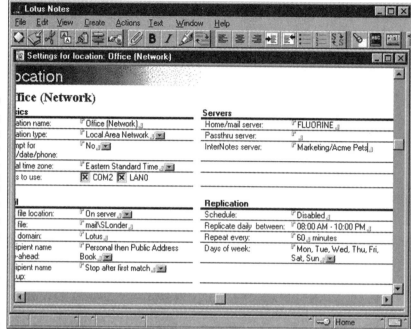

Figure 16-1:
To use the
Notes Web
Navigator,
enter the
name of
your
company's
InterNotes
server in the
appropriate
field in your
location
document.

Grab Your Surfboard . . .

Got your tanning lotion and blanket? After you've edited your location document, you can plunge right in to the Web. When you click the Open URL SmartIcon, you see the Open URL dialog box, as displayed in Figure 16-2.

Figure 16-2:
You can
enter the
address of
any Web
page in the
Open URL
dialog box.

When you enter an Internet address and click the <u>O</u>K button, Notes displays the page you requested.

So, what are you waiting for?

Of course, it isn't always that simple — so few things in life are, after all. When you click the <u>O</u>K button in that Open URL dialog box, you see the requested page, but how quickly do you see it? *That* is the $64,000 question.

The good news is that if you ask for a page that you (or anyone else at your company) has used before, you'll see it lickety-split. Every time someone at your company reads a Web page that hasn't been seen at your company before, Notes automatically stores the page in a special Notes database on your InterNotes server. So, if you're using a page that's been previously viewed, you don't have to wait very long to get it.

The bad news comes when you are the first person to ask for a given page at your company. In this case, Notes has to actually contact the Web server that has the page. This can take awhile, especially if the Web server in question is halfway around the world or if the page has lots of pretty pictures. Exactly how long you will have to wait is hard to predict because it depends on your company's network load, your company's Notes servers, the Internet, the weather in Timbuktu, the average stock price on the NYSE, and whether or not it rains in Indianapolis in the summertime. The wait shouldn't be unbearable, but you will definitely notice a difference between reading "old" pages and reading "new" pages.

If your InterNotes server has to go out to the Internet to get the page you asked for, you'll see the spinning globe (shown, but not spinning, in Figure 16-3) while you're waiting; you'll also see a progress meter in the status bar to tell you how things are proceeding. You can choose <u>W</u>indow to do something else in Notes while you're waiting for a Web page to arrive. You can also click the globe if you want to cancel the retrieval of a page.

Figure 16-3:
A watched
pot never
boils. . . .

Reading a Web Page

When you're in the Web, your screen is divided into two parts: the Web page itself (with pictures, text, and or links) and a special bar at the top of the window, with nine buttons that help you move around the Web:

Home	The Home button takes you back to the Home Navigator (further explanation on the way).
Open	The Open button produces the Open URL dialog box, so that you can open another page by entering the page's address. This button acts just like the Open URL SmartIcon.
◀	The Previous button returns you to the previous page in the History list.
▶	The Forward button goes to the next page in the History list.
History	The History button shows you all of the pages you have visited today.
Reload	The Reload button gets the latest and greatest version of the page from the original Web server (useful if the version of the page in the Web database is out of date).
Recommend	The Recommend button lets you score the page, so that it has a rating when it gets saved in the Web database.
Forward	The Forward button jams the page into an e-mail message, so that you can send it to another Notes mail user.
Bookmark	The Bookmark button adds the page to your Personal folder in the Web database so that you can find it again easily.

What's in a page: links, pix, and files

The content of a Web page varies wildly from one page to the next. Some are brimming with interesting information, some have lots and lots of network-clogging pictures and graphics, and some even have downloadable files.

The common denominator, though, of most pages is the *link*. A link on a Web page is just like your old friend, the Notes DocLink: it's a shortcut to related information. And you use a Web link the same way you would use a DocLink; you click it once to see a pop-up box containing the URL page where it's going to take you; you click it twice to go there. A link on a Web page is discernible from the rest of the text on the page because it's blue and underlined.

Sometimes, a picture acts as a link on a Web page. If you see a graphic on a Web page that's surrounded by a blue border, you know that the picture itself is a link, and you know that double-clicking the picture will link you up to something.

More and more Web pages are coming adorned with pictures. Pictures are certainly nice, and they most definitely jazz up the appearance of Web pages. Unfortunately, they take a long time to display. If you're trying to view a page that has a 254K photograph in it, and the page is on a server in Japan, and it's the middle of the business day, so the network is really busy. . . . Well, you can figure out the rest. Unfortunately, pretty pages often mean slow pages.

Some Web pages have a special kind of link that downloads a file. If the pop-up box for a link begins with the letters FTP instead of HTTP, you know that link will download a file. When you double-click an FTP link, Notes downloads the linked file, turns the file into an attachment, and then saves it in a document in the Web Navigator database. Then, if you want to put the downloaded file onto your computer's hard disk, you'll have to do two things:

✔ Find the File Archive folder in the Navigator database.

✔ Detach the attachment.

The next section of this chapter discusses the Web Navigator database; check out Chapter 10 to read about attachments.

Using the Web Navigator Database

Every time you open a new Web page, Notes stores that page in a special database on the InterNotes server. You can use this database to see the pages that you (and other people) have visited, and also to categorize, sort, and organize the pages. Because Notes stores these pages in a database, you can get to them very quickly without having to connect with the Web server that had the page in the first place. (Your administrator runs a program at night that makes sure all of the pages in the Navigator database are up to date with the latest and greatest information.)

The icon for this database appears in Figure 16-4; it's called the "Web Navigator," and you'll find it on your company's InterNotes server. Refer to Chapter 9 if you need to read about opening a new database.

Figure 16-4:
Use this database to see what pages people at your company are using.

Web Navigator

Big Brother is watching you! Every Web page you visit gets saved into your office's Web Navigator database. Keep in mind that the World Wide Web has many pages that aren't necessarily, uh, appropriate for the workplace. And if you visit one while using the Notes Navigator, everyone is going to know that you were goofing off on the job.

When you open the Navigator database, you see the page shown in Figure 16-5.

Figure 16-5:
The Notes Web Navigator's Home Navigator. Could we use the word "Navigator" a few more times in this caption?!

Use the Sampler part of the Navigator page to view Web pages that have been already sorted into the categories you see listed. Click any one of the pictures to see the pages. For example, if you want to see an up-to-date list of pages related to shopping, click the little picture of the shopping bag.

The lists available from the Sampler part of the Navigator are based on the entire Web, not just the pages that are already in your Navigator database. (This list is collected and compiled by a company called Yahoo!.)

When you click the oval-shaped button that says Our Home, you'll be whisked away to your company's Web page, if your company has one. If your company doesn't maintain its own Web page, don't bother with that button!

The five buttons at the bottom of the page help you find the documents that have already been saved in your Navigator database.

✔ Use the Database Views button to see all the different Web pages in the database.

✔ The Recommended button shows you the pages that your colleagues have deemed especially interesting or informative.

✔ The Directory Search button helps you find Web pages about any topic.

✔ The Open URL button works just like the Open URL SmartIcon: You enter the address of a page to view it.

✔ The last button, User's Guide, opens a special Help database for using the Notes Web Navigator.

Because the World Wide Web is so large, and because it has pages about so many topics, The User's Guide is a good place to start if you're new to the Web. As you can see in Figure 16-6, when you click the Directory Search button, you get a special search page. You enter the word or words that you want to look for in the `Enter topics to search` field, and then click one of the three icons (Yahoo!, LYCOS, or the SEC).

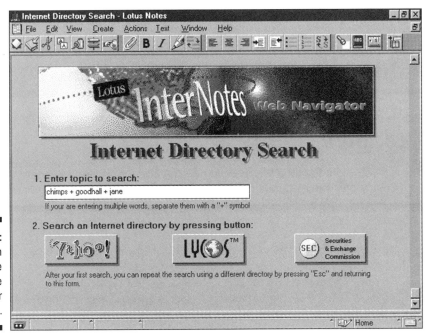

Figure 16-6:
You can search the whole Internet for any topic.

Each of those three companies maintains huge databases full of Web pages, so in no time you'll have a pretty big list of pages that contain the term or terms you asked for. You can click the links in the query results page to go to the page that was found. Figure 16-7 shows a sample result of searching for the word "Dummies."

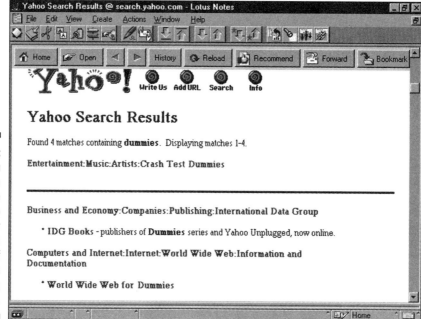

Figure 16-7:
When you search for a word, the Web Navigator produces a whole list of Web pages containing the term.

Three more things . . .

You should know a few more important facts before you can count yourself amongst the illuminati of the Internet. They don't fit anywhere else in this chapter, so we just piled them up here.

Your URLs

Have you noticed that Web page addresses always begin like this: `http://`? Well, Notes recognizes that, too. In fact, anytime Notes displays a document with a URL (Uniform Resource Locator — or Internet address), it automatically treats that URL as a link to the Web page.

Say you find a cool Web page, and you want to tell your friend about it. So you send her an e-mail, as displayed in Figure 16-8.

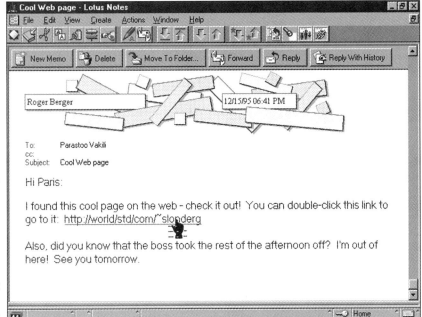

Figure 16-8:
You can
double-click
a URL,
anytime,
anywhere,
to open that
Web page.

As soon as Notes sees the `http://` business, it realizes that the text is a Web page address, and treats it as a Hotspot to that page. If you want to open the aforementioned Web page, double-click the URL Hotspot. Off you go! Notes automatically opens the Web Navigator, and automatically opens the page, just like any other DocLink.

Well, maybe. It turns out that you have to tell Notes that you want it to treat all the little http://s as Hotspots. Choose File⇨Tools⇨User Preferences, and then, in the Advanced options list, select `Make Internet URLs (http://...)` `into Hotspots` as we've done in Figure 16-9. Click OK, then you're done.

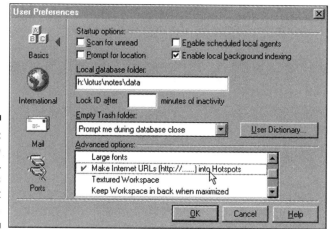

Figure 16-9:
Tell Notes to
treat URL
addresses
as Hotspot
links.

Mail Links

Sometimes, a Web link isn't intended to take you to another Web page. Rather, it acts more like a Notes button, in that it sends a mail message. (In The Business, such a link is known as a *MailTo* link.) The only reason we bother mentioning this is so you don't get surprised when you click a link someday, and find that the link opens a new mail message. Notes will automatically fill in the e-mail address of the person, all you have to do is write your message in the Body field and click the Send button just like a normal e-mail.

Your company must have an Internet Mail Gateway to send e-mail via the Internet, so check with your administrator if MailTo links aren't working.

Cruising from Home

If you want to set up a computer at home to connect to the Internet via your company's InterNotes server, you have to do two things:

- Edit the location document you use at home to enter the name of the InterNotes server you'll be using.

- Add a connection document to your N&A Book for the InterNotes server. You can learn how to use location and connection documents in Chapter 15.

Chapter 17
Data In / Data Out

. . . .

. . . .

*U*sing Notes has many advantages over your average, run-of-the-mill, do-only-one-thing programs. Unless you're just joining us, you're probably already aware of many of them — for example, that Notes works in Windows, OS/2, Macintosh, and UNIX. In all these environments, you can take information of all sorts from another application (Microsoft Word, for instance) and use it in Notes.

The business of getting the information from one application into another varies from the relatively simple to the relatively complex. Here are your choices:

✔ Copying to and pasting from the Clipboard

✔ Creating attachments

✔ Using File⇨Import and File⇨Export

✔ Linking

✔ Embedding

Where's the Glue?

Back in the good old days, when you wanted to include a picture, a chunk of text, a graph, or a table of data in something you were typing, you pulled the paper out of the typewriter after you finished typing whatever text you needed. Then you used scissors to cut out the picture/text/graph/table and found a bottle of glue to paste it into the blank space in the typed copy. This system is not very high tech, could be messy, and made it pretty hard to jam that piece of paper back into the typewriter if you needed to type some more.

But this is the future, the age of bread makers, laser-guided missiles, and (with the advent of the personal computer) cutting and pasting without using scissors or glue. You can use your friendly Clipboard to add objects — such as a graph from 1-2-3 for Windows, a paragraph from Word, or a graphic from Freelance — directly to your Notes documents. Here's how:

1. **Open the program and file that contains the object you want to snag for your Notes document.**

   Technical types call this program the *home program* or the *source application.*

2. **Highlight the desired object and copy it.**

   In most programs, you usually use the Edit⇨Copy command for this.

3. **Switch into Notes, position the cursor where you want the object, and choose Edit⇨Paste.**

   Unless the object was too big to fit in the Clipboard (for example, if you tried to copy 3,000 cells from a Lotus 1-2-3 worksheet), you see a copy of the original data in the Notes document.

If for no other reason, this system is preferable to the scissors-and-glue system because the page with the pasted item doesn't stick to all the other pages. It's also faster, it's seamless, and it gives you the ability to move the pasted object around or delete it completely if you change your mind. Besides that, you can edit the pasted object after you've pasted it into Notes.

This copy-and-paste system works fine as long as the source application supports the use of the Clipboard and you're able to open the source application to get at the information you want to copy. But keep in mind that, if the data in the source application changes, Notes cannot update its copy of the data. After you copy and paste something into Notes, Notes has no way to know what goes on in the source application.

Unlike most of the other techniques in this chapter, you can use the copy-and-paste method to copy data from one Notes document into another. Most of the other techniques only work with data and files created outside of Notes.

Throwing Out Your Paper Clips

What if you can't use the Clipboard? Your next weapon in the arsenal of using non-Notes data is *attaching* files to documents. It doesn't matter whether Notes supports the file format, whether the original application has ever even heard of the Clipboard, or what kind of laundry detergent you are using — in a rich text field, you can attach any file to any Notes document.

Place the cursor where you want a symbol of the attached file to appear and then choose File⇨Attach, or click the File Attach SmartIcon. Figure 17-1 shows the dialog box that appears. Use the Look in: box to find the file you're importing and choose the filename in the list box or enter its name in the File name: box. After you've found the file, click Create and, voilà, the file appears inside your Notes document.

Up one level   Create folder   List Details

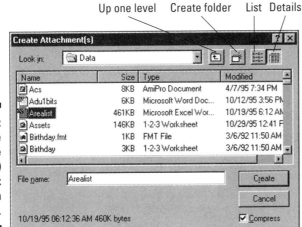

Figure 17-1:
Use the
Create
Attachment(s)
dialog box
to attach
a file.

 Notice in Figure 17-1 that you can see lots of fascinating information about the highlighted file — its size, the program in which it was created, and its date and time of creation — because we've clicked the Details button, one of the four buttons in the upper-right corner of the Create Attachment(s) dialog box.

 By default, the Compress box in the Create Attachment(s) dialog box is checked. This feature squeezes the file to make it smaller as it attaches it. The attached file may end up only 20 percent of its original size after Notes compresses it. That means the memo itself takes up less disk space and will take less time to send. (That's good.) The argument against compressing a file is that the attachment process takes a little longer. Your recipients won't know whether you compressed it or not, because the attachment automatically decompresses when it gets detached. So don't worry about someone complaining about receiving a squashed file.

If a memo has an attached file, all the reader will see is a symbol of the file in the memo. If possible, that symbol will be an icon of the original program. An Ami Pro icon, for instance, represents an Ami Pro file. Because you can attach any kind of file, sometimes the icon will not match the source application. For instance, if you attach a batch file or an executable file (one with the .EXE extension), Notes represents that file with what looks like a piece of paper with the corner folded over.

You can't see or edit the data from an attached file in a Notes document. The purpose of attaching a file is simply to give that file to others, not to use the data in your Notes document.

If you receive a memo or open a document with a file attached, you can choose to view it, launch it, or detach it. Find out more about each of these options under "Enclosed Please Find" in Chapter 6.

Importing and Exporting

Okay, so you want to include some information from another source into your document, but the original application doesn't support the Clipboard so you can't use copy and paste. And you don't want to *attach* the file because you want the reader to see the data rather than an icon. Your next option is to *import* the file from its native format into Notes. By the same token, if you can't copy Notes data to the Clipboard to paste it into the other application, you can *export* it.

Importing from non-Notes programs

Imagine that you're composing a Notes document and you need to include a bunch of pages that you've already typed in WordPerfect for DOS. This is a case where you can't use the Clipboard to include the document, because WordPerfect for DOS isn't even a Windows program and doesn't know anything about the Clipboard. If you attach the file, the people who will be reading your document won't see the actual text of the WordPerfect document, they'll see a crummy little icon.

What do you do? You *import* the WordPerfect file. Importing is how you convert a file from WordPerfect right into the Notes document you're composing and right into the rich text field in which you are typing. You could also convert files from lots of other programs, like Lotus 1-2-3 or WordStar.

How do you import something? Like this:

1. **Get your cursor to the spot in the rich text field where you want to insert the file.**

   (By the way, don't even think about importing a document into any kind of field other than rich text.)

2. **Choose File⇨Import.**

   You'll see a dialog box like the one in Figure 17-2.

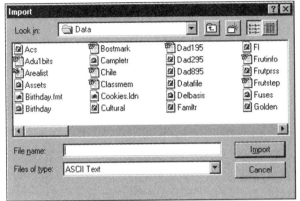

Figure 17-2:
The Import
dialog box.

3. **In the Look in: box choose the drive and directory where you think the file is.**

4. **Select which kind of file you're importing in the Files of type: drop-down box.**

5. **Either highlight the file name in the box or type it in the File name: box and then click Import.**

Ta-da. The file appears inside your Notes document.

When you do import a file, Notes converts it to regular text, so feel free to liven it up by changing the fonts, making some of the words bold, or whatever.

Using File⇨Import to include a foreign (non-Notes) file in a rich text field is your technique of choice if the file's source application either isn't installed on your workstation (maybe someone else gave you the WordPerfect file, but you don't have WordPerfect on your computer) or can't be copied and pasted via the Clipboard.

Although File⇨Import does convert foreign documents, try the Clipboard first when incorporating information from other programs. It's quicker and cleaner.

Here's a (long) list of the kinds of files that you can import into a rich text field:

Ami Pro	JPEG Image
ASCII	Lotus 1-2-3 Worksheet
Binary with Text	Lotus PIC
BMP Image	Microsoft Word RTF
CGM Image	PCX Image
Excel 4.0	TIFF 5.0 Image
Excel 5.0	Word for Windows 6.0
GIF Image	WordPerfect 6.0/6.1
Interleaf ASCII	

If you need to import a file that is not in the list, see whether the originating program can save the file in one of the formats that Notes supports. For example, if you need to import a Quattro Pro spreadsheet, you can use Quattro Pro to save the file as a Lotus 1-2-3 worksheet and then import the converted Lotus 1-2-3 worksheet into Notes.

Exporting: A document leaves home

You probably guessed that, just as you can convert documents from other documents to Notes, you can also convert a Notes document into a file that can be used by a different program. Perhaps you have a Notes document that you want to give to a colleague who doesn't have access to Notes (do they know what they are missing?!). You can convert the Notes document to, say, a Microsoft Word document and then deliver the file to your friend on a floppy disk.

In the information age of the '90s, copying a file onto a floppy disk and then walking down the hall to hand-deliver it is euphemistically known as using *Sneaker Net*.

To convert a Notes file into another format, follow these steps:

1. Find and open the Notes document that you want to export.

2. Choose File⇨Export.

This brings you face-to-face with the dialog box shown in Figure 17-3.

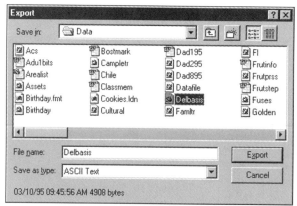

Figure 17-3:
The Export
dialog box.

3. Use the Save in: box to specify the location of the file you want to export.

4. Enter the name of the file in the File name: text box.

5. **Use the Save as type: drop-down box to tell Notes what kind of file you want it to be.**

6. **Click Export and you're done.**

    Now you (or your friend) can open the new file in the appropriate program.

Here's the list of the file types to which you can export a Notes document:

> Ami Pro
> ASCII Text
> CGM Image
> Microsoft Word RTF
> TIFF 5.0 Image
> Word for Windows 6.0
> WordPerfect 6.0/6.1

Just as with File⇨Import, only use File⇨Export if you can't transfer the Notes document to the other program via the Clipboard.

Documents come into view

Another way to bring information into Notes is to import not an individual document, but rather lots of documents at the same time. This method would be the appropriate choice if, for example, you have a Lotus 1-2-3 worksheet and you want to import it such that each row in the spreadsheet becomes a separate document in a Notes database. If your worksheet has 4,362 rows worth of information, you'll get 4,362 new documents in your Notes database.

First steps . . .

First things first: You have to use 1-2-3 to set up the spreadsheet in a very particular fashion. You have to remove all the fancy formatting, blank rows, and so on that are typically included in a worksheet. In fact, there are a couple of very specific rules for preparing a spreadsheet to import into Notes:

- ✔ The column headings for the worksheet must be in row 1 of the worksheet, and they must be the same as the field names in the Notes database. This is important, so call the person who created the database if you're not sure what the *exact* field names are in the Notes database.

- ✔ The rows of spreadsheet information must begin in row 2 of the worksheet and must be in a solid block. There can't be any blank rows in the middle of the spreadsheet, or else you'll get empty documents in your database.

Probably your best bet is to take the worksheet you intend to import and rearrange it to conform to the aforementioned rules. But be sure to save it with a different name so you don't replace the original worksheet.

If you need to import any other kind of file, such as a big text file or an Excel worksheet, you're best off converting *that* file into a Lotus 1-2-3 worksheet and then importing the Lotus 1-2-3 worksheet into Notes. No surprise that the easiest kind of file to import into (Lotus) Notes is from (Lotus) 1-2-3, right?

Second steps . . .

After you've gotten the worksheet all ship-shape, open the database into which you'll be importing the worksheet and choose File⇨Import. Make sure that you have a view on-screen when you choose File⇨Import. In other words, just open the database without opening one of the documents or trying to compose a new document. Otherwise, Notes will think that you want to put the worksheet into just one document.

Use the dialog box shown in Figure 17-4 to indicate the place to find the file (Look in:) and the type of file (Files of type:) and select the file, or type the name in the File name: box. In Figure 17-4 we chose a 1-2-3 worksheet.

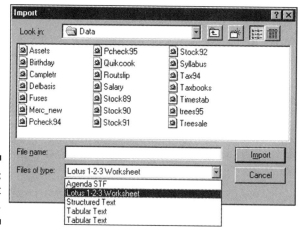

Figure 17-4: The Import dialog box.

When you click Import, Notes presents you with yet another dialog box, as you can see in Figure 17-5. Here, you can tell Notes how to import the rows of the spreadsheet. You need to decide whether you want Notes to import all rows or only selected rows as documents, and whether it should include the column heads in the new spreadsheet.

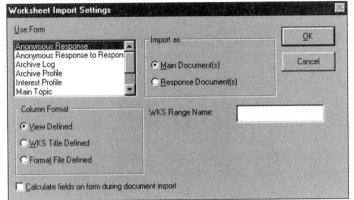

You have five decisions to make (roughly clockwise from the upper-left corner of the dialog box):

✔ Which form Notes will use to display the new documents

✔ Whether the new documents will be main documents or responses

✔ Which range to import from the spreadsheet — you can enter either the cell coordinates (like **A1 . . D341**) or a range name

✔ How the fields (columns) will be named

  Because you followed our advice and were careful to make the spreadsheet column heading match the field name, choose WKS Title Defined.

✔ Whether Notes should calculate any field formulas that have been defined on the form for each document as it is created

  If that's what you want, click the Calculate fields on form during document import box. If you're not sure whether you should check this box, consult the person who created the database.

Click OK and you're in business. Notes will import the worksheet and convert each row into a brand new document for your database.

As you've probably guessed by now, there are actually a couple of ways to import documents. We've only discussed importing a Lotus 1-2-3 worksheet because it's the most common kind of import and because the other kinds of view-level imports are pretty complicated. If you're convinced that you have to import a file that's not a 1-2-3 worksheet, you'll need help from the person who created the database or from your local Notes guru.

Hey view, make me a spreadsheet

Exporting from a view is even easier than importing into a view. The idea behind a view-level export is that you want to create a spreadsheet based on the columns in a view.

Although exporting a view to a spreadsheet is the most common kind of view-level export, you can actually export a view to any of the following four file types:

- ✔ A 1-2-3 worksheet, compatible with any version of Lotus 1-2-3 and also accessible by most other spreadsheet and database programs, such as Excel, dBASE, and Paradox

- ✔ An Agenda STF file, which is a file format used by a (discontinued) program from Lotus, so you can probably forget about this one

- ✔ A structured text file, which is an ASCII file that would then be imported into some other program

- ✔ A tabular text file, which is easy to import into other spreadsheet and database programs

To make a new spreadsheet file out of a view, follow these steps:

1. Open the database in question and switch to the view that will be the basis of the spreadsheet you are creating.

When you export a view, you will only export the fields that are in the view. If you need to export fields that are *not* in the view, you'll have to negotiate with the person who designed your database to add a column or two to display the additional fields, or you can create a private view or folder. See Chapter 11 for advice on how to do that.

2. If you only want to export some of the documents in the view, use the mouse or spacebar to check off the documents you want.

3. Choose File➪Export and watch for the dialog box shown in Figure 17-6.

4. In the Save in: drop-down list, select the drive and directory where the new file will be saved.

5. Click Export.

6. In the next dialog box, tell Notes whether you want to export all the documents in the view or just those that you selected in Step 2.

You also see a check box to Include View Titles, which will make each column heading in the worksheet match the database's field names. If you don't choose this option, the spreadsheet won't have any column headings.

Figure 17-6:
The Export
dialog box.

7. Click OK.

Notes creates a Lotus 1-2-3 worksheet for you based on the view that's open — and that's all there is to it.

If you intend to export data from a Notes view to a program other than Lotus 1-2-3, you should still export the view to a Lotus 1-2-3 worksheet and then use that other program to further convert the worksheet. Take it from us, using Lotus 1-2-3 is a lot (A LOT) easier than using the structured or tabular text formats.

Keeping Links to Home

What if you want to add something from another program to your Notes document, but you want it to retain its identity as data of the original application? You want a have-your-cake-and-eat-it-too way of bringing data into Notes. This data doesn't become native Notes data as it does when you choose any of the File⇔Import options we discussed in the preceding section.

A *link* adds information to your Notes document but keeps an eye on the original data so that, if you or anyone else changes the original, the copy in the Notes document will change, too. However, you can't use linking and embedding within Notes to link two Notes databases. Copy-and-paste or DocLinks are the way to do that.

What makes linking and embedding a bit confusing is the terminology; some words used for linking are also used in other Notes contexts. For instance, the program in which the original data was created is called the *server.* The program into which the data is placed is called the *client* (a term sometimes also used for *workstation*). Keep in mind as you read this section that we are not talking about Notes servers and Notes clients, but link servers and clients.

What's a DocLink?

Cufflinks for your favorite doctor? Sausage for physicians? Not in Notes-speak. A *DocLink* is a connection between one document and another.

Suppose that you are sending a memo to an associate about a report that is in another database. Rather than saying, "Find the document for yourself, you lazy bum," you can put a little icon of the report in your memo. When the lazy bum receives the memo, a mere double-click on the symbol opens the document.

The recipient must have access to the database and the document that you are linking in your memo. An error message appears on-screen if someone clicks a DocLink and he or she doesn't have rights to access the documents or the database itself or doesn't have access to the server that contains the database that contains the document that lives in the house that Jack built. One of the databases to which others do not have access is your own mail database, so you wouldn't even think of linking to one of your mail messages, right?

To create a DocLink, you first need to open (or highlight in a view or folder) the document *to which you are creating a* link and then choose Edit⇨Copy as Link⇨Document Link. Then switch to the document that will contain the DocLink and choose Edit⇨Paste.

When your recipients receive the memo, each can double-click the DocLink. The document itself opens before their very eyes. It beats typing the whole report all over again, doesn't it? Just for the record, you need to be in edit mode to add a DocLink to a document, but you don't need to be in edit mode to open a DocLink. And even though the example presented here is a mail memo, you can paste a DocLink into any Notes document in any Notes database.

Here's a tip: When reading a document that has a DocLink in it, choose View⇨Document Link Preview to see a little bit of the linked document (without actually opening it). It's just like previewing a document in your mail database.

To create a link, follow these steps:

1. **Open the server application and create or open a file containing the data to which you'll be forging a link.**

   If this is a new file, be sure to save it before trying to create the link.

2. **Highlight the data to link and choose Edit⇨Copy.**

3. **Switch to the Notes document and place the cursor where you want to place the data.**

4. **Choose Edit⇨Paste Special.**

   The dialog box in Figure 17-7 appears.

5. **In the As: list box, choose the format for the data to be linked.**

   You may choose the file's native file format (Microsoft Word in Figure 17-7), Rich Text (text arrives with all formatting), Picture (usually used for graphic objects), or Text (text arrives without formatting).

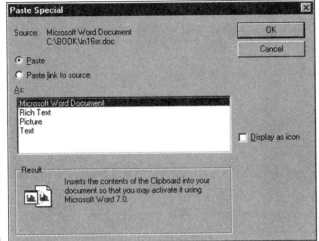

Figure 17-7:
This is
where you
choose the
original file's
format and
how it
should be
pasted.

6. **Choose** `Paste link to source.`

7. **Click OK to finish the job.**

After a few seconds, the data appears in the Notes document. If the
original selection contains multiple text formats, you may see an icon
rather than the actual text.

By making a link, you have created a *compound document,* a document with
multiple features, containing non-Notes data which keeps in touch with home.
You can't edit the linked data while you're in Notes. To edit the data, you need
to double-click the linked data or the icon. Notes opens or switches to the
server application and file, where you may edit the data. As you do the editing,
the changes are reflected immediately in the Notes document.

Not only can you edit the data, you can also edit the link itself. In the Notes
document, choose Edit⇨External Links. Watch for the dialog box you see in
Figure 17-8.

In the External Links dialog box, you may choose to use any of the following:

✔ **Update Now:** if the data in the Notes document is not up-to-date with the
server document

✔ **Open Source:** to edit the source document

✔ **Edit Link:** to use new data or a new file as the original document that is
linked into the current Notes document

✔ **Break Link:** to permanently sever the link between server and client

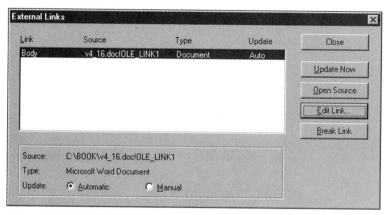

Figure 17-8:
The External
Links dialog
box.

In the External Links dialog box, you can also change the link from Automatic (the link will make changes immediately in the client when the server file changes) to Manual (you have to choose Edit⇨External Links and click Update Now to update links). You usually choose Manual if editing the server file slows down your computer's performance.

A link requires that you have a saved file *and* the server application available to Notes. Often, the server file itself will be on a network server (wow — both uses of the word *server* in one sentence) so that the same file is available to all users. If all users of the Notes document don't have the same directory structure for the server application, Notes will not be able to open the application to allow updating. Also, if the file is moved or renamed, everyone loses the link between the original information and the information in the Notes document. So watch it!

If You Can't Link 'em — Embed 'em

To the person reading your document, an embedded object will look the same as a linked object. Either one may be an icon or data, depending on the complexity of the data in the server file. The difference between the two is that data embedded in a Notes document uses the file itself, not a link, so changes to the original file are *not* reflected in the embedded file.

Why would you embed an object in a document? Here's an example.

Suppose you want people to enter expense reports in a spreadsheet format into a Notes document for storage in a Notes database. You could embed a 1-2-3 spreadsheet in a Notes form which contains the text and formulas users need to enter data. When users create an expense form in Notes, the embedded spreadsheet kicks into action and users find themselves in 1-2-3, where they fill in the data. When they save the work in 1-2-3, they return to Notes; the data is in the Notes document; they save the document and wait for the check to arrive. Get it?

To embed information in a Notes document, follow these steps:

1. **Open the original file in its original program.**

2. **Copy the information to the Clipboard.**

3. **Open the Notes document and position the cursor in a rich text field.**

4. **Choose Edit⇨Paste Special.**

5. **Make a choice of format under As.**

6. **Click Paste.**

You can also create a placeholder for an object that you will want to embed later, but which doesn't even exist yet. To accomplish this miracle, choose Create⇨Object and, because it's a new embedded object, select Create a new object as we did in Figure 17-9. Select the application that will be the server under Object type: and then click OK. Notes starts the program for the type you picked. Then you enter data which becomes part of the Notes document.

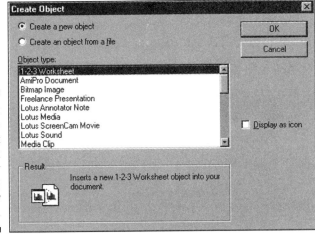

Figure 17-9:
The Create
Object
dialog box
for
embedding
a new
object.

On the other hand, if you want to embed an existing file, click on Create an object from a file, select the file, and choose OK. The dialog box you'll use looks like Figure 17-10. Notes embeds the file in the Notes document.

Embedding doesn't require that the readers of the Notes document have access to the original file, because they have their own copy of the file. However, they do have to have the *server application* so that they can use it to edit the original data. To edit the original data, double-click the embedded data, and both the server application and the file open. Any changes to the embedded file on one user's version of a document may not be reflected in other users' copies of the document, depending upon whether the documents are replicated to all other users.

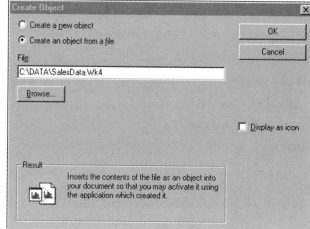

Figure 17-10:
The Create
Object
dialog box
when
you are
embedding
an existing
file.

Searching for text, covered in Chapter 18, is a valuable tool. Both linking and embedding will allow your readers to search for text as long as you follow two rules:

✔ You must link or embed the data as text or rich text.

✔ The data must be visible (it can't be represented by an icon).

This business of embedding and linking used to be called OLE and DDE (and still is by people who speak in abbreviations, use pocket protectors, and whose glasses slide down their noses). OLE (pronounced Spanish style: *o-lay*) stands for *Object Linking and Embedding;* DDE stands for *Dynamic Data Exchange*. Don't lose any sleep over which one you're using. It doesn't matter. That's something for Notes to worry about behind the scenes.

Chapter 18

Full Text Search — Finding Facts in a Flash

· ·

In This Chapter

▶ Introducing Full Text Search

▶ Using the Search bar

▶ Setting search conditions

▶ Setting search options

▶ Using Query by Form

▶ Building your own index

· ·

*D*atabases crowd your servers, documents pile up in each one, and mountains of data are there for the reading. Now you need to find some important piece of information that someone entered somewhere on a form in a database. All you have to do is read every document to find it. Cancel your plans for the weekend, you have a lot of reading to do. Or do you? Since we live in the age of electronic miracles, isn't there some way to find some text without having to read every document in every database?

Rest assured we wouldn't raise the issue if there were bad news to answer that question. The answer is *Full Text Search,* a slick way to let Notes do the digging. Take our word for it, no matter how many speed reading courses you took, Notes can find information faster than you could ever hope to.

What Is Full Text, Anyway?

You just got a new job, and you're going to be taking business trips once or twice a month. The first thing you need to do is find out your company's policies for travel — what airline should you use, what hotels can you stay in, and, most important, do *you* get to keep your Frequent Flyer miles? So you open up that trusty Human Resources Policies database, but there must be at least 700 documents in it. How are you going to find all the documents that have the word "travel" in them?

It's Full Text Search to the rescue. *Full Text Search* is a way for you to find all of the occurrences of a word (or of a couple of words) very, very quickly. You can search a huge database in no time at all. Most searches don't take more than two or three *seconds*. And, when you ask Notes to search for the word "travel," it finds *all* the documents for you, no matter where (or how many times) the documents contain the word "travel." Notes calls this Full Text Search, not because it finds full text (there's no such thing), but because it is full of neat features.

Hide and Go Seek with the Search Bar

You begin your search for text by choosing <u>V</u>iew⇨Search <u>B</u>ar. The Search bar is what you use to enter the criteria for your search. It appears at the top of the View window, as shown in Figure 18-1.

When you perform a search, Notes only searches the documents that are in the current, open view. So you have to be careful to choose the right view before you start your search. If the view you have open only shows documents from the first half of the year, your search will not look through the documents from the second half of the year.

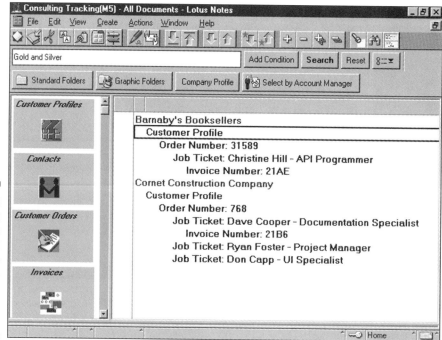

Figure 18-1:
The Search bar contains "Gold and Silver" — words we want to find in the database.

The magic FTI

A text search is faster than a speeding bullet and more powerful than a locomotive when the database is *Full Text Indexed*. To get a database indexed, you need to contact your trusty Notes administrator or the person who created the database, or you need to create the index yourself. To do that you must be a manager or a designer of the database, or you must have a copy of the database on your local (non-Macintosh) computer. Read the section at the end of this chapter called "Creating Your Own Index" for more information about a do-it-yourself index.

If the database isn't Full Text Indexed, you have a different option in the Search bar: a Create Index button replaces the Add Conditions button. That's because you can't add conditions until there's an index. Even if the database is not indexed, you can still search for text. It's just that a lot of options aren't available to you.

One more thing, the index may be outdated — until it's updated, newer documents may not be included in the index and therefore won't be found when you conduct a search.

The big, blank box

The Search bar contains several important parts. Starting from the left, the blank box is where you type the text you want to search for. Here are the types of things you can enter:

- **A single word:** For example, type **gold** to find all documents containing the word "gold."

- **A phrase in quotes:** For example, type **"gold and silver"** to find documents containing the phrase "gold and silver."

- **Words connected by and, without quotes:** For example, type **gold and silver** to find documents with both the word "gold" *and* the word "silver" in them.

- **Words connected by or, without quotes:** Type **gold or silver** to find documents that contain either the word "gold" or the word "silver" — maybe both, but at least one of the two.

Get into conditions

Next to the text box in the Search bar is the Add Conditions button which, when clicked, produces the dialog box in Figure 18-2.

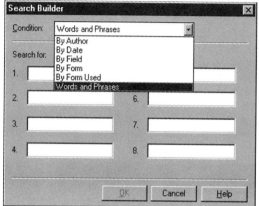

Figure 18-2:
The Search
Builder
dialog box
— click the
Add
Conditions
button to
see it.

Rather than entering words or phrases you want to find in the text box, you can enter them in the numbered boxes in the Search Builder dialog box. Hidden by the drop-down list near the top of Figure18-2 are the words Any and All. (We opened the list so you could see what it contains.) Choosing Any is like using the word "or" in the text box between "gold" and "silver"; the resulting search will find all documents containing any of those words. Choosing All finds documents which contain every word in the list.

Clicking on the drop-down list next to the Condition box allows you to change the search from just Words and Phrases to looking for the following:

- **By Author:** A new dialog box appears for you to enter a name of someone whose documents you would like to see.

- **By Date:** A dialog box appears so you can enter a date and tell Notes to find documents which are newer or older than that date.

- **By Field:** A dialog box appears for you to enter a field and the data you want that field to contain in the documents you want to find.

- **By Form:** This allows you to look in specific fields in a specific form. This is the famous Query by Form, explained in further detail later in this chapter.

- **By Form Used:** A dialog box appears for you to tell Notes to look only in documents composed with a specific form.

On your mark, get set, search!

After you have entered the text and set your conditions, it's time to start the search itself. That part's easy — just click the Search button. You may have to wait a few minutes, even though Notes is fast. If you have a lot of documents in the view, it's going to take a couple of minutes to find them. Of course, if it's a database with three small documents, the search won't take any time at all. The point? The amount of time a search takes depends on three factors:

✔ The size of the documents in the database

✔ The number of documents in the database

✔ The complexity of the conditions you have set

Resetting the stage

When you've read the documents that interest you, click the Reset button to clear the search to return all documents to the view and end the search.

If you want to conduct another search, it isn't necessary to click Reset first, just type in a new bunch of text and set your conditions; then click Search and off you go. Typing a new search word makes Notes forget all about the old search, and returns only documents which satisfy the new set of criteria. It's really only necessary to use the Reset button when you're completely done searching.

The nameless options

The next button doesn't have a name, just an arrow to show that you can click on it to see more, and a couple of dots which may mean that there are options from which to choose or that it's catching chicken pox. Let's assume the dots represent radio buttons next to a series of options.

As a matter of fact, if you click on this unnamed button, you do see a list of options, shown in Figure 18-3.

Figure 18-3:
This is the
list of
options for
the search.

Because a paragraph is sometimes worth a thousand pictures, we'll save several thousand pictures by explaining each and every item in the list.

✔ **Include Word Variants:** tells Notes that you want to look for other forms of a word as well as the one you typed in. Use this feature when you type the word **write**, for example, but you want to search for variations such as wrote, writing, and writes.

✔ **Use Thesaurus:** tells Notes to use not only the word you typed, but also its synonyms. So, if you type "hunt" in the text box, Notes looks for "search" and "look" and any other synonyms it can find for "hunt." Depending on the word you enter, this feature may take a while and return a lot of documents.

✔ **Sort by Relevance:** means that you want to see the documents arranged by weight, the ones with the largest number of examples of your criteria are at the top with the darkest part of the bar in the marker column.

✔ **Sort by Oldest First** and **Sort by Newest First:** causes the documents with the earliest composed date or the latest composed date to head the list Notes gives you.

✔ **Maximum Results:** sets the highest number of results you want to see. The default is 250, but if you expect the search to take too long, set the number lower.

✔ **Save Search As:** is a tool only a designer or manager of a database can use. You choose to save a search if you plan to use it frequently. If you have any saved searches, they'll appear at the bottom of this drop-down list, right below Delete Saved Search.

✔ **Delete Saved Search:** is also only for designers and managers. It probably comes as no surprise that you use this option to delete one of the saved searches.

The arrow keys allow you to find each occurrence of the search text in an opened document. The right arrow takes you to the next occurrence, the left arrow to the previous one.

Seek and Ye Shall Find

When the job is finally done, Notes changes the view to show only the documents in the view which contain the text you're searching for and which meet the conditions you set. If you want to see all documents, even those which do not satisfy the search, choose View⇨Show⇨Search Results Only. All documents are again visible to the naked eye, or one with clothes on. The documents that satisfy the criteria are checked in the left column.

Notes lists the documents that match your criteria in order of their weight. Now Notes doesn't measure a document's weight in grams or pounds or even bytes. Rather, in this case, *weight* refers to the degree to which each document satisfies the search criteria. It first lists the documents that have the most occurrences of your criteria and then the documents that have fewer occurrences of the criteria. The vertical bar, called the *marker bar,* at the left-hand side of the view represents the relative frequency of your criteria in each document. The darker the bar, the more occurrences in that particular document. You can see the effect in Figure 18-4.

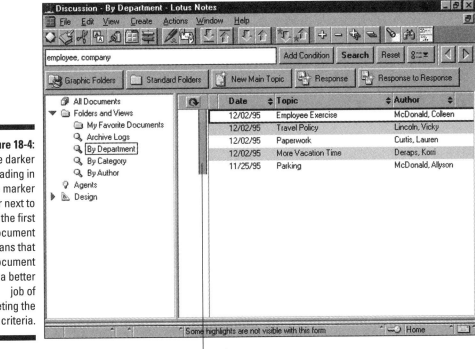

Figure 18-4:
The darker shading in the marker bar next to the first document means that document did a better job of meeting the criteria.

Marker bar

In the Options drop-down menu, you can choose to sort documents by age rather than by weight. Be sure you make the decision before the search.

You open a document uncovered by a search the same way that you open any other document: double-click it or highlight it with the cursor keys and press Enter. When you do, Notes shows you the document and highlights (in little red boxes) the words you asked it to find, as you see in Figure 18-5 (minus the red).

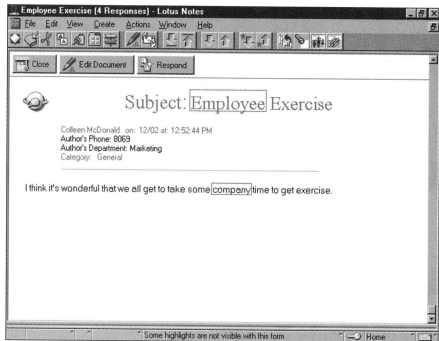

Figure 18-5:
A box
appears
around each
occurrence
of whatever
text satisfies
your criteria.

As you read a document retrieved by a Full Text Search, you can jump quickly to the next occurrence of the search word by pressing Ctrl++ (that's the Ctrl key and the plus sign). You use Ctrl+- (Ctrl and the minus key) to jump quickly to the preceding occurrence of the word.

If your hand is already on the mouse, click on the arrowheads at the right end of the Search bar, rather than switch to the keyboard to move to each occurrence of the word. The right arrow takes you to the next occurrence of the word, the left arrow takes you to the previous occurrence.

Query by Form

A way to make your life easier is to do a *Query by Form*. That means that you use one of the forms in the database to tell Notes which words you're looking for, and in which fields you want to find them. This method narrows and refines your query substantially.

Imagine that you want to search through a personnel database for a person's name, but that person is the author in many documents in that database. You aren't interested in documents the person wrote, only in documents where the person's name is mentioned. You can use Query by Form to tell Notes to be sure that the name occurs in the Body field of a particular form. (Of course, the name of the field may be different in the form you're using.)

Here's how you make a Query by Form:

1. **Click the Add Conditions button in the Search bar.**

2. **In the Search Builder dialog box, click the down arrowhead to the right of Condition:.**

3. **From the drop-down box, pick By Form.**

4. **Click the down arrowhead to the right of Form: to see the list of forms.**

5. **Pick the form you want to use and Notes gives you an empty version of the form.**

6. **Move the cursor into the field where you want to find the word or phrase and type the text you want Notes to find in that field.**

    In Figure 18-6 we entered "Vacation" into the Subject field to find all documents with that word in the subject field.

    Tired of picking and clicking? Sorry, one more.

7. **Click OK to close the dialog box, and then click the Search button in the Search bar to find the documents.**

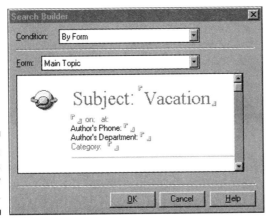

Figure 18-6:
This is
Query by
Form.

Indexing a Database All by Yourself

A search for text is much more speedy and offers tons more options when you have *a Full Text Index* (a behind-the-scenes list of text and documents), which the search uses to find documents with the text you want to find. If you're a manager or designer of a database, or if you have a copy of the database on your own computer, you can create your own index. How about indexing your mail database? That way, you can easily find all those old messages that have your customer's names in them or quickly put your hands on all the messages that are about a certain project.

Yeah, but ...

You must consider a few issues before indexing every database in sight.

Issue #1: Disk space

Indexing a database takes up more disk space — maybe an additional 50 percent (or more) of the database's size. In other words, if your mail database takes up, say, 10 megabytes of disk space, indexing could increase the size to 15 megabytes. It's hard to predict exactly how big the index is going to be, because that depends very much on the type of database you're indexing. If you have a database that has a lot of pictures in it and a relatively small amount of text, that database's index won't be as big (percentage-wise) as it would be for a database that's almost all text.

Of course, if the database you're going to index is on a Notes server, rather than your own computer, you won't be as conscious of the disk space requirements because you're not going to use any of *your* hard disk space — the index is stored with the database on the server.

Don't let your administrator read that last paragraph, because administrators are *extremely* concerned about disk space on the server. That's their job.

Issue #2: Maintenance

Like a beautiful lawn or a good haircut, indexes have to be maintained. As people add and remove documents to and from the database, the index has to be periodically updated to stay abreast of the new and deleted documents. Who's going to do the work to keep up the index?

Here again, if the indexed database is on the server, maintaining the index is more your administrator's concern than it is yours. In fact, the indexes are automatically kept up-to-date if the databases are on the server.

On the other hand, if the indexed database is on your computer's hard disk, *you* have to be responsible for keeping it up-to-date. (More about maintaining the local indexes in a minute.) It doesn't sound like much, but this maintenance takes time — how much time depends on how many documents have been added to the database since the last time you updated the index.

The bottom line is that if you index a database that's on your computer (as opposed to one that's on the server), you have to be prepared to sacrifice some disk space and remember to keep the index up-to-date.

Issue #3: Operating system

You cannot index a database that's on your own computer if you have a Macintosh. Mac users can create indexes for databases that are on the server, and Mac users can certainly use the indexes for the databases on the servers. They just can't create an index for a database that's local.

Index Building 101

To create a new Full Text Index for a database, activate the database's InfoBox by clicking the Properties SmartIcon and then clicking on the Full Text tab in the InfoBox. The Full Text tab looks like Figure 18-7. You can see in the figure that this database has never been indexed because it says `Database is not full text indexed` right in the InfoBox. The Create Index button is right there for the clicking. But you have one more dialog box to deal with first, shown in Figure 18-8.

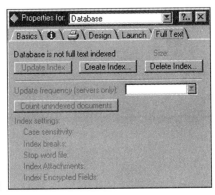

Figure 18-7:
The Full Text tab of the Database InfoBox tells you that this database hasn't been indexed.

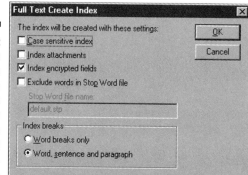

Figure 18-8: You have some decisions to make before you can create the full text index.

You have several choices to make in the Full Text Create Index dialog box. Your decisions can really affect how long the indexing process will take and the size of the FTI (that's a TLA — Three Letter Abbreviation — for Full Text Index).

- ✔ **Case sensitive index:** means a search will separately list upper and lower case occurrences of a word. This is a definite space hog.

- ✔ **Index attachments:** means Notes actually reads all the files attached to each document and includes their contents in the Full Text Index. Wanna guess what happens to the size of the index?

- ✔ **Index encrypted fields:** reads and includes the contents of encrypted fields in the index. If the search finds a document with the search text in an encrypted field, it includes that document in the results — even though you may not be able to read the document.

- ✔ **Exclude words in Stop Word file:** tells Notes that you want every word in all documents included in the index. If you select this option, you can search all your documents for such strategically important words as "the," "my," "a," "an," and so on. It's a space hog and usually a waste of time.

The last two choices have to do with how Notes deals with individual words:

- ✔ **Word breaks only:** just makes a list of all the words in a document.

- ✔ **Word, sentence and paragraph:** makes it possible to find words in a document even when they're in the same paragraph or sentence as other words in a search. This feature tells Notes to remember not only the word: but where it occurs. Space hog!

We didn't get into word and paragraph breaks when talking about setting search criteria because that gets a bit complicated. A search formula you write to take advantage of sentence and paragraph breaks looks like this:

```
("gold" sentence "silver") paragraph "diamonds"
```

Here we look for the words "gold" and "silver" in the same sentence and in the same paragraph as "diamonds." In this formula, the words sentence and paragraph are not text the search is looking for; rather, they're actually part of a search formula.

If the database is on a workstation, you must answer one more question before you start the indexing process. The question appears in Figure 18-9, and the answer is usually "Yes, of course I want to create the index now, that's why I did all the keystrokes and made all the selections."

Notes just wants to remind you that, if this is a workstation-based database, you'll have to index it manually whenever you need the index updated. This questions is Notes' subtle way of reminding you.

Add this to your daily chores: maintaining the index

Creating an index takes a while because Notes has to index every single document in the database that first time. The good news is that updating the index after that first time won't take so long because Notes only has to update the index to reflect the changes (new, deleted, and edited documents) that have occurred since the last time you updated the index.

Figure 18-9:
Choose <u>Y</u>es
to create
the index.

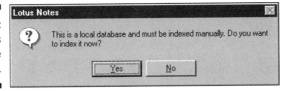

You can get an idea of how long the process will take, or at least how necessary it is, by clicking the Count unindexed documents button on the Full Text tab of the Database InfoBox. In Figure 18-10, you can see in the middle of the page that there's only one unindexed document. That's not too bad. You may decide not to bother updating the index because it's not too out-of-date. On the other hand, you may decide to go ahead with the update because the process won't take very long for just one document. It's your call.

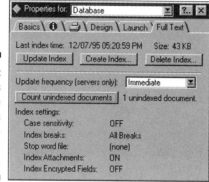

Figure 18-10:
This
database
contains
only one
unindexed
document.

If the indexed database is on a Notes server, maintaining the index is a job for your administrator. That's one less thing you have to worry about! Your administrator controls the frequency with which Notes updates the index — whether it's instantly, hourly, or daily. The more often the update, the slower the server will be, so you might have to do some negotiating (or resort to bribery) to get your administrator to agree to an index that updates the instant that the database changes.

On the other hand, if the database is on your workstation, *you* have to update the index. On the Full Text page of the Database InfoBox, click the Update Index button.

If you decide that you don't need a database to be indexed after all, click the Delete Index button. Why would you want to do that? Perhaps because you're running out of disk space or you simply never do a search for text and so don't want the index. These reasons aside, an index is a handy thing to have around.

Part VI

The Part of Tens

The 5th Wave   By Rich Tennant

"Hey-who created this full moon icon?"

In this part...

You've got your ten small toes to wiggle in the sand, ten idle fingers snap at your command, now you've got a bunch of chapters that present ten (more or less) groups of things we thought you would find useful, or interesting, or perhaps even necessary.

Don't consider these chapters to be frills, icing on the cake, or lace on the shirt-front of life. No, these chapters are the result of hours and hours of list making on the part of the authors, and we'd like to think that you will be glad we included the information.

Chapter 19

Ten Features New to Notes Release 4 and Useful to You

. . . .

. . . .

*E*very time a company releases another version of its product, that new release contains new features (otherwise, why bother with all the work and hype?) with the possible exception of boxes of laundry detergent that scream, "New and Improved!" We doubt that anyone honestly thinks you'll do a load of laundry and see some improvement over all the loads of laundry you did with that old stuff.

Lotus Notes Release 4 truly is *New! Improved!* But how, exactly, is it different from the previous version of the program? This chapter lists some of the improvements the crafty geniuses back at Lotus have made to Lotus Notes. Lotus would undoubtedly list many more such new-and-improved features, but this chapter consists mainly of the features that we, as regular folks, are most likely to appreciate and use.

Setting the Location

You probably work in several different places, and you may also have a different computer at many of those places. One such location, of course, is the office, where you work on the network; another is at home, where you may be connected to the office via a modem; you may also work in other places where your computer is generally not connected to the network or a phone line, such as in your car. (Have you noticed that more and more drivers seem to think that computing, combing their hair, and talking on the phone are the primary reasons for being in the car and that driving — especially if it actually involves looking out the front window — is nothing more than a rude interruption?)

With the earlier version of Lotus Notes, you had to perform a bunch of commands to tell Notes that you were at the office with your laptop and that, therefore, it could connect directly to the network without using the modem. Then you had to tell Notes that you were in a hotel, and you first had to dial 9 and then wait before dialing the office number. And then you had to tell Notes where your mail file was located, and so on. In other words, every time you worked in a new place, you had to put off getting any work done until you told Notes about your surroundings.

No more. Now you can define a series of *locations* so that such factors as the location of your mail database, the number you need to call to connect to the office, whether you're hooked up to the network, what port you're using, and what you had for dinner can all be defined in advance. Just click the location section in the Status bar to see the list of locations shown in the example in Figure 19-1, select the name of the place where you are currently working — and then get to work!

Figure 19-1:
Using the
Status bar
to choose
a new
location.

You define each of these locations yourself by choosing File➪Mobile➪Locations and then editing an existing (or creating a new) location document. In Figure 19-2, we're editing our Home location document (with fictitious information — in case anyone steals your book and tries to use our calling-card number).

For more information on location documents, read Chapter 15.

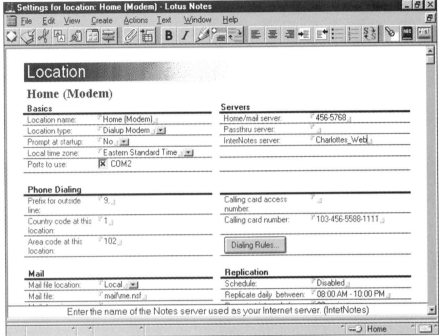

Figure 19-2:
This screen
shows the
(fictitious)
information
for a home
location.

My, How the View Has Improved!

Take a look at Figure 19-3 and notice the following features, all new to Release 4
of Notes. If you're a veteran user of Release 3, you can tell at a glance that
you're seeing a *big* change.

- ✔ Alternate rows are *colored* so that your eyes won't stray from one row into
  the next. (If you ever looked up someone's name in the phone book and
  then moved your gaze to the next line by accident while seeking the phone
  number, you know how valuable such an aid is in helping you stay focused
  on the correct line.)

- ✔ The first column contains a little *double arrowhead*, indicating that you can
  re-sort the column — in other words, you can put it in reverse alphabetical
  order.

- ✔ The *vertical line* indicates that you are taking advantage of your new
  option to change the width of columns (thoughtfully provided by the
  generous view designer). Not every column can be resized — only those
  the designer designates as resizable. (Now what would you pay for this
  handy program? A thousand dollars? Ten thousand? But wait — there's
  more!)

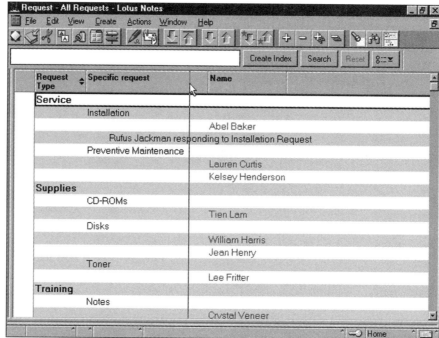

✔ The first column heading has the word "Request" on one line and "Type" on the other, showing that you can have multiline rows in the heading and in the view. You can even tell Notes to give the row just enough lines to show all the data . . . and no more.

For more information about using these exciting features in views you create, see Chapter 11.

Electronic Manila Folders

Views are great — no question about it. Yet views do offer one problem: You can't decide what goes in them, so a view may contain lots more stuff than you want. Unfortunately, the only way to get a document *out* of a view is to delete the document from the database. And that's a bit of a problem — first, because you probably can't delete documents from a database (few people have the right to do that), and second, because, even if you could, deleting a document permanently from a database just because you don't want to see it in a view is a *bit* heavy handed, don't you think?

Folders (one of the cool new features of Notes Release 4), which look much like views, let you put documents into them and take the same documents back out again. So, if you have a bunch of documents in a database that all relate to a particular subject, just create a folder (or use an existing one) and click and drag whatever documents you want into it. After you no longer need a document in a folder, you can simply remove the document without deleting it from the database.

For more information on folders, see Chapter 5 (for how to create and use folders in your e-mail database) or Chapter 9 (for general folder-holder tips).

My Opinion — in Flaming Red

Your task, should you decide to accept it, is to read a plethora of documents in a Notes database and add your comments. The problem is that, if you write your comments right in the text, no one can distinguish what *you* wrote from what the original author wrote.

In Release 3, every time you wrote a comment, you had to click a load of SmartIcons and menu items to change font, color, and other characteristics of your text so that it would stand out. And you had to take these steps for *every* comment you made. Pretty soon, you'd probably stop making comments entirely (which would be a tragedy for everyone). So how does Release 4 remedy the situation?

 Introducing — ta *daaaa!* — the *Permanent Pen*. You, the person making the comment, define how you want your words to look — red, bold, italics, 15-point, Times New Roman — and assign those characteristics to the Permanent Pen. Then you click anywhere in the document to position the cursor, click the Permanent Pen SmartIcon, and write your comment. Your comment magically appears in the special characters you chose and stands out from the surrounding text. It's just that easy.

For more information about the Permanent Pen, see Chapter 12.

Go Ahead — Type-Ahead

In Release 3, you addressed a memo by typing people's names in the To:, cc:, and bcc: fields, and if the names you entered weren't exactly right, you received a heartfelt greeting from Notes suggesting that you either pick from a list of possible alternatives or try on your own to find the correct name of one or more addressees. This if-at-first-you-don't-succeed method of addressing memos could potentially become very time consuming.

Now, compliments of the Name and Address Book, you can start to type a person's name, and, as soon as Notes recognizes the name, it *types ahead* and finishes the name for you — and does it right the first time.

If your type-ahead feature isn't working, check the Mail section of your location document. There, you have three choices: Disabled, Personal N & A Book only, and Personal then Public.

And Now, Showing in a Pane Near You . . .

The division of the Notes screen into *panes* is new, improved, and more convenient. You can now display the *Preview pane.* Unfortunately, this pane doesn't appear automatically; you must choose View⇨Document Preview from the menu bar to access it. Then you can highlight a document in a view and review its contents in the Preview pane without actually opening the document. If you've been counting, you probably noticed that, once you've enabled the Preview pane, viewing the contents of a document involves one step: highlighting it. Compare that to closing one document, highlighting another in the view, and then opening the new one.

Taking Action against a Sea of Troubles

Also new to Release 4 is the *Action bar.* The Action bar is that strip of buttons appearing across the top of your screen. The Action bar's biggest claim to fame is that it lets you forego using the menus. Sometimes you just can't remember exactly which menu command to use for a certain task; the attractive and graphical Action bar solves this problem quite handily.

Notice the two buttons in the Action bar in Figure 19-4? One simply saves and closes the document; the other helps you add extra information to the document. This latter function is especially handy, because adding that information by other means involves remembering how to edit the document, what keys you press to use Keyword fields, and a bunch of other stuff you probably would rather not have to think about.

InfoBoxes — Chock-Full of Neat Things

 Once upon a time, if you wanted to make a series of changes to a paragraph or some selected text, you needed to click all over the place in the menu to find where all the different attributes were located. Now, however, InfoBoxes offer convenient places to change most — if not all — characteristics of whatever you highlight. Just place your cursor in a paragraph, for example, and then click the Properties SmartIcon. Poof! An InfoBox appears. Right there, on the tabbed pages, are all the paragraph attributes you can think of, as well as some you probably never thought of. Figure 19-5 shows an InfoBox for a paragraph.

Action bar

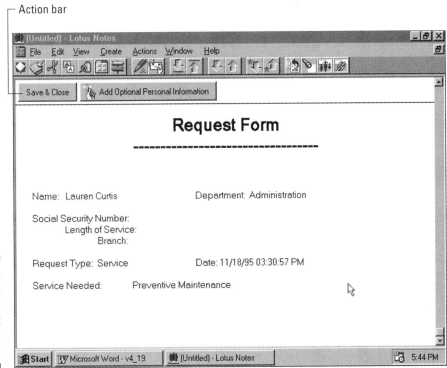

Figure 19-4:
The Action
bar for this
document
has two
buttons.

Figure 19-5:
This InfoBox
for Text
enables you
to change
all sorts of
attributes
of the
characters
and the
paragraph.

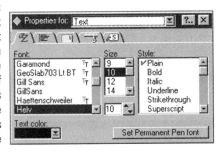

The InfoBox stays on-screen until you choose to dismiss it. So, if you highlight something else, such as a graphic, a button, or a field, you can change the properties of the newly selected item immediately.

Cruising the Web

When you get Notes Release 4, you also get — without additional cost and without any obligation whatsoever — the most convenient, the most handy, and the easiest-to-use Web cruiser imaginable. Yes, friend, you heard me right. Notes now has a *fully integrated, absolutely free* World Wide Web browser that works seamlessly with Lotus Notes. Now you can forward Web pages or documents, link them into a Notes document, or just cruise the Web without ever leaving Notes and without navigating through a lot of difficult commands to integrate Web data into Notes.

For more information on the Notes Web Navigator, see Chapter 16.

@Sum Thing New

This feature is so new, so revolutionary, that it's certain to be welcomed by database designers from all corners of the globe — at least it would be if the globe had corners. In Notes, one of the most difficult tasks facing database designers is writing formulas. Some formulas are easy to write; others are killers. The whole job, however, is much easier now because of a group of preprogrammed functions that you can paste right into formulas. These functions are called, aptly enough, *@functions*.

In Release 3, right near the top of the list of formulas everyone hated to write, was one formula that added multiple values in one field. You could tell whenever someone was writing one of these formulas, because the hapless writer had empty coffee cups all around his desk, and the poor creature would sometimes not go home for days at a stretch. And the monitor screen was full, from top to bottom, with thousands of strange little characters.

Several new @functions are available in Release 4. We don't talk much about them in the rest of this book because @functions are mainly used by database designers, and this book is mainly for users. The reason we mention this feature here is because you may someday become a database designer, and then you may regard the addition of @functions to Lotus Notes as very good news. Even if you don't plan to design a database, and even if the preceding paragraphs don't make a bit of sense to you, whenever someone asks you about the new features in Release 4, you can simply raise one eyebrow just a little, sniff, and say significantly, "Well, you know, they've added @Sum." (By the way, you pronounce that *at sum*.)

Chapter 20

Ten (Okay, Nine) Cool Tricks to Impress Your Friends

. . . .

In This Chapter

▶ Close windows in a flash

▶ Check for new documents in just one step

▶ Privatize a document

▶ Make new music when your e-mail arrives

▶ Tell Notes to send e-mail replies for you while you're away

▶ Create your own letterhead

▶ Tell Notes to pipe down

▶ Add additional addresses to your Address book

▶ Use the function keys

. . . .

*I*f you *really* want people to think you that know what you're doing, read this chapter to discover the ten best secret tricks Notes has up its sleeve.

Close the Window — Faster

Whenever you want to close a document or view, pressing the Escape key is faster than choosing File➪Close. If you've been editing or composing the document in the window, don't worry, Notes asks whether you want to save the document before dismissing it from the screen.

You can also double-click the right mouse button to close a window (except on a Macintosh), just as you could in Release 3, but you must enable that feature first. (To enable the capability to close a window by double-clicking the right mouse button, choose File➪Tools➪User Preferences and then, under Advanced options: in the User Preferences dialog box, click the option that reads `Right double-click closes window.`

Press Tab to Check for New Documents

If you're in the workspace (in other words, if you don't have any windows open), you can press Tab to start checking each database on your workspace for new documents. Pressing Tab at the workspace is really just a shortcut for choosing Edit⊏ᐣUnread Marks⊏ᐣScan Preferred.

Make a Document Private

If you're composing a document in a database on a server, you can decide that you want only certain people to see the document. By creating a *Read Access List,* you can be very specific about the names of the people who get to read your contribution. Your fellow users who open the database but whose names are *not* in your Read Access List cannot see your document at all. In fact, they can't even find the document in the view!

To make a document available to only a subset of the people who can use the database, follow these steps:

1. **Press Alt+Enter to activate the InfoBox for the document you are composing.**

2. **Click the page tab that has a picture of a key.**

3. **Deselect All readers and above.**

4. **Click the icon at the right (the one that looks like a silhouette) to select from the Name and Address Book those people whom you are enabling to read your document.**

Make sure that you include your own name in the Read Access list; otherwise, you won't be able to read the document yourself.

If you know your document will replicate to another Notes server, you must also include the name of the server in the list of "people" who can read the document.

Change the Music That You Hear When You Get New E-Mail

If you use Windows, you can have Notes play a WAV file to tell you when new e-mail has been delivered instead of using the boring old "beep beep beep" message. To tell Notes to play your special tune, add the following line to your NOTES.INI file, substituting the appropriate filename and path for the WAV file that you want to hear:

NewMailTune=c:\windows\tada.wav

To hear this change, you must have a speaker on your computer that can play music. Assuming that you do, prepare for a real symphonic delight!

NOTES.INI is an ASCII file full of configuration information, and it's (usually) located in your Windows subdirectory. You can edit it by using either the Windows Notepad or SysEdit program.

The bad news: If you don't use Windows, you can't perform this neat trick. Sorry!

Automatically Reply to Incoming Messages while You're on Vacation

If you expect to be out of the office for a while, and you won't be checking your mail by modem, you can instruct Notes to automatically send a form letter to people who send you messages, telling them that you're on vacation, won't be back for a couple of weeks, will respond to their message then, and so on.

To get Notes to send automatic e-mail replies, open your mail database, and choose Actions➪Mail Tools➪Out of Office, and then fill out the form that appears on-screen.

After you return from your vacation, remember to choose the Actions➪Mail Tools➪Out of Office command again to access the form you need to turn off your automatic replies.

Check out Chapter 7 for more information about this and other advanced mail options.

Change Your Letterhead

Have you noticed all those pretty pictures and graphics at the top of your e-mail messages? You can pick any of these — and more — for your e-mail from a big, long list of exciting and attractive designs. Won't your friends be jealous when they see your pretty messages? Why, you'll be the talk of the entire block. . . .

To change your letterhead, open your mail database, and choose Actions⇨Choose Letterhead. From the list, select the picture that best expresses your own individual personality and *joie de vivre* and then click the Done button on the Action bar.

Turn Off New E-Mail Notifications

This trick won't necessarily wow your coworkers, but it may make you much more popular if you work under, shall we say, *crowded* conditions. If, every few minutes, someone's computer plays that catchy little tune signifying that they have new mail, the office can sound like a nursery full of little kids playing those annoying toy pianos.

To silence the constant "beep beep beep" signal that Notes uses to alert you that new e-mail has been delivered, choose File⇨Tools⇨User Preferences, and then click the Mail button. After the mail page appears, click the box next to the Check for new mail every [ ] minutes option. You can always change your mind later and turn on this option again if you decide that you miss those "beep beep beep" alerts.

Automatically Add People to Your N&A Book

If you receive an e-mail from someone with a particularly nasty and hard-to-remember e-mail address (usually from the Internet), select or open the message and then choose Actions⇨Add Sender to Address Book. Notes automatically adds the person's name to a Person document in your personal Name and Address Book. That way, you don't need to remember the address; Notes remembers it for you. After you use the Actions⇨Add Sender to Address Book command, your new friend is in the list.

Use the Function Keys

Table 20-1 lists the Function key commands you can use in Notes for Windows and OS/2.

Table 20-1	Function Keys
Key	*Windows and OS/2*
F1	Open context-sensitive help
F2	Enlarge text to next available point size
Shift+F2	Reduce text to next available point size
F3	Go to next selected document
Shift+F3	Go to previous selected document
F4	Go to next unread document
Shift+F4	Go to previous unread document
Alt+F4	Exit Notes
F5	Lock ID
Alt+F5	Restore Notes program window to default size
Ctrl+F6	Cycle through open windows
F7	Indent first line in a paragraph
Shift+F7	Outdent first line in a paragraph
F8	Indent entire paragraph
Shift+F8	Outdent entire paragraph
F9	Update all fields in current document, view, or workspace
Shift+F9	Rebuild all views in current document, view, or workspace
Ctrl+F9	Minimize active window and cascade other active windows
Ctrl+F10	Maximize all open Notes windows
Alt+F10	Maximize the Notes program window (OS/2 only)
F10 or Alt	Access Menu

Chapter 21

Ten Things You Should Never Do

In This Chapter

▶ The ten worst things you can do when using Notes

▶ The reasons why you should never, ever do them

▶ What to do if you've already blown it

*U*sually, we encourage you to be adventurous, try new things, check out menus that you've never used before, and generally live on the edge of life. But, just as the nascent mycologist has to learn to eschew certain dangerous and poisonous mushrooms in favor of the edible ones, you need to know about the ten things in Notes that you should never, ever do.

Don't Change Your Notes Name

Maybe you just changed your name. Maybe you just got married and you're going to start hyphenating your name with your spouse's — from now on, it's "Bill Rodham-Clinton." Or maybe you have to change your name because you got a new job at your company — instead of "George Parker/Consulting/Acme," now it's "George Parker/Support/Acme."

Of course, you want your name in Notes to change, too, so that the new messages you send and the new documents you compose have your new name.

As tempting as it may be, you should never, ever choose File⇨Tools⇨User ID⇨More Options⇨Change Name. If you do (and you won't, because we told you not to, right?), you will be able to change your name, but in the process you'll lose all your certificates.

If you've never even heard of *certificates* before, prepare to learn all about them real quick if you change your name, because, without a certificate, you will no longer be able to access any of your company's Notes servers.

If you really want to change your Notes name, you should choose File➪Tools➪ User ID➪More Options➪Request New Name. This way, your administrator can change your name but make sure that you don't lose your certificates.

If it's too late, because you already did choose File➪Tools➪User ID➪More Options➪Change Name, your only recourse is to call your administrator. There isn't anything *you* can do to fix the problem.

Don't Delete Your E-mail Database

You probably have Manager Access to your e-mail database. That's good, because you want to be able to customize your mail forms, change the way your folders work, and generally do anything you want to your e-mail database. But it can also be bad, if you're not careful, because as Manager, you can use the File➪Database➪Delete command to completely, totally, irreversibly, forever, we're not kidding here, delete your *entire* mail database. And when we say entire database, we mean it; this command will delete every last e-mail message!

So *don't delete your e-mail database!*

If it's too late and you've already deleted your e-mail database, call your administrator. Be prepared to grovel, and hope that your administrator has a back-up copy.

Don't Save or Send a Message without Spell-Checking It First

As the olde saying goze, yOu oneley have one chanse to maik a good furst impresssion — so don't blow it by e-mailing or posting documents that are full of typos. What excuse do you have for sending e-mail with spelling errors when you can always use Edit➪Check Spelling to correct your errors? Shame on you!

Don't Remove Your Password

Passwords are important in Notes for two reasons:

✔ First, you don't want anyone else to read your e-mail, and you don't want the casual passerby to sit down at your desk and compose a few messages (full of four-letter words) under your name, right?

✔ Second, you have an obligation to your company not to let anyone use your USER.ID. If someone from your company's competition gets his hands on your USER.ID, that person can act as you — in fact, as far as Notes is concerned, he *is* you. So that nasty person can read all the company's confidential databases that only you are supposed to be able to access.

So don't even consider removing your USER.ID's password. As long as your USER.ID has a password, someone could steal your computer, but you (and the rest of your company) wouldn't have to worry about the thief getting any unauthorized access.

If it's too late and your (un-password-protected) USER.ID has been compromised, you should contact your administrator *immediately*.

If your USER.ID came without a password, you should set one *right now* by choosing File⇨Tools⇨User ID⇨Set Password.

Don't Forget to Press F5 When You Go to Lunch

Did you read the previous section? The same security concerns apply to an unattended Notes workstation, even when your USER.ID does have a password. So, before you leave your workstation unattended, remember to always press F5. That way, scoundrels trying to use your computer will be prompted for your password, and they'll be locked out when they can't give it.

Don't Let Temp Files Pile Up

Notes has a problem that can cause it to fill up your hard disk with temporary files. It puts temporary files on your hard disk whenever you launch an attached file. Sometimes Notes remembers to delete these files when you're done with them, and sometimes it doesn't. If you find any of these files lying around, you can *always* delete them to recover some valuable hard-disk real estate.

Every once in a while — maybe once a month — you should look in your Windows program directory, your Notes data directory, and your TEMP directory for files whose filename begins with a tilde (which looks like this: ~), or whose extension is TMP. If you find 'em, you can delete 'em.

Don't Forget to Consult the Manuals

Sure, we know, everybody hates to read computer manuals, but the Notes manuals really aren't as bad as some. They're not exactly the most exciting things you'll ever read, but they do contain useful, even vital, information about how to use the program.

So, when you're stumped, consider a perusal of your nearest set of Notes documentation. As they say in the computer business, when all else fails, RTFM. (That stands for **R**ead **T**he **F**lippin' **M**anual.)

Don't Forget to Save Early and Often

Notes is like any computer program; unexpected power interruptions can be tragic. It's important to get into the habit of saving your work early and often. You can choose File➪Save, use the Save SmartIcon, or just press Ctrl+S.

Don't Forget to Switch Back to the Proper Location When You Return to the Office

If you use the same computer when you travel as you do in the office, you know to use File➪Mobile➪Choose Current Location to have Notes accumulate your outgoing mail until you make a phone call to your home server.

Don't forget to use File➪Mobile➪Choose Current Location when you plug your computer back into the network upon your return to the office. Otherwise, your outgoing e-mail will never leave your workstation; it'll just keep piling up in your workstation's MAIL.BOX.

Refer to Chapter 15 for more information about using Notes while traveling.

Don't Talk to Strangers

And don't believe everything you read, either.

Chapter 22

Ten Neat Things You Can Buy for Notes

In This Chapter

▶ Some fun Notes extras that can make your life easier

▶ Where you can get these extras

*I*n addition to the core product, a number of Notes add-ons exist — some are called *Companion Products* — that you or your administrator can purchase for Notes.

The Lotus FAX Server

Lotus FAX Server is a program your administrator installs on a Notes server to enable you to send and receive faxes right from your e-mail. If someone wants to send you a fax, the person uses a regular fax machine to call your Notes server (instead of your fax machine), and the server converts the incoming fax to an e-mail message that you receive right along with your regular messages in your mail database. If you want to send a fax to someone (or fax any Notes document from any Notes database), you just send it as an e-mail message with a special address.

The Notes Pager Gateway

If you carry an alpha-numeric beeper, your administrator can buy and install a gateway from Lotus that sends your (specially addressed) e-mail messages right to your beeper. If you have the gateway installed at your company, you can also create agents that automatically forward the subject line of your incoming e-mail. Neato!

InterNotes

Although Notes automatically works as a World Wide Web navigator, Lotus also sells a product called InterNotes. This little jewel takes any Notes database and makes the documents in it available to non-Notes users via the WWW.

CompuServe

CompuServe has been providing dial-in services for years and has now started to make Notes servers available, too. For a fee, you can use your Notes work-station to call into these servers, where CompuServe has set up some public discussion databases. It's also a great way to be able use Notes mail between people at different companies. Additionally, CompuServe hosts a Lotus Notes-related forum where you can ask questions, get information, download data-bases, and generally talk to a bunch of Notes geeks. (The authors of this book have been known to put in an appearance there, too, but we're not geeks.)

If you subscribe to CompuServe, use **GO LOTUSCOMM** to access this forum.

WorldCom

WorldCom is a company that lets you use their Notes servers while paying for the amount of time you're dialed in to them. WorldCom offers lots of public discussion databases, Internet groups, and some news services (databases that get daily feeds from wire services) and is also a good way to send Notes mail to users who don't work at your company. WorldCom is a great place to ask people any questions that you have about using Notes, too.

If you want to really see what's going on with other Notes users around the world, consider subscribing. You can reach WorldCom in the United States at 800-774-2220.

A Mail Gateway

A mail gateway is a program that your administrator can buy and install that allows you to send e-mail to people who use other systems for their e-mail — cc:Mail, DaVinci, or even the Internet.

The Lotus Notes Network

LNN is a Notes-based news subscription service that's available for a yearly fee. You tell the service what kind of stories interest you — maybe you want information about certain products or business, your competitors, the World Wrestling Federation, and so on — and it scours a ton of news services from all around the globe and then sends you the results every day via Notes. Real state-of-the-art Information Superhighway stuff.

You can reach this service at 800-357-0051.

Memory

Like any program, Notes is happiest when it has lots of memory, so installing some more RAM can never hurt.

Phone Notes

Phone Notes is a program that does two things: It embeds a phone message in a Notes document, and it reads a Notes document to you over the telephone, using one of those cheesy computer-generated voices. It's still pretty neat, though. Imagine getting your phone mail messages sent to you as e-mail!

More Copies of This Book

We're sure you agree that no Notes workstation is complete without at least one copy of *Lotus Notes Release 4 For Dummies,* right?

Chapter 23

The Ten Most Common Problems

. . . .

In This Chapter

▶ The ten most common problems you (may) encounter while using Notes

▶ The ten easy ways to avoid the ten common problems

. . . .

*H*ey, you can't expect everything to work perfectly all the time, and Notes is no exception. In this chapter, we discuss the ten most common problems — and their ten matching solutions.

Your Laptop Doesn't Connect to Your Server

Problem: You're trying to use Notes remotely, but every time you try to make a call, you get an error message that says `Modem could not connect dial tone`.

Solution: Did you know that two kinds of telephone lines exist? One is called *analog,* and the other is *digital.* You don't need to know the difference between the two — you do need to know, however, that Notes (and any computer program, for that matter) can use only analog lines with its modem. If you get the aforementioned error message as you try to call in, the problem may be that the phone line you've plugged into the modem is digital instead of analog. Most offices (and many hotel rooms) are equipped with digital lines, and that causes all kinds of problems for Notes.

The bottom line is that you must find an analog line to use your modem with Notes. It figures that you can't tell the difference between an analog line and a digital one just by looking at the jack in the wall, doesn't it? You'll probably need to ask someone. Good luck explaining this to most hotel operators!

If all else fails, you can plug your modem into the phone line being used for the closest fax machine, because fax machines use analog lines, too.

You Can't Edit a Field

Problem: You're trying to compose (or perhaps edit) a document, and you can't edit a particular field. You've tried the arrow keys, the Tab key, and even the mouse, but you can't even get the cursor into the field.

Solution: This problem is one for your administrator (less likely) or the database designer (more likely) to solve. Notes has many security features, and they're all under the control of the designer and administrator. Call one or the other of them and explain the problem. The one you call can offer a solution.

You Can't Use a DocLink

Problem: You double-click a DocLink icon, but you can't open the target document.

Solution: Tell the person who composed the document in the first place. Most likely, that person created a DocLink to a document that's in a database on a server that you don't have access to.

Your Server Isn't Responding

Problem: You double-click a database icon, but in response see the error message `Server (servername) is not responding,` or `Network operation did not complete in a reasonable amount of time,` or perhaps `Remote system is no longer responding.`

Solution: Each of the above error messages indicates a network problem, over which you have no control. (*Your* job isn't to keep the servers in good working order!) As is often the case, the solution to this problem begins with a call to your administrator.

You Don't Have the Right Certificate

Problem: Whenever you try to access a server, you see the error message `Your ID has not been certified to access the server.`

Solution: Call your administrator and explain the problem.

You Can't Open a Database

Problem: Whenever you try to use a particular database, you see the error message You are not authorized to access that database.

Solution: Once again, call your administrator and report that the Access Control List is incorrect for the database in question.

Call the Access Control List the "ACL" when you talk to your administrator to sound as though you know what you're talking about.

You Can't Use Full Text Search

Problem: You are trying (unsuccessfully) to create a new Full Text Index.

Solution: If the database that you're trying to index is on a Notes server, the problem is usually that your administrator has set up the server not to allow Full Text Indexes. Indexes take up lots of disk space, and sometimes administrators get stingy.

You Can't Delete a Document That You Composed

Problem: You composed a document in a database, and now you want to delete it — but you can't, no matter how many times you press Delete.

Solution: Call your administrator and/or the database designer and ask the one you reach to check that the database is properly recording author names in the documents and that the Access Control List enables you to delete documents.

You Can't Launch an Object

Problem: You double-click an embedded object's icon, but you can't get the other program to load.

Solution: To open an embedded object, you must have installed on your computer the program that was used to create the object in the first place. If the object is an embedded Lotus 1-2-3 worksheet, but you don't have 1-2-3 installed on your computer, you *cannot* launch or edit that object. (You may also need to install a newer version of Notes; contact your administrator, who knows what to do.) Even if you don't have the program necessary to launch an object, you should be able to view it — just select View instead of Launch in the Object dialog box.

You Don't Know Who Your Administrator Is

Problem: You've read this book, and it seems that everytime we discuss a potential problem, we use the "Call your administrator" cop-out. The problem is that you don't know who that is!

Solution: Ask your manager or someone else in your office, or consider changing jobs so that *you're* the administrator — and then call yourself.

Part VII
Appendixes

"He may not type so fast, but boy can he remember those hotkeys!"

In this part...

The term *appendix*, an anatomically useless yet troublesome vestige of some forgotten stage in the development of humans, seems a poor label for such a valuable section of a book. The appendix about installing Notes, for example, is not useless, and ignoring it may be more troublesome than reading it. The descriptions of the Notes templates may save you hundreds of hours of work if you decide to create a database. The tips for remote use and those for Macintosh users are too valuable to be ignored, and the glossary is as complete a list of useful Notes terminology as you'll find this side of the Orinoco River. So we don't think that the following chapters should be called *appendixes* (or even appendices, for the sophisticated).

However, if we named them after some more valuable organ, like the kidney or the brain, no one would know what they were, and a statement, like "Please refer to Kidney B in the back of the book," would sound really strange. So the next section of the book contains (gulp) the appendixes. . . .

Appendix A
Installing a Notes Workstation

• •

1 f you don't have Notes installed on your computer, this appendix had better be one of the first things you read, even though it's near the end of the book. The information here is for installing Notes as a *workstation,* or *client.* (If you are a Notes administrator planning to install Notes as a server, many large tomes full of complicated technical information are available for you to use, all of which you get when you buy Notes.) The purpose of this appendix is to hold your hand and guide you as you sit blinking before flashing screens and bewildering options, afraid that making the wrong choice may cause your computer to burst into flames.

Although we hope this appendix contains everything you need to know about installing Notes, anytime you want more information about a choice, click the Help box to get specific, helpful, warm, friendly advice. Whenever there's even the slightest chance you may need help while you're installing, a button labeled Help appears somewhere in the current dialog box.

Installing Notes as a workstation is no more complicated than installing any other software (which doesn't necessarily mean that the process is easy); the trick is understanding the choices you need to make.

1. **Find the disks or CD-ROM labeled "Lotus Notes."**

   Note: The disk or CD-ROM may also be labeled "Client Install."

   Make sure that the disk or CD-ROM is appropriate for the platform onto which you are installing Notes: Macintosh, Windows, UNIX, or OS/2. If in doubt, ask your Notes administrator.

2. **Insert the Lotus Notes / Client Install disk in the disk drive (or CD-ROM in the CD reader) and start the install program.**

   To install in Windows, choose Run⇨Install. Depending on whether you're using a disk or a CD-ROM, and depending upon whether your computer runs Windows 3.1, Windows 3.11 for Workgroups, Windows NT, Windows 95, or UNIX, you may need to select from several subdirectories the appropriate program for your operating system. Check with your Notes administrator or the information supplied with the disk or CD-ROM.

   To install in Macintosh, close all open applications, insert the Notes Install disks, and then double-click the Install Lotus Notes icon.

3. **When you get the heartfelt Welcome screen, type your name and your company's name (see Figure A-1). Then click Next> to go to the next screen.**

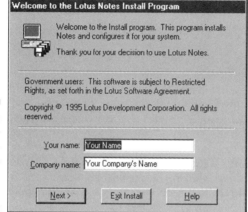

Figure A-1:
The friendly
introductory
screen for
Notes
installation.

4. **Click Next> to reveal a second dialog box confirming that you spelled your name and your company's name correctly (see Figure A-2).**

    If you did, choose Yes; if you did not, choose No to go back and fix the spelling. (We told you this stuff would be tricky!)

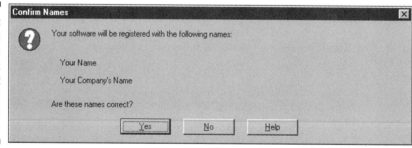

Figure A-2:
The Confirm
Names
dialog box
ensures that
you spelled
everything
correctly.

Any time you think you goofed or you want to change a choice you made earlier, you can choose <Previous to go back through the install dialog boxes. If you're satisfied with progress so far, click Next> to continue.

5. **After mastering the Confirm Names dialog box, you move on to the Install Options dialog box, shown in Figure A-3, where you get to decide what you want to install.**

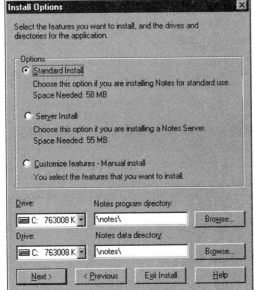

Figure A-3:
In the Install
Options
dialog box,
you decide
what to
install and
where.

You have the following three choices: Standard Install, Server Install, or Customize features - Manual Install. Our advice is to stick with the first choice, Standard Install, because this option allows the experts back at Lotus to decide what to install. Definitely do *not* choose Server Install — first, because nothing in this appendix can help you figure out what to do next, and, second, because users do not install servers for their own personal use.

You may choose Customize features - Manual Install if you need to conserve disk space, because Notes takes a lot of disk space (it tells you right in the dialog box how much). By selecting only the parts you want installed, you can cut down on the amount of disk space Notes uses.

6. If you have several hard disks, choose the one with the largest amount of available disk space in the Drive and Drive drop-down lists.

Notes takes up more space on your hard disk as time goes by. Several files grow like weeds the more you use Notes. Remember that if install says Notes is using 55MB of your hard disk space, and you have only 55,000,001 bytes free, you'll be hurtin' for certain real soon.

You may wonder what in the world is the difference between Drive and Drive, besides the underlined letter. The first refers to the drive and directory where the Notes *program files* are placed; the second refers to the place where the *data files* are kept. (The distinction between program and data files is not important to us. The distinction *is* fascinating to those who reconfigure their CONFIG.SYS files on Saturday nights for fun and excitement.) The best bet is to accept the Notes defaults, unless you are running out of disk space and need to separate the two sets of files.

7. Click the button next to the choice you want and click Next>.

If you decide on the Standard Install (wise choice), skip on to Step 9; if you choose to Customize, go to Step 8.

8. Decide what you want to install and then click Next>.

Your choices appear in the Customize dialog box, shown in Figure A-4.

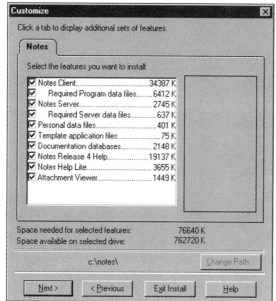

Figure A-4:
Customize your Notes installation by choosing only the features you want to install.

Click the boxes next to the features you want to install on your hard disk. Make sure that the ones you want are selected and the ones you don't want are not selected. (Remember: an X in the box means that the item is selected.) The following list is a brief description of each group:

- **Notes Workstation:** You need these files to run Notes — that says it all. Without this group of files, you do not have Notes on your computer. Don't deselect this choice unless you like doing an install several times, you have already installed these files in an earlier install, or you are using a public network copy of Notes.

- **Notes Server:** You don't want these. Period, end of subject, have a nice day.

- **Personal Data Files:** These files are the ones that tailor Notes to your own personal use. Regardless of where you are installing Notes, you need these files. Deselect this group only if you are reinstalling Notes and know that the files already exist on your computer.

- **Template Application Files:** These are empty database shells that you can use as templates for databases you may choose to create later. Included are Customer Tracking, Correspondence, Discussion, Document Library, Mail, News, Service Request Tracking, Status Reports, Meeting Tracking, Reservation Scheduler, and Things To Do database templates. They are all described in Appendix B. You may want to deselect this group if you are sure that you don't intend to create your own databases and you want to save about 1MB of disk space.

- **Documentation Databases:** These are databases containing information about the following rather technical aspects of Notes, such as how to upgrade from previous releases, Notes administration, and how to install. (Think about that last one for a minute: You must install these files to get information about installing?!) You can probably do without these files.

- **Notes Release 4 Help:** If you are new to Notes, you ought to install this so that any time you run into unfamiliar territory, you can summon Help. This Help system may already be installed for all users on the network, in which case you don't need it on your own disk. You need to ask the Notes administrator about this one.

- **Notes Help Lite:** This Help system is for installations on computers where disk space is at a premium, such as on laptops. You don't need both Help and Help Lite, because the latter is a subset of the former.

- **Attachment Viewer:** This feature enables you to view files attached to Notes documents, even if you don't have the original application.

9. **Decide where you want the Notes icon to appear.**

Notes Install presents you with a list of program folders (groups) in which your operating system displays the Notes icon. (Figure A-5 shows the Windows 95 display.) Click your choice or create a New Folder, and then click Next>.

10. **Install those files.**

You now see the Begin Copying Files dialog box. This box may look like the one shown in Figure A-6 if you're using Windows 95, slightly different if you're using a different operating system. Close down any open applications, return to the dialog box, and click Yes to begin installing files on your hard disk.

Your work is almost done. If you are installing from disks, don't leave your computer; although Install does most of the rest of the work, it pauses occasionally to ask you to insert the next disk. Pop the requested disk into the disk drive, press Enter, and sink back into a reverie until you receive the next disk request. Helpful little screens appear showing you how the installation is progressing, touting the virtues of Release 4, and, in general, making you feel like an absolute genius for (1) deciding to use Notes and (2) actually managing to install it.

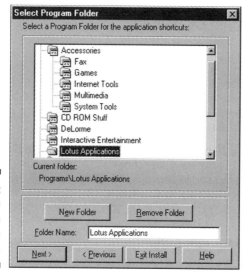

Figure A-5:
Decide here
where to
place the
Notes icon.

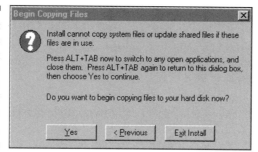

Figure A-6:
In this
dialog box
you set the
stage for the
transfer of
files to your
hard disk.

After the directories are all created, the files are transferred, and the icons
are in place, a message box like the one in Figure A-7 appears, congratulating
you on your accomplishment and your entry into the world of Notes users.

11. Because you're done, you can now click <u>D</u>one.

If your workstation is connected to a LAN (local area network), now's a good
time to read Chapter 2; otherwise, you should read Appendix C and then
Chapter 2.

Figure A-7:
When you
see this
message,
you're done.

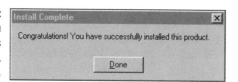

Appendix B
The Lotus Notes Database Templates

*W*hy reinvent the wheel? The time may come when you need to create a database for your own use, or (if you're a truly generous and helpful person) a database for lots of your coworkers to use. Databases come in many different flavors. Most are one-of-a-kind, created at a particular organization for some purpose unique to its function. However, some databases are put to use in many organizations.

The generous and helpful folks at Lotus determined the most common databases and created templates for them. Now, rather than people at every Notes-using company in the world starting to build a database from the ground up, they can simply retrieve a template, tailor it to their own needs, and alacazam — they're done.

If you want to use any of these templates, make sure that you install them during the Notes set-up process. While you are installing Notes, you see a list of file groups that you may install with Notes. The Template Application Files group is selected by default, so all you have to do is not deselect it. In other words, leave the X in the box next to Template Application Files, and Notes will install the templates.

If you already installed Notes and chose not to install the templates, start the install program again and select only the Template Application Files. See Appendix A for more information about installing Notes.

Putting the Templates to Work

To create a database using one of Notes' prefab templates, choose File⇨ Database⇨New. In the New Database dialog box shown in Figure B-1, select the template you want from the list box below the Template Server button, and then click on OK.

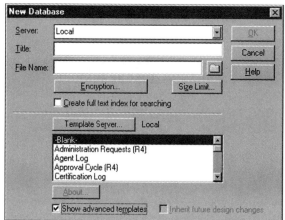

Figure B-1:
Use the
New
Database
dialog box to
choose a
template for
your new
database.

Click on the <u>A</u>bout button to see the About This Database document describing the template's use and design features. Select `Show advanced templates` to see more templates from which you can choose.

Here is a list and brief description of the more important database templates available in Notes. We don't describe all of them, because some are just used by Notes for its own working databases and are not really meant for regular folks like us.

Approval Cycle

A database created with this template allows you to build a standard approval cycle into any database, using a subform containing approval logic which you can add to forms in other databases, such as Purchase Requisitions, Time Sheets, and Expense Reports. This template also includes an agent to manage overdue approvals.

Discussion

A database created with this template allows workgroups to share their thoughts and ideas. This template allows the archiving of older documents, which in turn allows users to mail themselves document links to topics of interest automatically, using an *Interest Profile*.

Document Library

A database created with this template allows the creation of an electronic library for storing reference documents. This template includes a review cycle and archiving capabilities.

This template is also available for Lotus SmartSuite, Microsoft Office, and Novell PerfectOffice. Databases based on this template automatically launch, store, and support review cycles of documents created with suite products that include word processing and spreadsheet applications.

Personal Journal

A database created with this template allows creation of a database in which individuals can write and organize private ideas and documents, like a diary. This template includes graphic navigators and instructions for customizing the design.

Room Reservations

This template allows you to create a database that includes group schedules and tracks the use of conference rooms. You can also customize this database to track such shared resources as portable computers or audio/visual equipment.

Shared Template Components

This template allows you to create a database that you use primarily as a repository for design components that are inherited by several other standard application templates, such as Document Library and Discussion.

This template contains the following shared components:

- **Forms:** Archive Log, Archive Profile
- **Views:** Archive Logs, ($All), ($Profiles)
- **Agents:** Archive Selected Documents, Edit Archive Profile, Mark Document As Expired, Periodic Archive

Appendix C

Setting Up to Work
Away from the Office

● ●

*A*t the beginning of Chapter 2, we discuss the steps for starting Notes for the very first time, but we make one big assumption — that your computer was connected to the network.

In this appendix, we discuss what you do if the computer you use isn't connected to the network, either because you always use it away from the office (and connect to your Notes servers with your modem), or because it's a so-called *stand-alone* workstation that's never connected to a server.

Before You Start . . .

This appendix assumes that you have successfully installed the Notes program on your computer's hard disk and that you are ready to set it up for the first time. If that is not the case, stop right here and refer to Appendix A, and don't come back until you have the program installed!

This appendix is divided into two sections: "Setting Up a Remote Workstation" and "Setting Up a Stand-Alone Workstation." Read the first section if you are installing Notes on a computer that's going to occasionally connect to a Notes server via a modem. (Maybe it's the computer you have at home that you'll be using to dial in to your company's servers, or maybe it's a laptop that's connected to the network when you're at work, and connected to a modem when you're at home.) Read the second section if you are installing Notes on a computer that will never connect to a server.

Setting Up a Remote Workstation

When you start Notes for the very first time, you need to have some information handy that only your administrator knows. Call your administrator and ask for the answers to the following questions:

The Question	**The Answer**
What is my password?	( )
What is my exact User Name?	( )
What is the name of my Home Server?	( )
What is my Home Server's telephone number?	( )
What's my time zone?	( )
Do we follow Daylight Savings Time?	( )
What kind of modem do I have?	( )

When you start Notes for the first time ever, the program is smart enough to figure out that it has to set itself up, so you'll see the dialog box shown in Figure C-1.

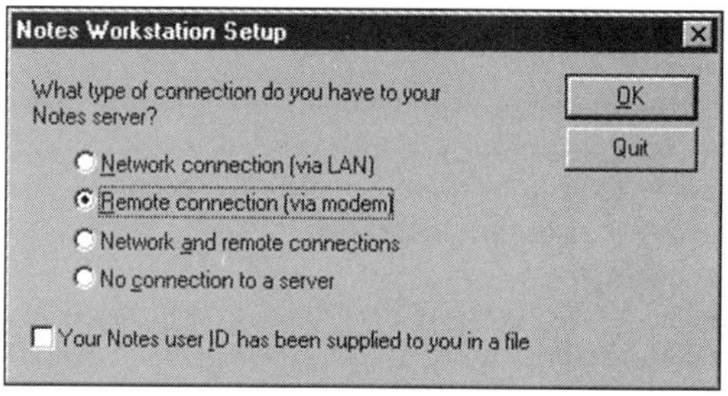

Figure C-1:
The Notes
Workstation
Setup
dialog box.

Because you are setting up remotely, choose Remote connection (via modem).

When you click OK in the Notes Workstation Setup dialog box, Notes presents you with another dialog box, shown in Figure C-2.

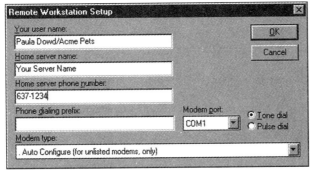

Figure C-2:
In this
dialog box,
fill in the
information
you got
from your
administrator.

Using the worksheet full of answers that you got from your administrator, fill in all the appropriate fields: your name, the server's name, and the server's telephone number.

You also have to tell Notes what kind of modem you have by choosing it from the Modem type: drop-down list.

If your modem's name is not in the list, choose the first one in the list (Auto Configure).

Use the Phone dialing prefix field if you have to dial 9 to get an outside line, or if you have to enter *70 (for push-button phones) or 1170 (for rotary phones) to disable Call Waiting. (The beep that Call Waiting uses to tell you that there's another call will wreak havoc when your computer's trying to call your server.)

Make sure that you have selected the correct Modem port — most likely, it's COM1, but some computers have the modem plugged into COM2.

When you click OK, Notes places a call to the server to get a copy of your mail database and to get your User ID. So make sure that your modem is connected to the computer, and that the power is turned on!

The last dialog box that you have to deal with during setup asks you about your time zone. Pick the appropriate time zone, tell Notes whether you observe EST (Eastern Standard Time — not ESP, Extra Sensory Perception), and click OK.

Once you've completed the call and answered the questions about time zones, the setup process is complete and you can begin to use the program. Congratulations and welcome to the wonderful world of Notes!

If you're new to Notes, refer to Chapter 2 to get more information about how to use the program in general. Refer to Chapter 14 for more information about using your new remote workstation.

Setting Up a Stand-Alone Workstation

When you start the program for the first time ever, Notes is smart enough to figure out that it has to set itself up, so you'll see the dialog box shown in Figure C-3.

Because you will not be connecting to a server, choose `No connection to a server`.

When you click <u>O</u>K, Notes presents you with another dialog box, shown in Figure C-4. Enter your name and click <u>O</u>K again. Notes creates a User ID for you and then asks about your time zone.

After answering the questions about your time zone, you're done! That wasn't so bad, was it? Refer to Chapter 2 for more about how to use the program.

Figure C-3:
You see this
dialog box
when you
start Notes
for the
first time.

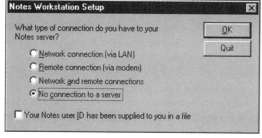

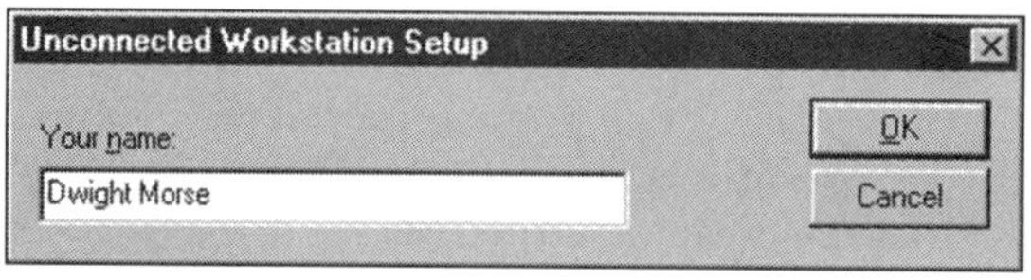

Notes Workstation Setup

What type of connection do you have to your
Notes server?   <u>O</u>K

                                                  Quit

○ <u>N</u>etwork connection (via LAN)
○ <u>R</u>emote connection (via modem)
○ Network <u>a</u>nd remote connections
◉ No <u>c</u>onnection to a server

☐ Your Notes user <u>I</u>D has been supplied to you in a file

Figure C-4:
Hey, good
looking,
what's *your*
name?

Unconnected Workstation Setup

Your <u>n</u>ame: <u>O</u>K

Dwight Morse   Cancel

Appendix D
Macintosh Tips

As they say at Lotus, "Notes is Notes is Notes," which is their (not-so-funny) way of saying that Notes is *cross-platform*. In other words, Notes works the same way regardless of your workstation's operating system. Using Notes on a Windows PC is no different from using Notes on a Macintosh — the commands are the same, the menus are the same, the colors are the same — everything is the same. Well, almost.

In this appendix, we explore the relatively few (and relatively insignificant) differences for Mac users. If you're not a Mac user, don't bother reading this appendix.

No Right Mouse Button

On a Windows PC, you use the right mouse button to bring up a context-sensitive shortcut menu. Bad news: there's no way to get that shortcut menu on your Macintosh. You're stuck using the regular menus.

Command instead of Ctrl

On a Windows PC, many of the menu commands have keyboard shortcuts — for example, to open a new database, you can choose File⊃Open Database or press Ctrl+O. Because Macintosh keyboards don't have a Ctrl key, you use the Command (⌘) key instead.

Command Key Combinations

While we're on the subject of the Command key, it's worth mentioning that many of the menu shortcuts are different on a Mac. For example, to close a document on a Windows PC you press Ctrl+F4, but on a Macintosh you press ⌘+W.

Don't worry — all the keyboard shortcuts are listed right in the menus.

Dialog Boxes

If you sometimes use Notes on a PC and you sometimes use Notes on a Mac, you'll notice small cosmetic differences between the dialog boxes and menus. These dialog boxes and menus work the same way; they just look a little different.

Notes Data Folder

On a Macintosh, all the modem command files, local databases, and so on are stored in a folder that's referred to as your Notes Data Folder. On a Windows PC, it's called your Local Data Directory. Same things, just different words.

NOTES.INI

Windows workstations have a file called NOTES.INI stored in the Windows subdirectory. On a Mac, the analogous file is called Notes Preferences and is stored in your Preferences folder.

No Underlined Menu Options

In Windows, you can choose an option from a menu by typing the underlined character — like the F in File or the O in Open Database. Mac menus don't have underlined characters, so you always have to choose options from a Mac menu with the mouse.

Balloon Help

To see SmartIcon hints on a Macintosh, you have to choose Help⇨ Show Balloons.

Appendix E

Glossary

@Function A formula element containing preprogrammed calculations that make writing a formula much easier. Examples are @Sum, @UserName, @Now. The following are not examples of @functions: 3 Doz @ $2.99, @ Home, @ Choo.

Accelerator key A keystroke combination used to accomplish the same thing as choosing a menu item. Ctrl+Z is the accelerator key for Edit⇨Undo.

Access Control List The part of every Notes database that determines who can do what in that database. See also *No Access, Depositor, Reader, Author, Editor, Designer,* and *Manager.*

ACL An abbreviation for Access Control List.

Actions Tasks which normally involve several keystrokes and which are assigned to buttons and/or a special menu, then associated with views, forms, and folders so you can easily perform them. Actions are what happen when you click buttons in the Action bar.

Administrator The person who is in charge of running the Notes servers at your company and to whom you should turn if you have questions or problems.

Agent A mini-program or set of instructions which automates tasks in Notes. (Formerly called *macros.*)

Application designer The person at your company who created the database(s) you use. Also known as *Database manager* and *Application manager.*

Application server (1) A Notes server that is only used for application databases — in other words, it does not have anybody's e-mail database on it. (2) A computer application used to create data linked or embedded into Notes documents.

Archive A special copy of a mail or another database containing documents selected for storage away from current active documents.

Archive Log A summary of the documents that have been put in an archive database.

Archive Profile A special form used to set the criteria for determining which documents should be put in an archive.

Attachment A file (Lotus 1-2-3 worksheet, Microsoft Word document, and so on) that has been included in a Notes document. You can only put attachments in a rich text field.

Author (1) The person who composed a document and (usually) the only person who can edit it or delete it. (2) A level of access you can have to a database. As an author, you can read documents, compose new documents, edit your own documents, and delete your own documents. (3) Someone like the fine people who wrote this book.

Balloon help The things that show you what each SmartIcon does.

Banyan The company that makes Vines.

Browse The official, more dignified term for surfing or cruising the Internet. Call it what you want; it means you're looking for information or just wandering around (electronically, of course) to see what there is to see.

Button A rectangular picture resembling a button which, when clicked with the mouse, launches some action or task.

cc:Mail Another program from Lotus Development Corporation that's used for e-mail. At many companies, some people use Notes for e-mail and other people use cc:Mail.

Certificate A special "stamp" for your USER.ID that your administrator gives to you. You have to have a certificate specific to your company to use the servers at your company.

Clipboard A section of memory used to hold something you have copied or cut, and plan to paste somewhere else.

Common name The part of your Notes User Name that sounds like what your mother calls you. For example, if your User Name is Stephen Londergan/Lotus, your common name is just Stephen Londergan.

Compound document A document containing information from more than one program.

Connection document A document in your personal Name and Address Book that tells your workstation when and how to call the server.

Database In Notes, a collection of Notes documents, folders, views, agents, and other design elements. In general, any organized collection of information.

Database template A shell of a database that you use as a starting point to create your own database. Saves you lots of work.

DDE Dynamic Data Exchange. A copy of a document created in another application and placed in a Notes document. It retains a link to the original document so that changes to the original are reflected in the copy.

Default A decision about an action or condition the program makes for indecisive users or users who have not expressed a specific preference. Default text color, for instance, is black.

Delivery report A return message that tells you when a message you sent was delivered to the recipient's mail database.

Depositor A level of access that you can have to a database. As a depositor, you can only add documents to a database. You cannot read, edit, or delete them.

Designer A level of access that you can have to a database. In addition to having all the rights that editors have, designers can change the database's forms and views.

DESKTOP.DSK The file on your workstation that keeps track of what databases are on your workspace and which documents in them you have already read.

DocLink An icon in one document that you can double-click to quickly go to a different document.

Document (1) An individual item in a Notes database. In other database programs, a document would be called a record. (2) A piece of paper with stuff written on it.

Domain (1) All the Notes servers at your company. (2) What a king is in charge of.

Editor A level of access that you can have to a database. Editors can read documents, compose documents, and edit documents, even if they didn't compose the documents in the first place.

Electronic signature A special, numeric code added to a document that proves it really was written by the person who sent it.

E-Mail An electronic mail message.

Embedded object Information included in a Notes document that came from another program. You can double-click an object to edit it, if you have the originating program on your computer.

Encryption A procedure in which a document or part of a document is scrambled, except when opened by a person who has the proper decryption key.

Encryption key The numeric code used to scramble and unscramble a document or part of a document.

Error message A dialog box that Notes shows when you make those all-too-frequent mistakes.

Export A way to turn Notes documents into files for use in other programs, like Lotus 1-2-3 or WordPerfect.

Fax A process of sending a picture of a document over a phone line. Didn't I hear the phone ringing? Just the fax, Ma'am.

Field A place in a database form for specific individual pieces of information. *First Name* might be a field in a personnel data form.

Folder A database element which lists documents in a database. You put documents in and remove documents from a folder.

Footer Text that appears at the bottom of every printed page.

Form What you use to compose, edit, and read documents.

Full Text Index Part of a database that locates words and phrases in all documents in a database so that you can later search for text in those documents.

Full Text Search Searching for text or phrases in documents in a database.

Gateway A special program that runs on a Notes server and converts Notes e-mail messages that are destined for other mail systems, such as the Internet, or even a fax machine.

Group A collection of users' names, defined in either the public or your personal Name and Address Book. Using group names saves having to type the individual names of people in a group when sending them e-mail.

Groupware Software that enables several people to work together on computers.

Header (1) Text that appears at the top of every printed page. (2) What you take when you fall over something.

Help document A special collection of tips about how to use a database.

Hierarchical name A User Name that includes not only your common name but also your organization and the level or department in that organization.

Home page Another name for a Web page. (You'll have to look that up near the end of this glossary).

Home Server The one and only Notes server that has *your* e-mail database on it.

Hotspot (1) A place where you shouldn't sit. (2) A location in a form or graphic, which, when clicked with the mouse, launches an action.

Icon A graphic used to represent a database, a program, or an action.

Import What you do when you want to turn a foreign file, like a Lotus 1-2-3 worksheet, into documents in a Notes database.

InfoBoxes Sometimes also called Property Boxes, they are dialog boxes usually containing several pages which allow you to change many aspects of the selected item (database, text, paragraph, field, spouse).

Input validation formula A formula included in a form that checks to be sure that you entered data in a field and that it's the right data type.

Install A process or program that places a usable copy of a program on a hard disk.

Internet A huge collection of computers that are all connected in a vast global network.

InterNotes A special Notes server that connects you to the Internet.

LAN An acronym for Local Area Network. Rhymes with "man." It's really just a bunch of wires that are used to connect your computer to other computers.

LAN workstation A computer that (1) has Notes installed on it and (2) is plugged into the network.

Letterhead Fancy graphics you can include in mail database forms.

License A right to use Notes. There are four types of Notes licenses: Server, Regular, Notes Mail, and Desktop.

Link A graphic representation in one document of another document, database, or view. Click the link to open the other document, database or view.

LMBCS Lotus Multi-Byte Character Set: A set of characters including standard keyboard characters and characters not found on keyboards.

LN:DI Abbreviation for a program called Lotus Notes Document Imaging. Pronounced *lindy,* this special program lets you include scanned images in a Notes document.

Location A name and accompanying data that defines the places where you use Notes, such as on the LAN at the office, on a modem at home, or not connected at all in the shower. *Locations* are defined in *location documents* in your personal N&A Book.

Lotus Notes The program that this book is about.

Macro A mini-computer program of Notes commands. This is the old name for what are now called *agents.*

Mail database The database that holds all your incoming and outgoing e-mail messages. No one but you can read the documents in your mail database.

Mail server A Notes server that has mail databases on it.

MAIL.BOX A special kind of Notes database that holds messages that are pending delivery.

Manager The highest level of access available for a database.

Modem Hardware that lets you use your Notes workstation to place a phone call to your Notes server. Useful if you need to read your e-mail and other Notes databases when you're at home or on a business trip.

Modem command file A special ASCII file that Notes needs to use a modem. Every brand of modem has its own modem command file.

Mycophile A fungus fancier.

Mouse A device that moves a pointer around your screen so you can make selections without using the keyboard.

N&A Book Name and Address Book. See *Personal N&A Book* and *Public N&A Book*.

Navigator (1) A program used to find Web pages on the Internet. Notes has a built-in Navigator. Navigators are also available from other companies including Microsoft, Netscape, and America Online. (2) A database element which substitutes graphics and associated commands for normal menu items, making use of a database more user friendly.

NetBIOS The most commonly used protocol for Notes. Pronounced *net-BYE-ose*.

Network A collection of computers that are connected by wires and that use a network operating system.

Network operating system A type of software used to connect computers. Some common network operating systems include Novell, Banyan, and Pathworks. Sometimes called NOS.

Newsletter A special memo which is automatically generated to notify users of new documents in a database.

NLM An operating system that's used only on some Notes servers but never on workstations.

No Access A level of access to a database. If you have No Access to a database, you can't use that database. Period!

NOS Acronym for *network operating system.*

Notes data directory The directory on your computer's hard disk that has your local databases, DESKTOP.DSK, and modem command files in it.

Notes data folder The folder on your Macintosh that has your local databases, DESKTOP.DSK, and modem command files in it.

Notes log A special Notes database that keeps track of all the phone calls you've made from your remote workstation — if you've made any, that is.

NOTES.INI An ASCII file on every Notes workstation that holds configuration information for that workstation.

Novell The most popular network operating system.

Object See *Embedded object.*

OLE Acronym for *Object Linking and Embedding*; it's that part of the operating system that lets you include information from other programs in a Notes document. Pronounced *OLAY.* See *Embedded object.*

OLE object See *Embedded object.*

Operating system The program that runs your computer. Notes runs with the Windows, OS/2, UNIX, and Macintosh operating systems.

OS/2 An operating system that you can use on Notes workstations and servers.

Page break A code you insert in a long document that instructs Notes to print subsequent text on a new sheet of paper. Normally page breaks are not visible.

Pane A section of a Notes window (window pane, get it?). The number, name, and purpose of the panes varies depending on the context.

Password A secret code that you have to enter every time you use your USER.ID.

Permanent Pen (1) A unique font used to make editorial comments in a document. (2) A writing implement specifically designed to stain your clothes permanently.

Person document One kind of document in a Name and Address Book. In the public N&A Book, there's a Person document for each user at your company. You can also compose a Person document in your personal N&A Book to give one of your friends an e-mail nickname, or to help you remember someone's complicated e-mail address.

Personal N&A Book A database on your computer's hard disk in which you can enter person, group, and connection documents.

Platform Another fancy computer word that means the same as operating system.

Policy document A document that describes the purpose of a database and the rules for its use. (Also called the About This Database document.)

Pop-up A part of a Notes document that has hidden text associated with it. You view this hidden text by clicking on the word.

Port The name for the part of your computer where your network or modem is plugged in. Some computers have more than one port; yours might have one port for the network and one port for the modem.

PowerBook A portable Macintosh computer.

Power tie A knot tied around the neck symbolizing extreme corporate fealty, but mistaken for a symbol of corporate authority.

Preferences document The Macintosh equivalent of NOTES.INI.

Private key The part of your User ID that's used to decrypt your encrypted mail messages.

Private view A view that's only on your workstation.

Protocol A techie-term for the part of your network operating system that is used to connect your Notes workstation with your Notes servers. You might hear about protocols called NetBIOS, SPX, or TCP/IP. Then again, you may never hear protocols mentioned.

Public key The part of your USER.ID that other people use to encrypt mail messages for you.

Public N&A Book The database on the Notes server that defines all the Notes users, servers, groups, and connections at your company.

Query Builder A dialog box you fill out that makes it easy to define the criteria for a Full Text Search.

Query by Form A way to enter the criteria for a Full Text Search, using the same form that was used to enter the document in the first place.

Read Access List A way to control which people can read a document that you compose. You set a document's Read Access List in the Document InfoBox, on the page with the key tab.

Reader A level of access that you can have to a database. As a reader, you can only read the documents that other people have composed; you cannot compose your own.

Relational database A database program that allows the full sharing of data between databases and between forms within databases.

Remote workstation A Notes workstation that is not connected to a Notes server via a network. Instead, remote workstations often use a modem to talk to the Notes server.

Replica ID A special serial number that every database has that identifies it as the same database, even if there are copies of it on other servers.

Replication The process used to synchronize two copies of a database between two servers or between a server and a workstation.

ResEdit The program you use on a Macintosh to edit your Notes Preferences document.

Return receipt A special kind of e-mail message that tells you when a recipient read an e-mail that you sent.

Rich text A special field type that can include more than one font and formatting (like bold and italics), and can contain embedded objects and attachments.

Ruler The part of the Notes screen that you can use (if you choose to display it) to set margins and tabs in a rich text field.

Selecting (1) Designating text or data to be deleted, copied, or changed in some way. (2) Choosing documents in a view for such group-treatment as categorizing, printing, or deletion.

Selection formula A Notes formula used to designate which documents will be replicated.

Search bar The dialog box at the top of the screen (if you choose to display it) that allows you to specify the text to search for and rules for the search.

Section Part of a Notes form or document with its own fields. It may be *collapsible,* meaning the user can choose to display or conceal its contents, and it may have *restricted access,* which means only designated important people can edit its fields.

Server A shared computer that stores Notes databases.

Server-based mail A setting you use that causes Notes to send off your messages immediately; the opposite of workstation-based mail.

Signature Also called an *electronic signature*; a way for you to guarantee to the recipient of a message that it really, honestly, absolutely came from *you*.

SmartIcon A picture representing an action you can take. Click the SmartIcon to initiate the action.

SmartIcon palette A collection of SmartIcons.

Sort (1) To put items in a list in order. (2) To match your socks.

SPX A protocol made by Novell.

Static text Text in a form that doesn't change. The title of a form is an example of static text.

Stationery A template of various types of messages you might send.

Status bar (1) A line of information at the bottom of the Notes window, part of which you can use to change parts of your document. (2) A drinking establishment on Main Street where they have cold beer and hot tunes. Closed Sundays; shoes and shirt required.

Subform A section of a form with its own fields, text, graphics, and design, which designers can use in multiple forms.

Styles Named collections of paragraph attributes which you can assign to a paragraph all at once.

Tables (1) Small spreadsheets that you can insert into Notes documents. (2) A place to put your cold beer while you're listening to the hot tunes at the Status Bar. Closed Sundays; shoes and shirt required.

TCP/IP A protocol.

Template A special kind of Notes database used to create other Notes databases.

Type-ahead The ability in Notes to start typing the name of an addressee of a memo and have Notes finish it for you.

UNIX An operating system that you can use on Notes workstations and servers.

Unread marks Stars or colored text used in views to show you which documents you haven't read yet.

URL Uniform Resource Locator, the address of any particular Web page.

Vacation Profile Special agent used to reply automatically to messages you receive when you are on vacation or playing hooky.

View A summary of the documents in a database. Most databases have more than one view.

Vines (1) A network operating system. (2) Places where grapes grow.

WAN (1) Wide Area Network: a bunch of computers connected in some other way than by network cables. Most frequently used are phone lines, satellites, broadcast, and tin cans with string. (2) How you look when you don't take your vitamin pills.

WARP Release 3 of OS/2.

Web page A document on Web servers which can contain graphics, links to other documents or pages, text, attached files, and multimedia features.

Web server A computer somewhere in the world on the Internet which holds Web pages.

Windows An operating environment that you can use on Notes workstations and servers. Current versions are Windows 95, Windows NT, Windows 3.1, and Windows for Workgroups

Workspace (1) The first Notes screen you see, the one containing the tabbed pages and database icons. (2) Any Notes window. (3) The place where your boss lets you work when you're good.

Workstation The computer at your desk, or (if you have a laptop) the computer in your briefcase. It's the computer that each person uses to work with Notes.

Workstation-based e-mail A setting that you use when your computer is not connected to a LAN, which causes Notes to queue up your outgoing e-mail until you place a phone call to a Notes server.

WorldCom A company that lets you use its Notes servers for an hourly fee.

World Wide Web A collection of computers on the Internet that have special pages (see *Web pages*) you can use.

WWW A TLA (Three Letter Abbreviation) for the World Wide Web.

Index

• *G* •

• *H* •

IDG BOOKS WORLDWIDE REGISTRATION CARD

RETURN THIS REGISTRATION CARD FOR FREE CATALOG

Title of this book: **Lotus Notes® Release 4 For Dummies®**

My overall rating of this book: ❑ Very good [1] ❑ Good [2] ❑ Satisfactory [3] ❑ Fair [4] ❑ Poor [5]

How I first heard about this book:

❑ Found in bookstore; name: [6] _____ ❑ Book review: [7] _____

❑ Advertisement: [8] _____ ❑ Catalog: [9] _____

❑ Word of mouth; heard about book from friend, co-worker, etc.: [10] ❑ Other: [11] _____

What I liked most about this book:

_____

_____

What I would change, add, delete, etc., in future editions of this book:

_____

_____

Other comments:

_____

Number of computer books I purchase in a year: ❑ 1 [12] ❑ 2-5 [13] ❑ 6-10 [14] ❑ More than 10 [15]

I would characterize my computer skills as: ❑ Beginner [16] ❑ Intermediate [17] ❑ Advanced [18] ❑ Professional [19]

I use ❑ DOS [20] ❑ Windows [21] ❑ OS/2 [22] ❑ Unix [23] ❑ Macintosh [24] ❑ Other: [25] _____
(please specify)

I would be interested in new books on the following subjects:
(please check all that apply, and use the spaces provided to identify specific software)

❑ Word processing: [26] _____ ❑ Spreadsheets: [27] _____

❑ Data bases: [28] _____ ❑ Desktop publishing: [29] _____

❑ File Utilities: [30] _____ ❑ Money management: [31] _____

❑ Networking: [32] _____ ❑ Programming languages: [33] _____

❑ Other: [34] _____

I use a PC at (please check all that apply): ❑ home [35] ❑ work [36] ❑ school [37] ❑ other: [38] _____

The disks I prefer to use are ❑ 5.25 [39] ❑ 3.5 [40] ❑ other: [41] _____

I have a CD ROM: ❑ yes [42] ❑ no [43]

I plan to buy or upgrade computer hardware this year: ❑ yes [44] ❑ no [45]

I plan to buy or upgrade computer software this year: ❑ yes [46] ❑ no [47]

Name: _____ Business title: [48] _____ Type of Business: [49] _____

Address (❑ home [50] ❑ work [51]/Company name: _____)

Street/Suite# _____

City [52]/State [53]/Zipcode [54]: _____ Country [55] _____

❑ **I liked this book!** You may quote me by name in future
IDG Books Worldwide promotional materials.

My daytime phone number is _____

IDG BOOKS

THE WORLD OF
COMPUTER
KNOWLEDGE

 # YES!

Please keep me informed about IDG's World of Computer Knowledge. Send me the latest IDG Books catalog.